A LIFETIME OF BEING AN ACE: MAKING ASEXUALITY VISIBLE
DAVINA A

'A lifetime of being an Ace – making asexuality visible'
Copyright © 2023 by Davina A.

All Rights Reserved

No part of this book may be reproduced in any form or by any electronic or mechanical means including information storage and retrieval systems, without permission in writing from the author.
The only exception is by a reviewer, who may quote short excerpts.

Disclaimers

This is a memoir about the discovery of an asexual orientation, where I have recounted events from memories, personal letters, old journals, diaries, and study documents.

This book is a work of non-fiction with some changes in personal details to protect privacy. Therefore, to keep anonymity of individuals, I have named people with fictitious initials and altered some identifying characteristics.

This book may supplement existing knowledge on the topic of asexuality, but it is not intended to be a textbook to advise or counsel readers on their own sexual orientations.

Cover design by Nifty Ness Designs.

Interior layout by Cecily Potter.

Printed in Australia

First Printing 2023

Paperback ISBN- 978-0-6457690-0-5

E book ISBN- 978-0-6457690-1-2

Hard cover ISBN- 978-0-6457690-2-9

A Welcome and a Warning

Given that sex is such a crucial factor in our lives, I ask – what would it be like if you never experienced sexual desire?

Would you feel lonely or think you had won the trump card of finding you were an *'Ace'* (an asexual person), who loves people, but in a unique way?

Firstly, a *welcome* and a *warning*.

Welcome to my sex-life excursions that led me to discovering the *invisible* treasure of *'asexuality.'*

I invite the reader to embrace sexual diversity without fear and delve deeper into the complex world of sexual orientations, which can be a pathway to gaining wisdom about our humanity.

Warning! I am presenting a personal story that is bluntly revealing, and where there is no shying away from openly talking about sex or encounters with disappointed lovers.

I have interwoven this memoir with other matters that affected my sex life, such as social attitudes, religion, coping with failures, and philosophies about love and romance.

My asexual revelation does not gently unfold as I chronicle through personal journals that lurch towards sexual self-discovery with many lessons learnt along the way, such as understanding the mystery of a 'core-gasm' or discovering various kinds of marriage partnerships. In order to understand and clarify my life history, I wrote these journals after consulting old diaries, former study essays, and dominant memories of life events.

So be prepared to share in my colourful rainbow quest, where, like Dorothy in *The Wizard of Oz*, love was 'at home' within myself the whole time.

- Davina A. 2023

Contents

Introducing the 'Pretend' Heterosexual	1
Childhood Sexuality	13
Early-Life Education	23
High School and Teenage Years	35
Dancing Days	50
Socialising and a Boyfriend	66
Wedding and Honeymoon	77
Marriage and Pregnancy	84
The Birth Experience	93
Divorce	103
Single Life	110
University Life	120
Planning for Relationships	139
Marriage and Divorce No. 2	157
A New Man and a New Life	174
Living Alone	189
How I Found Asexuality	197
The Process of 'Coming Out'	211
Scientific Asexuality Research	222
Asexual Relationships	234

Learnings About Love	250
Humour and Asexuality	268
Summary and Outcomes	280
Appendices	286
2021 Better Together Conference Report	287
The Equality Project Australia	289
Bibliography	291
Acknowledgements	292
About the Author, Davina A	294

INTRODUCTION

Introducing the 'Pretend' Heterosexual

Throughout much of my life, I tried to behave as a 'normal' heterosexual woman looking for love. How wrong I was! It took an act of serendipity to learn I was an asexual and always had been. It was a shock, a relief, life changing, and thank goodness I lived long enough to realise I was not only normal, but exceptional! In the following journals and reflections, I will explain how and why it took years of misguided sexual behaviour of trying to emulate other people.

I came across my real sexuality accidentally when I undertook a casual Google search for the meaning of the word *'asexual.'* I expected the answer to be, *'abstaining from sex,'* and to an extent I was right. Then, I noted the additional information that *'Asexual individuals may still experience attraction, but this attraction does not need to be realised in any sexual manner.'* This statement inspired me to investigate further, until I stumbled across a website that made all the pieces of my life finally click into place. I *was* one of these people. Yes, I was an asexual, and better still, it was a legitimate way of being. I was overcome by the euphoria of feelings – including relief, and a renewed sense of self-identity.

Like all true serendipitous stories, the definitive answer of my own asexuality happened because of my earlier research into sexual topics. It was good to have previously studied a lot about sexuality, so I could realise this latest information as being significant. Therefore, it was fortunate I had enough knowledge to understand the relevance of my finding and intuitively know the term *'asexual'* applied to me.[1]

After keeping this secret to myself for a time, I felt the natural desire to tell someone but knew *'coming out'* about one's sexuality could be an awkward process. Besides, I wondered if anyone would be really interested in a *non-existent* form of sexuality. However, because I had spent so much of my eighty plus years in vague sexual confusion, I certainly did not want other people like me to waste their precious time searching for a sexual pathway that did not exist. So, I decided to write about the complicated journey of how I finally managed to discover my real identity.

First, I wanted to research the subject of asexuality and examine how any facts might relate to me. After only minimal research, I had lightbulb moments and could see why I had made past unwise life decisions and persisted in exploring heterosexuality so seriously. I asked myself tough questions, then began the therapeutic process of recording my former sexual beliefs and experiences in a rather haphazard fashion. At times, it was painfully embarrassing with a few shameful, guilt-ridden moments relating to my past efforts of sexual pretence. On the bright side, this writing began to generate a certain level of self-forgiveness.

To make further sense of myself, I decided to seriously redraft the story covering the different eras of my life. I even considered looking for a sexologist or research expert, who could contribute or support my writings. Sadly, I could not find such a person, so my first writing

---

[1] Definition of serendipity – An act of serendipity is the happy event of discovering something by chance or accident. One finds science is full of such serendipitous discovery stories. Most importantly, it takes a 'prepared' mind to recognise the incident as being significant. For example, Christopher Columbus unexpectedly found new land, but he did not at first recognise it as a vast continent – so here his mind was not fully prepared.

attempt resulted in a series of conversations between myself and a pretend counsellor. This served to get all the facts on paper, but it was still like a stream of consciousness, making sense to only me. At least this first try enabled me to express facts with a degree of honesty and provided the inspiration to rewrite something more understandable – just in case others might want to read it.

Journals

With some kind encouragement from the informative AVEN asexual online community (AVEN – Asexual Visibility & Education Network), I felt motivated to write what evolved into a form of chronological journals.[2] These journals allowed me to 'talk' to someone – even if that someone was only another part of myself. I developed a real fondness for my journal writings, which became a form of counselling. It also helped to define the cultural and behavioural issues that had influenced me throughout the unfolding chapters of my life. Beginning in childhood, through the teen years, career endeavours, marriages (yes, two actually), parenthood, and relationships, my *Dear Journal* became a friend, confidant, and teacher. The writing took place over four years, giving me valuable time to digest thoughts and emotions along the way. In all, it became a life saga that revealed those barriers which had kept me on the heterosexual search-path for so long.

Although the journals gave me a chance for honest appraisal of past events, I was aware of the pitfalls of inaccurate recall and realised I would be writing with my 'present-day' mindset. Even if I had hazy details of past events, at least I trusted the emotional memories would hold true. Hindsight is a wonderful thing when reinterpreting one's history, and it was hard to revisit decisions which had been made with

---

[2] Asexual websites: AVEN https://www.asexuality.org or asexuality – https://www.wiki how.com

limited knowledge, or where I was behaving according to 'hidden' social scripts. As a result, I have been able to construct a new, alternative life story, rewarding me with a contented *'I'm-okay-after-all'* kind of feeling. I might add, my story is not how I *failed* at being a heterosexual, but more about how I was not one in the first place.

I knew the journal writing would be a liberating process for my own benefit, but I questioned whether other people could gain anything from my strange sexual confessions. Then, I decided other asexual people might find comfort to hear the story of an older female who was able to live well, despite not understanding herself until she was over 80 years of age. Even knowing other asexuals would have lived through different circumstances, I thought they might glean something from someone who had lived in ignorance for so long.

Then again, I wondered if heterosexual folk might also be curious as to what being asexual means. I also believed a wider public knowledge of such a little-known sexual orientation would be beneficial. In fact, when recently watching a TV show, I saw one poor participant who was showing signs of asexual behaviour put under pressure to engage in physical sexual intimacy.[3] Although 'relationship experts' supervised this show, they either lacked knowledge about asexuality or ignored such a possibility.

This made me think about people in partnerships who may be suffering *'sexual disharmony'* and might not have considered asexuality as a factor. Besides, I suspect older psychologists and sex therapists may still regard lack of sexual desire as being a physical or psychological disorder – depending on whether they kept up with current knowledge and research. Therefore, it is not easy to find people with a good understanding of the asexual orientation,

---

[3] I refer to 'reality' television shows such as *Married at First Sight*, which present the emotional difficulties of people 'searching for love.'

especially considering asexuality represents only a small percent of the population. If one cannot find a friend or therapist with whom to discuss asexuality, a book or the internet could be the next best thing.

With the encouragement from the online asexual community to 'come out' beyond the scope of just my friends, I decided that now being in my eighth decade, I have nothing to lose. At my age, I believe older people should be brave enough *not* to 'retire' their voices but put their stories 'out there' for anyone who cares to listen. Who knows, if my writing only entertains, educates, or helps a handful of people, it could be worthwhile. Nevertheless, sex is a topic with a taint of bad press from religious and cultural interpretations. This means it can invoke negative emotions, including suppression of desire, layers of guilt, and worst of all, shame.

I found a sense of freedom from self-examination and research, where I could honestly admit to past uninformed choices and inappropriate behaviour. This meant I was able to acknowledge those unhealthy decisions with a sense of self-forgiveness. Of course, there were those realisations about seemingly unwise judgements that fortunately resulted in *good* outcomes. For example, a marriage that blessed me with a child.

The following journal writing is not a complete autobiography, as it only follows one thread of personal experience relating to my sexual memories and life-explorations. Along the way, the reader will gain some idea about my interests, values, and beliefs, but this writing will not fully reflect all the other successes and rewards in my life. Therefore, I have omitted stories that would have revealed more about satisfying friendships, vibrant working-life, joys of motherhood, or interesting travels. Although it is a record about the struggles and agonies towards understanding my sexual past, I cannot recall a time when I felt truly alone or devastated. For that good fortune I am grateful to family and friends for their loving care. To protect privacy of people in my life, I have used the pseudonym 'Davina A.' which is also my internet name for conversing with online colleagues.

Reflections

After writing each journal entry, I found myself reflecting on key issues that arose out of a particular topic or period of my life. Therefore, there are extended themes written after each journal entry where I felt the need to summarise or to further clarify insights. So, these interspersed reflections explore what topics each journal raised for me.

But before beginning my first journal, I will clarify some asexual terminology and definitions so people will know what I am talking about.

Asexuality and Related Definitions

What is Asexuality?

Like most people, I did not know what asexuality was or what being an asexual really meant. After some research, my basic definition settled on: *'the lack of sexual desire towards other people.'* My first investigations produced the following insights:

- o   Asexuality is different from celibacy, which is a choice.
- o   Asexuality is not where people abstain from sex for a certain time period due to physical, psychological, or circumstantial reasons.
- o   True asexuality is a lifelong, enduring lack of sexual desire that steadfastly stays as a core way of being. Therefore, it is a

- person's basic orientation or 'default' position on the sexual spectrum.
  o Being asexual is not a selected choice, nor is it a feigned sexual viewpoint or excuse for not wanting to express love in a sexual way.

Orientation

Originally, I confused the terms *'orientation'* and *'gender.'* I now define *orientation* as referring to the *inherent way of sexually wanting to connect with another person.*[4] For example, we are born either right or left-handed; one way feels right, and the other feels plainly wrong. Conversely, my father was born left-handed but was able to change to right-hand dominance by methods of repetitive use, which retrained his brain. In my ignorance, I also tried to alter my 'given' sexual way of being, but I dismally failed all attempts. Why? Because sexual orientation is enduring, and I think results from an early complex interaction of biological elements. Therefore, despite emulating heterosexual behaviour for years, it did not alter my true orientation.

Also, asexuality cannot be changed by psychological techniques such as *'conversion therapy,'* which is a treatment method intended to change someone's sexual orientation or gender. I consider this intended 'cure' to be unscientific, in the same category as torture, and a violation of human rights.

Gender

A person's gender is their inner concept of being male or female. Some can also feel both male and female or express no gender at all. Again, physically you might be male but emotionally desire to live as

---

[4] Definitions of gender and orientation have altered over time, so these are my interpretations.

a female. These strong feelings seem to occur from birth, showing that brain structure and hormones must play an underlying foundation in the development of gender. I recognise how hard it must be for those who have the desperate need to change the gender that was physically assigned to them at birth. As for me, I know I am female (but with a few male personality traits), and asexual in orientation.

Gender Expression

Gender *'expression'* is communicated through one's culture as seen in actions, mannerisms, dressing, and even in the use of vocal style. It is therefore easy to realise how the society in which we live drives the creation of male or female behaviour. Society's influence on gender is obvious in marketing, male/female fashion, the workplace, and particularly how significant people like parents, teachers, or peer groups subtly endorse the expected behaviour of males and females.

Asexuality Invisibility

Asexuality has been unseen and hidden – probably because it does not overtly breach accepted human behaviour. Under certain circumstances, such as within some religious contexts, not engaging in sex can be considered a virtue. But, within intimate relationships, asexuals can often hide, only receiving criticisms that they might have a low sex drive or need medical help.

Therefore, a constant lack of sexual desire is often not acknowledged, and in my own experience, it was certainly 'invisible' even to me. I had no knowledge of asexuality, so in such ignorance, there was no explanation for my lack of sexual thoughts and feelings. Also, being a female, it was easier for me to remain undiscovered, as I could engage in 'pretend' sexual behaviour that did not reflect my inner inclinations.

In the previously mentioned website that goes by the acronym of AVEN for *'Asexuality Visibility Education Network,'* the word *'visibility'* is most important. Obviously, David Jay, the founder, felt the title needed to highlight the hidden nature of asexuality to bring it into focus.[5] To complicate things, we humans are such complex creatures in that no two individuals are alike. Therefore, asexuals also have a variety of individual behaviours and preferences resulting in diverse ways to experience connections with other people.

Attraction

In certain cases, asexual people can feel an *attraction* to another person that is romantic, aesthetic, intellectual, or even sensual, while not wanting to express those feelings sexually. For example, I sometimes feel 'attracted' to men where I would be happy to show affection by hugging or kissing, but where it would not cross my mind to sleep with them. Again, I like seeing male aesthetic bodies and find attraction to them in terms of physique for dance, sport, or as a handsome fashion model – although this type of physical attraction does not 'turn me on' in a sexual way. I have also experienced intellectual attraction, where one looks to connect with someone because of their knowledge or inspiring ideas.

Arousal

Here I refer to a degree of physical libido where some asexuals feel a need to masturbate and yet not associate these feelings as needing sex. Therefore, I believe there can be physical sexual responses that asexuals interpret as only a pleasant bodily function, and it is *not* associated with feelings of longing for a sexual partner.

---

[5] David Jay – Asexual activist born April 24th, 1982, from St Louis, Missouri. He founded the AVEN website and has worked tirelessly for public acceptance of asexuality and the development of a supportive online community. (David Jay Wikipedia)

Sense of Identity

I am sure sexuality is bound up with our sense of identity, relating to people's concepts of themselves. Originally, I was not comfortable with my sexual self. At first, I was often aware of my lack of sexual feelings but had no comparison with anyone else who felt the same way. Much later in life, I stopped bothering about sex and just accepted myself until I finally found the explanation of asexuality – it was only then I felt a fully integrated sense of truly belonging in this world.

Asexual Untruths

It is problematic when others give uninformed opinions or guess as to the probable causes of asexuality, so I will summarise the popular misconceptions.

- o Asexuality is not a medical or psychological condition needing treatment.
- o Asexuals are not reacting to negative feelings towards other sexual orientations.
- o Asexuality does not necessarily develop from past sexual or abuse experiences in childhood.
- o Asexuals are not acting out of guilt, shame, or desire to fulfil an idea of 'purity.'
- o Asexuality does not develop out of unhappiness about one's appearance.
- o People do not become asexual because they are too busy with no time for sex.
- o Asexuality is not a new fad or trendy topic, although the term 'asexual' is now becoming more frequent in the public domain.

Asexual People are Not...

- waiting to meet the 'right person'
- fulfilling a religious ideal or going through a phase
- necessarily lonely (solitude does not always equate with loneliness)
- unemotional, frigid, or hiding desire
- trying to be selfish or 'being a tease' in relationships
- trying to avoid having children or are deliberately avoiding sex
- needing to be 'fixed' with therapy
- living uncomplicated lives – as asexuals, too, can have busy, complex lives.

Gay/Queer LGBTIQA+ Community Terminology[6]

For years I used the term 'gay' to describe anyone who was homosexual and liked its connotation of the word 'happy.' Today, the umbrella term of 'queer' is used to cover all sexual diversities. I am still getting accustomed to this word, as to me, it originally meant 'odd' or 'bizarre.' Therefore, I still tend to use both gay/queer. Here I am reminded of how language constantly changes. Once I choreographed a children's musical production titled *The Little Gypsy Gay*. However, the school was uncomfortable with the title and so changed it to 'The Happy Gypsy'!

The first four letters are well known, but the IQA+ often need a little more explanation. These alphabetical symbols are difficult to

---

[6] The alphabetical letters LGBTIQA+ stand for **L**esbian, **G**ay/queer, **B**isexual, **T**ransgender, **I**ntersex (those born with both male and female physiology), **Q**uestioning (including non-binary gender identities falling outside of being strictly male or female; gender fluid, where gender identity or expression changes over time; and gender queer, as not following static categories of gender), **A**sexual (with little or no sexual desire), and + (plus) standing for other forms of sexuality.

pronounce, and I am never sure about the order of letters. Just like naming the seven dwarfs in the 'Snow White' story, I always forget one. The order I have chosen is LGBTIQA+, as used by The Equality Project (Australia) – an organisation that supports gay/queer people.

Because sexual orientation and basic gender is set from birth, I consider my asexuality as a fixed part of my identity and would not want to change or be any other way. Therefore, the following journal writings and reflective summaries will reveal the challenges of this asexual discovery – one that occurred much later in life. But, I am so grateful it happened at all!

JOURNAL 1

Childhood Sexuality

Dear Journal,

In this writing, I hope to gain clarity in retelling remembered life events and see how my asexual ignorance has caused so much confusion along the way. Firstly, what was I like as a child? From photographs, memories, and letters written by my mother, I was outgoing, energetic, and empathetic – although quite content with my own company. At about the age three, I became far more subdued after a bout of near-fatal pneumonia. It was then I became hospitalised, and the nursing staff removed me from my parents – after which I became a chronically bronchial and far timider little child.[7]

From then on, I am sure this health change made me less outwardly adventurous. I say outwardly, as inwardly I still fantasised about growing wings or flying with a billowing cape like a comic-book hero. In my imagination, I was a traveller who liked rainbows, a Native American who rode horses bareback, or a superwoman who saved people. I loved nature, wanted to be a dancer, and my favourite game was pretending to be someone else like an actor. In truth, I lived indoors, spoke in breathy short sentences, and could not even walk fast, let alone run without wheezing for breath.

---

[7] There used to be a practice of not having parents visit their hospitalised children. Staff considered children became upset when parents left, and thought it was better if they remained passive – where in reality, children became traumatised. 'Hospital trauma' is now a recognised condition.

Being asthmatic created a sense of guilt, as if I were somehow responsible for my own ill health. Consequently, I felt being sick was my fault, so I hated my lack of stamina and the fact I missed so much schooling with doctors always confining me to bed rest. In those days, there was little understanding about such chronic conditions and there was no standard medical treatment. Childhood was a strange experience of trial medical 'cures,' applications of adrenaline throat sprays, bouts of hospitalisation, and having myriads of injections to detect allergies. Despite this, I never gave up hope that I would eventually become stronger, especially after always hearing *'she will probably grow out of it one day'* – so with childlike optimism I chose to secretly believe in a healthier future.

Growing up in the World War II era also meant I led a sheltered, isolated life on a farm. Other than hearing stories about other parts of the world, my actual world was small and quite devoid of any visual sexual images. So, when did I first have any childhood experiences that later equated as something to do with sex?

On the Matter of Penises

One occasion I now recognise as being related to early sex education was probably when I saw a penis for the first time. This happened when my mother was giving my baby brother his first bath; a ritual that took place on our large kitchen table. Looking at his tiny male body naked on a towel, I noted with curiosity that his anatomy was different from mine. I said something like, *'He has a funny tail up top,'* and before Mother could reply, an arc of urine went over the baby's head into a vase of flowers. This brought forth screeches of laughter from me and an equally amused mother, who was also learning that boys' bodies behave differently. Later, after comparing his body to mine, I thought I looked much neater and tidier. In fact,

CHILDHOOD SEXUALITY

I felt sorry for him having extra body bits hanging between his legs – so certainly there was no Freudian *'penis envy'* on my behalf!

A couple of years later, I remember another washing ritual where my brother and I were taking a bath under our grandmother's supervision. I thought it strange when my grandmother insisted that my brother turn his back to me when she was towelling him. Her actions revealed that I was not supposed to see his exposed penis. She muttered something about not showing his rude bits. Here, the message conveyed was that a five-year-old girl should not view certain parts of male anatomy. I then felt sorry for my brother, who not only had an untidy piece of anatomy, but now my grandmother labelled it as rude! This only proves how childhood experiences play a part in creating attitudes towards our physical selves.

Still on the topic of penises – it was always amusing that boys invented so many names for this anatomical organ. Since I have a son and grandsons of my own, I like to think they have always been comfortable about their bodies, especially as they were taught proper names for body parts. Therefore, a penis was called a penis. I still remember when my grandson came home from school and was unusually anxious to tell me what he had learned that day. He realised that other boys did not call a penis by its normal name and thought it hilarious they used names like, *'Johnny Thomas'* and *'Doodle'*!

I also wondered why males often referred to the penis as if it had a separate identity. (Like their special mate.) I could only conclude that as a reflex sexual organ, the penis had a virtual life of its own, and so thus developed the trend of giving it a personalised nickname.

Of course, the thing I did envy was how boys could urinate easily without having to sit or squat – especially convenient for country roadside stops or picnics. I was also envious of the fun young boys had urinating against walls in competition to see who could spray the highest. Yet, I never wanted to be a man with an appendage that dictates physical desires and demands attention, so not having a penis has always been a relief.

Talking of Birds and Bees

The first information relating to sexual knowledge occurred when my mother gave me the fundamental *'birds and bees'* talk. I know this took place just before my tenth birthday when she told me how babies were made. What she imparted was quite a revelation, as previously I had believed a flying stork delivered babies to a hospital during the night. The night was my invented idea, as despite being on the lookout, I had never seen a flying stork during the day. Of course, I never saw such a bird at night-time either, and so I assumed stork-deliveries must have happened when I was asleep.

My mother revealed babies could be born after you were married, and she related how mothers and fathers loved each other in a 'special' way. She then revealed some strange facts about the father putting his penis in the mother to sow a seed to grow a baby. This was surprising, as I thought a penis was only for urinating, and now it could plant seeds as well! At first, I wondered whether this revelation was in the same category of Father Christmas and Tooth Fairy stories, both of which, according to my school mates, were false. Then again, Mother's serious tone suggested that she was telling the truth and this baby-making stuff was for real.

Naturally, like many other children, I thought adult intercourse only happened for the sole purpose of creating babies. As for how childbirth happened, I imagined mothers went to the hospital where they hatched the baby like an egg, which was then put in a crib or incubator like our farm chickens. I did not bother to ask about the physical details of giving birth, believing hospital nurses somehow dealt with the delivery.

To me, this baby-making information was not gross – only weirdly interesting! On our farm I had seen pregnant sheep getting bigger and knew it meant they were having a lamb. Certainly, I did not relate this to humans or even think how the lamb actually came into the world. Later, with more knowledge about the actual birthing process, I thought it was just another odd bodily function. I imagined it would be a strange procedure, but it did not occur to me it could be painful, as then there was no television to depict agonising birth dramas.

Ignoring the physical process of giving birth, the idea of being a mother and caring for a child was appealing. I loved tending to my baby cousins and always imagined one day having a child of my own. Even my poor pet cat had to tolerate the indignity of wearing a baby bonnet and being wheeled around in a toy pram. The only odd thing about pregnancy was your stomach growing strangely larger, but I presumed the body returned to normal after the baby was born. In the meantime, I had bigger things to worry about, such as coping with schoolwork, which I struggled to keep up with the rest of the class on because of the chronic asthma.

Dear Journal, I will now confess to feeling alarmed about the other bit of information that related to the bodily function of 'becoming a woman.'

Menstruation

My mother also explained that at a future stage I would get something called a 'period' every month. She told me that I would shed a 'few' drops of blood because it meant I could have a baby when I was married. However, she did not explain that 'a few drops of blood' could also be a 'virtual flood,' nor was I told anything about symptoms of stomach pains. No kid likes the sight of blood, so this sounded gross, and I hoped this seemingly awful bodily function would not really happen to me.

However, it was still a surprise when my first period appeared only two weeks after my tenth birthday. Consequently, I knew her prediction was right, but I hoped it would only happen a few times. Being a skinny, sickly child, the look on my mother's face told me that she was even more stunned than I was. Years later, my mother confessed she was shocked when her physically underdeveloped, wan little daughter had started menstruating so early. To her credit, she convinced me I was now suddenly 'grown up' and was becoming a real woman. This idea pleased me, but I still had my doubts whether this event was really a good thing.

Then came the unwelcomed introduction to the ritual of folding flannel cloths to absorb the 'drops' of blood. In those days, there was the discomfort of wide waist belts and big safety pins to secure them, as no neat sanitary pads or tampons existed then. Along with this unexpected early entry into puberty, I had to wash the said flannel squares each night for further use. This was not a happy chore for a child, and I remember fantasising about becoming a comic-book hero like Mary Marvel, who I was sure would not suffer such inconveniences.[8]

After the initial bleeding experience, I decided this monthly menstruation business was incredibly frustrating – especially as I was instructed not to swim, wash my hair, or eat chocolate. Unbelievable! Such was the weird conventional wisdom that mothers foisted on young women in those days. How I hated those times, where on a beautiful summer day at the beach, my young brother would call me

---

[8] Mary Marvel was my favorite hero in the *Captain Marvel* comics in the 1940s. Created by Otto Binder and Marc Swayze, she was my first image of a woman who expressed strong elements of bravery and physical action.

a 'wimp' because I was not allowed to swim! Then, there was the anxiety of being at school while menstruating, as at this early age, none of my classmates seemed to be coping with such a thing. So, it became a secret from school friends during those first years.

Despite my original distaste, I eventually treated menstruation as an annoying, female bodily function, and I resigned myself to another nuisance factor of growing up. Nevertheless, I did want to be an adult, so if having a monthly 'period' was part of the deal, I adopted a weary acceptance of my female lot in life. I still do not know what my hormones were doing with menstruation happening before any other obvious physical development. Despite this, in those primary-school years, I still had a childlike optimism of believing I would live 'happily ever after,' just like most storybook endings.

Female Development

I grew to like my androgynous body shape, so at the age of thirteen, I was uneasy at the first sign of breasts. I knew they were for feeding babies and would have preferred they just grew for the baby and then deflated like a pregnant stomach. Though all my friends were excited, I just played along with their delight when they wore their first bra. Secretly, I preferred my body not to change and wished the chest 'bumps' would go away.

Luckily, my body development granted me a lifetime of small breasts, and even to this day, I cannot understand the desire of so many women wanting to enlarge themselves. In fact, I could happily live without breasts after they served their breast-feeding purpose. To me, the ideals of larger breasts, buttocks, and high heels to enhance female sexuality only seem to make women into odd-looking, stilted creatures, resulting in a peculiar posture and walking gait. I have always thought sexualised fashion impeded women's natural body movements, with spiked heels making ungainly clunking sounds on floors and pavements.

Being asexual, I do not care if my body is not sexually desirable, but I sympathise with other women who worry about losing breasts because of cancer. I realise they could feel less attractive, so I appreciate how reconstructive surgery would be important for their well-being.

Early Sexual Education

Children learn other 'facts of life' from their siblings or close school friends. Unfortunately, I did not always have a best friend because of so many absent days with illness. This meant that any possible close companion would often find another girl who frequented school more often. So, I do not remember any whispered or secret conversations with fellow students behind the school bicycle shed.

At school I also had a poor social image – particularly with the nickname of *'Cowardly Custard.'* The unflattering name inferred I was a bit of a physical weakling, who, on asthmatic days, moved exceedingly slowly. This meant when selecting team members for any running game, I was the always the last choice. On the annual sports day, my job was to rake the sand in the long-jump pitch to help me feel involved. In truth, I just felt humiliated. In that era, the medics considered that being chronically asthmatic was a psychological problem caused by an overprotective mother – an idea which fortunately, my parents considered as rubbish!!

Hence, outside my immediate family, I did not get sympathy for my constant ill health. But despite this, I was a child who lived in a household full of mirth surrounded with caring parents, grandparents, and extended family. Therefore, I am aware just how much I learned from them and how important a positive family atmosphere was for my educational and social development. This has made me reflect more deeply on what I gained from my home life, and how it gave me the emotional strength to support me in adulthood.

Reflection

Social Influence of Family

Looking back on this childhood era, I realised it was my parents, maternal grandmother, and aunts who were my first teachers relating to sexual matters and the gender behaviour of how to be a girl. Also, in those days, nicely illustrated books with titles like *Where Did I Come From?* did not exist, nor did I see any overtly sexual marketing images in this pre-television world.

Thanks to my brother, I knew something about the mysteries of being male, but he was always outdoors engaged in male-dominated activities with my father, while I was indoors, usually reading in my sickbed. We were both shy children, and our relationship was one of a friendly reserve without having an enormous amount of play adventures or verbal interactions together; in fact, we did not even quarrel like other siblings.

I can see how children become educated through the home atmosphere. I know my early learning came from watching how parents behaved, listening to the emotional tone of their voices, noting visual communications, plus absorbing the attitudes that abound in family life. For me, it was fortunate that home life was happy, supportive, and devoid of conflict.

Being born in 1938, we children grew up under the influence of World War II restrictions, where lack of petrol meant we were all isolated, particularly on a farm. There was no such thing as preschool, few social outings, and even a shopping trip to the nearby local town was a rare occasion.[9] Therefore, like other children in those days, my brother and I invented imaginary playmates, with mine being a genderless little elfin creature called *'Pippin.'* This pretend friend accompanied me everywhere and held many regular conversations with me. In addition, she/he guarded me at night – along with a couple of extra imaginary angels.

As parents were such powerful teachers, the next journal writing entry examines how family and early home life became such a vital influence – including those transmitted attitudes towards gender and sexuality.

---

[9] World War II life in Australia created social and economic restrictions. Throughout the war the government rationed food, clothing, and petrol, which made life extremely frugal. In 1939, there were ten preschools in our state, for only disadvantaged children. (https://www.samemory.sa.gov.au Learning and Education)

JOURNAL 2

Early-Life Education

Dear Journal,
The purpose of this entry is to relate memories about home life and the family members who inspired my interests, instilled their attitudes, and shaped my world view.

Parents

My father was born with laughter in his blue eyes and could recount (in an Australian-accented, gravel-toned voice) compelling and funny stories – particularly against himself. Whereas I would cringe if I made a silly mistake, he just relished in any of his own blunders as they were fodder for his funny, side-splitting yarns. I also learned from him that females should always be treated with respect, and that he admired women who dressed in an elegant style. Father always preferred the tailored dressing of the 1950s where females wore clothes accentuating a small waist and fitted bodice to highlight feminine curves. His admiration of my mother was unquestionable, and I will always remember their visible devotion to each other.

I can see how my mother complemented my father, by discreetly encouraging his humour while presenting herself as a gracious woman – one who became accomplished in all the feminine arts. She was a proficient self-taught pianist, a brilliant writer of letters, could sew, arrange flowers, cook, and was also a wonderful ballroom dancer. From her I learned that females should be ladylike, shine with personality, and be a bit 'out there' with a touch of glamour. I never thought I could match her natural talents or have her ability to be such a friendly, outgoing person. Indeed, any aptitudes I eventually did develop were through painful, laboured efforts, while my mother was seemingly born with innate skills and intelligence.

Both parents inferred that young women with personality would always be socially successful. I was never sure what this 'personality' thing was, but I decided it had something to do with frequent smiling, in order to be seen as an engaging, friendly person. Being a timid child, I often purposely tried to smile about nothing in particular, to give the appearance of having an attractive personality. Other than getting a face-ache from this false-smiling countenance, I did not invite any special attention, and it only reinforced my inclination to act and pretend my way through uncomfortable situations in life.

Nonetheless, my parents had 'star' qualities and engaged with many friends in their social world. They also genuinely admired each other and shared a deeply sustaining friendship. Therefore, I am convinced they enjoyed all aspects of their lives – sexual, social, and working together as a team. I would hear them discussing everything, sharing their concerns, praising each other's achievements – and they certainly laughed all the time. Our house continually echoed with laughter. No wonder I thought being married to someone who loved you would create a happy life. Later, in my teens, I also believed that such devoted love would magically create sexual desire. So, I presumed that married life was an ultimate state and divorced people only lived in Hollywood.

In our home, adults did not openly discuss sexual matters, although I was aware of some humorous mysterious knowledge that children were not supposed to hear. Being social people, my parents often entertained, and I would delight in hearing the adult party noises from my bedroom. At times voices would suddenly quieten, and there would be an intense hush, followed by mumbled sentences, and then hoots of laughter. If I asked the next day, '*Why were you all laughing last night?'* I always got that one-day-you-will-understand look with the reply, *'We were just telling funny grown-up stories.'* Obviously, sexual jokes must have abounded on these occasions.

Thinking of my parents, I realised I must have been a severe obstacle to their sex life. Because I was a consumptive child, my parents slept in a bedroom opposite mine with their door open so they could hear if I developed breathing problems. Having listened to many old fairy stories, including those about dragons and wolves that 'huffed and puffed,' I often woke imagining I could hear these characters making noises in the dark. I would instantly call out to my father, who eventually appeared holding out a glass of water, and with weary patience insisted that I was *'just having a bad dream.'* To my ears, a squeaking mattress was most certainly a monster creeping towards my bedroom at an ever-increasing pace!

I am sure they kept their sex life alive, and I remember the story of my father taking Mother to an exclusive lingerie shop in the city. Here he lounged in a shop chair while she tried on pieces of satin and lace in the dressing room. When Mother said to the assistant, *'I will ask my husband whether he approves of my choices,'* the assistant gave her a wink and said, *'Do not worry, dear – we never get husbands here – so just enjoy this chap. If he wants to spend money on you – just take advantage while you can. I would.'* My parents retold this story many times, of how a shop-assistant mistook my father for a 'Sugar Daddy.' But, the fact he was unashamed to purchase sexy underwear for his wife tells its own story.

Whereas Mother seriously gave me basic facts about sex, my father's only sexual information imparted to me was by way of a naughty poem. Evidently, as a young man, he had been inspired to learn quite a long risqué rhyme or what was known as a 'bawdy ballad.' Occasionally, he would start reciting this poem to me and then stop in paroxysms of giggles, saying I was not old enough to hear the rest – yet! It was not until I was in my early twenties that I finally heard every verse, as at the rate of only hearing a few lines per year, it was a long wait. Interestingly, I could always see what was humorous in a sexual joke, but I always understood it more from a rational/visual point of view, as I never felt any sexual, emotional, or physical reactions.

One incident involving my father does stand out as my first lesson relating to differences in gender education. On this occasion, I found my young brother receiving instructions from him about the interesting intricacies of how a car engine worked. With their heads bent under the car bonnet, I could hear explanations about cylinders, pistons, valves, and spark plugs. Being the eldest, Father had taught me skills, such as how to ride a bike or fly a kite, but he never instructed me on the mysteries of mechanics. I remember feeling quite hurt he had not thought to give me this knowledge when I was my brother's age. On the other hand, he did teach me to waltz and polka, while I am sure he did not instruct my brother on these kind of dance moves. Hence, I realised that in life, there was an expectation that boys were to learn different things compared to girls.

Yet, my father did tell me something about same-gender relationships. On one occasion he was most upset over the suicide of one of his regular fishing companions. The friend hanged himself and left a note saying that he could not live with the terrible secret of being gay/queer. Father explained that some men wanted to express love to a man rather than a woman, and that they could not help feeling that way. My father said, *'Poor chap! If he had told us, we would have understood, and he would have always remained our friend.'* Hence, I learned early on that 'gay/queer' men were different and not always accepted by everyone.

Maternal Grandparents

The other teachers were my maternal grandparents who moved to live permanently in our home during World War II. They were an unassuming, industrious couple, who chuckled more than laughed and gave my brother and me continual wise guidance and companionship. They were respectful and loving towards each other, but a tad Victorian with their genteel 'never-put-your-elbows-on-the-table' good manners. I also noted when Grandma was serving food at mealtimes, she always insisted my grandfather and father got the best lamb chops on their plates. To me, having the best chop was a symbol of the males being the important heads of the family.

I adored my grandmother, who was a quiet, gracious, and kindly woman. She particularly admired British royalty but thought the film star, Betty Grable, displayed too much of her legs. Despite being a tad conservative, Grandma loved romantic novels, which she often read aloud to me. Here, I pestered her if she tried to skip paragraphs relating to death or descriptions of love scenes. From her, I gathered that loving your husband required tenderly romantic behaviour, and bedroom activities were secret. Regarding relationships, Grandma's manner always showed that men were the leaders and women the followers. She had given birth to seven children, and her eyes lit up when my grandfather came into the room – so I saw a loving couple who were quietly comfortable in their lives together.

Once Mother related an occasion when Grandma had instructed her and her sister about a sexual matter from a book. Mother told me that Judy, her younger sister, came home from work and repeated a new phrase she had heard in the office. To put it to use, Judy said to my mother, *'Oh, you are so slow. You are just like a wet dream'*. My grandmother was horrified and at once produced a medical dictionary where it gave the definition of a *'wet dream'* as being *'nocturnal emissions.'* That left Mother and Judy with *two* phrases they did not understand and so were even more confused. Finally, their boyfriends were able to enlighten them about men ejaculating as a result of having a nightdream.

These maternal grandparents were calm, patient people, and I always felt emotionally safe with them. They loved nature, shapes and colours of trees, wildflowers, picking mushrooms, or watching spiders spin webs. My grandmother helped me plant my first garden, taught me to respect animals, appreciate music, not to be afraid of the dark or thunderstorms, and where to find star patterns in the night sky. These skills would be vital for me, as in the future, a 'love' of nature would partly replace my lack of the physical 'libido' love that I was not able to experience in human relationships.

The other grandparents on my father's side were far more removed from my life. They lived in the city, and it was obvious that my step-grandmother (Nana) did not have patience with children. Although I was fascinated by city life with its trams, tall buildings, neon lights, and shop escalators, I did not like staying in Nana's house. Here, my brother and I had to eat dried prunes, never interrupt her with silly questions, and reading quietly was our only approved activity. I will admit she introduced me to the magical place of the city children's library, and I have loved books, bookcases, and libraries ever since. In fact, it was Nana who first gave me a *Winnie-the-Pooh* book by A.A. Milne. I just loved these stories and admired the gentle, wise humour of the 'toy' characters, who forever reminded me of people in real life.

On the other hand, my paternal grandfather was quiet, but he appeared to like my brother and me in his own gruff way. I also noted he slept in the closed-in veranda and not in Nana's bedroom. In those days, there were quite a few lonely men who bedded in enclosed veranda spaces, which people called 'sleep-outs.' Overall, married couples tended to remain together rather than face the public shame of divorce, usually compromising with separate sleeping and living arrangements under the same roof.

Aunts

My 'second mother' was my mother's sister, who was also important in my life. This aunt was fun, made me laugh, and liked to compose silly poems. She also encouraged me to play in old 'dress-up' clothes, which further awakened the desire to pretend to be other people, and I am sure laid the foundation for my later drama pursuits. I also enjoyed playing on her old typewriter, and to this day, I still like the sound of tapping on a keyboard. Then, there was the skill of another great-aunt who encouraged early attempts at oil painting, and so I began to develop an eye for colours and became a lover of art galleries. All these activities would have an important effect in my adult life as a replacement for my lack of libido.

Conclusion

I felt in awe of the adults in my childhood and did not think I would live up to their expectations or ever reach their level of talents. In hindsight, my farmer-father worked hard to gain financial security. But, I considered he was always rich in other ways with his generosity of spirit, along with the care of family and people in the local community. My mother was naturally intelligent and could have taken her writing talents further, so I am sure she regretted not becoming an author. Both parents were curious about the world and broad in their thinking, despite having little opportunity to travel or obtain tertiary education.

My parents presented a kind of marriage partnership that I thought I should emulate, so this became the false ideal I pursued for years. However, I have felt blessed with valuable life lessons from a vibrant family that would sustain me in ways I would never have imagined.

Reflection

Family Life Lessons

So, what did I learn from family? Looking back on the earlier journal entry only confirmed how children learn physically, mentally, emotionally, and socially from their parents.

Sexuality and Femininity

As a female, family influences taught me how I should behave in a feminine way and that domestic accomplishments were important. In addition, looking elegant and attractive while also being socially acceptable were vital elements towards gaining a boyfriend. The standard practice of the day was to marry and be pregnant before you were twenty-five. Adults also presented me with vague ideas of sexuality as being a bit naughty, but nice secret fun that I would one day enjoy in the adult world of matrimony.

Home Cooking

Being happily married and a good cook were things I wanted to achieve, to fulfil the social expectations of the day. Despite believing I should try to excel in the kitchen, the hot mess of woodstoves and stress of cooking were areas I never enjoyed. Later in life, even though I failed in cooking enthusiasm, I did delight in efficient kitchens where nutritious food could be easily prepared. On the contrary, the lack of interest in complicated cake baking fortunately encouraged a healthy diet with little effort. Besides, I always appreciated home-grown vegetables and fruit, thanks to my grandfather's extensive home gardening efforts.

On the other hand, my family loved dining out in city restaurants and hotels amid the interesting array of silver and wine glasses. Here, our parents encouraged my brother and I to explore the menu, try new foods, and understand the etiquette involved. The other aspects of fine dining were the sense of occasion and the special intimacy of conversation, as I noted people were more relaxed when attentive waiters effortlessly brought the food and poured the wine. I still love dining with friends where I equate the experience with a romantic atmosphere that can induce personal connections. Therefore, I can well understand how sexual foreplay can take place over a dining table, despite it only working for me as a precursor for deeper platonic friendships.

Approach to Work

Family attitudes inspired me to appreciate the rewards of challenging work, experience the joy of achievement, accept the differences in people, to be community minded, and pursue lifelong learning. All family members had a strong work ethic with my father espousing a three-step work rule…

1. Do the worst job first. (The 'worst' being the task you dislike or want to avoid.)
2. Do it at once – as soon as possible and with no procrastination.
3. Do it to the best of your ability.

I can also remember being proud when my grandfather told me in his old-world English accent that I would make someone an excellent wife because I was a good little 'werker' (meaning worker). This Protestant work ethic came from the stoic survival attitudes of former family generations, where they had experienced the challenges of pioneer migration, two World Wars, The Great Depression, and knew the ravages of illnesses such as scarlet fever,

Spanish flu, TB, and in my time, poliomyelitis. Again, it was these attitudes that would give me the will to achieve in many areas of adult life.

Education

My parents set a good educational example, as they were always engaged in self-learning, asking questions, and were curious about the world (these days people use the term *'lifelong learning'*). Despite my parents' lack of opportunity for extensive schooling, our family valued new knowledge, research, and problem solving. They often consulted dictionaries or encyclopaedias and conferred with other people to gain their expert advice. My parents did not have the opportunity or means for extensive travel, so radio and newspapers were vital in bringing a wider knowledge of the world. Around our large kitchen table, my parents held spirited philosophical discussions on topics such as hypocrisy in religion, the plight of Indigenous people, or our place in the universe. They also regularly played the card game bridge, where memory and tactics as well as chance made it an intense mental activity. Having played fourteen different versions of the card game patience to relieve boredom in my sickbed, I did not follow their interest in playing bridge.

This atmosphere of learning created by family members inspired my interest in books, music, dance, art, drama/acting, typing/writing skills – even to cosmology, astronomy, and science. Although I was not to become expert in all these areas, the wealth of avenues for thoughtful activity and learning provided me with a rich internal world. Therefore, I have never felt lonely, and later, it was these educational interests that gave me a full life despite my lack of sexual desire.

Sport

Sadly, I did not ever reach the sporting skills of my parents. Failure in sport was not only due to chronic childhood illness, but also my non-competitive nature. The following school sports day story illustrates my lack of will to be a winner.

I lined up with my fellow students to partake in what the teachers called 'a running race.' It was one of those rare days when I did not have breathing problems, so somehow, I found myself running well ahead of my classmates. To my parents' amazement, I then stopped, turned around, and ran back down the track to join my 'friends' so we could be at the finishing line together! For me, it was obviously more important to be a part of the group than it was to be a winner. I can still remember my parents saying it was the funniest thing they had ever seen, and I became highly embarrassed whenever I heard the story retold!

With great enthusiasm, Father did everything he could to give my brother and me a good grounding in sporting skills. To that end, he constructed a full-sized tennis court in the front of our farmhouse for his children's benefit. I imagine it was disappointing for him to realise that neither of us could ever fulfil his expectations. My brother had once fallen on a rotten old tree stump, resulting in many operations to remove infected splinters from his leg. This accident meant he was never to be an agile runner, and with my chronic asthmatic lungs, our tennis skills did not reach any notable standard. Nevertheless, I have always appreciated sporting prowess, and my future dance activities would give me plenty of physical activity.

Attitudes

I now see my family's greatest gifts were: encouraging the spirit of enquiry, adhering to inner passions, to '*have a go,*' not to be upset by failure, and to follow one's individual chosen path. They also awakened many interests, which would give me the happiness that I could not feel in sexual relationships. Through their influence I always felt encouraged to examine the thorny questions of life and embrace one's unique individuality. It was these attributes of enquiry that would lead me to finally understand my asexual self.

Undoubtedly, it was my parents' vivacity with their personal support that sustained me through the coming years. When my heterosexual relationships did not work out, it was their encouragement in the arts and unconditional love that emotionally upheld me. Indeed, I thank my parents for giving me the ingredients for an enriched life that would serve me so well in times of isolation. The life interests awakened by my family saved me from the kind of loneliness and depression that I know other asexual people have experienced.

Following the education influences of my parents and home life, the next journal will examine those telling teenage years, where education continued away from home and when sexual development should have come to the fore.

JOURNAL 3

High School and Teenage Years

Dear Journal,
In the beginning, I approached secondary education with eager anticipation. I was to attend a city all-girls boarding school where I imagined having lots of '*jolly*' friends as described in the Enid Blyton 'schoolgirl' stories. ('*Jolly*' was Blyton's word meaning fun.) I also thought it would be the era where I might get the urge to have a boyfriend. Instead, I know this journal entry will bring back painful memories of homesickness, as in the 1950s, boarding-school life was highly regimented, severely spartan, and not at all 'jolly'! It was a time when country parents believed a British style of boarding-school education would provide a character-building independence and an experience of city living.

Boarding-School Experience

My parents also thought this experience would give me the educational advantage they had not been able to have themselves. As a result, I found myself at the age of twelve sleeping in a large dormitory of adolescent girls, with our lives dictated by a myriad of institutional rules and stern-faced teachers. It only took two days to feel dreadfully homesick, but it was not 'cool' to cry, so I muffled sad tears into my bed-pillow most nights. At the six o'clock clang of the rising bell, my stomach would be contracting into squeamish knots as I rose to face the rigid day ahead. During the long twelve-week term, the only contact I had with my parents was through lovingly descriptive letters written by my mother.

Limited Male Contact

It was an exclusively female world, and there were hardly any opportunities to have contact with the other sex. In fact, we only saw two males on a regular basis: one being the old school gardener, and the other our adored music teacher. The girls liked this teacher so much they regularly giggled in classes to get his attention, not because he was handsome, but because he was the only significant male in the whole school.

At this time, there also developed the growing realisation that I was not sexually 'in tune' with my fellow school girlfriends. Somehow, I could not share their excitement when it came to talking about boys. Although adolescence held many unspoken mysteries around sex, I approached the teen years with enthusiasm about becoming more 'grown up.' Being an adult meant you would be confident in male/female relationships – or so I thought! However, I did not feel grown up when it came to relating to the other sex.

Once a year there was an organised party with a nearby 'brother' school, and even this rare contact with boys did not give me cause for excitement. These social occasions were painfully stilted affairs where teachers selected our partners for the evening. They gave lists to the boys' school with information such as, '*Davina – short in height, quiet in manner*' – so I would become partnered with a '*Mervyn – short in height, socially shy.*' There were basic ballroom dances and games with a supper of sandwiches, biscuits, and cordial. My partners were usually shorter than me, could not dance, and our conversation was limited to comments like, 'Gee! You have cold mitts' (meaning hands).

During the final years, social parties with the boys caused more feverish excitement. Girls were particularly delighted if the boys followed the party with a Sunday visit to see their partner again, or they mailed short '*I like you*' letters, which must have taken hours to pen. The anticipation of visits or letters gave rise to giggles and whispered conversations at bedtime; including whether they were able to make physical contact during the ritual visit. Holding hands or stealing a kiss on the cheek was difficult when trying to avoid roaming teachers, whose job it was to make sure boys and girls were not sitting too close on garden benches.

Teenage Sex Discussions

In my last year, we were all approaching the age of sixteen and often discussed the phrase '*Sweet sixteen and never been kissed.*' This gave rise to conversations about petting and what kind of caressing had taken place on some of their hometown dates. The girls described lots of kissing techniques, and to me, tongue kisses did not sound at all salubrious, but I pretended they might be exciting! Up to this age, my only physical contact with boys was ballroom dancing, where they smelled of Lifesaver sweets and Brylcreem hair oil. There was also the occasional cinema date in my hometown during holidays. Such outings often entailed holding hands with a sweaty-palmed boy, which, although not enjoyable, at least gave me something to tell the girls back at school.

As for sex, there were discussions about the social crime of getting pregnant before marriage, along with the question of whether giving birth would be a painful affair. Despite having some knowledge, we were all still curious and wanted more information about human procreation. I remember my fellow students being in a high state of anticipation when our science teacher reached the Human Reproduction chapter in our textbook. We all hoped for some new sexual insights, but the lesson only entailed learning boring anatomical names for the weekly exam. In all, I did not share the excitement about sexual matters, and I only approached the topic as basic knowledge that could be useful one day.

Our school was geared to training girls to become homemakers. Therefore, one strand of the curriculum included subjects such as sewing, cooking, and domestic arts. Girls were also taught basic biology for future family health care and botany to facilitate with growing flower gardens. (Physics and chemistry subjects were only available at the boys' schools.) We also all attended a short course of 'mothercraft' lessons, where a nursing practitioner showed us how to bath a baby and fold a cloth baby-napkin. As it happened, this was the only practical knowledge I possessed when later in life, I did face motherhood. Even in 1960, there were no childcare books available, so we only had our mothers and old mothercraft school notes to guide us.

Sexual Orientations

Despite living with the closeness of other young females, the idea of sexual activity with another girl did not enter my head, and I did not even know what the term lesbian meant until well after I left school. Meanwhile, during my time in boarding school it was fashionable to have a crush on an older girl. This meant choosing a girl who had the kind of poise and style you wanted to emulate. It entailed trying to develop a bit of a friendship that only resulted in chatting to her about once a week. The chosen girl behaved as a big sister, who I think found it flattering to have the admiration of a younger girl. Certainly, there was never a hint of anything sexual about these liaisons. Of course, the rules dictated that we could not get into another girl's bed, and as the beds were so narrow, it was not even a comfortable consideration. Indeed, I am sure many people did not believe that female homosexuality even existed in those days.

What girls *did* talk about was falling in love and how you might know when it was the kind of real love that led to marriage. Nevertheless, under certain circumstances, I experienced emotional sensations of love that often felt like a warm wave of happiness. This occurred on occasions when I saw poignant films, art book illustrations, theatrical performances, or people being empathetic to each other. I did not feel great floods of affection with any boy I knew personally, although I admired male film stars if they had a good physique or expressed a kindly demeanour. I realise now that my early sensations of 'love' were never really sexual.

Passion for Theatre and Dance

One special school experience was attending the theatre where I saw my first ballet performance. It was the romantic *Sleeping Beauty* performed by the Borovansky Ballet Company in a beautiful city theatre. From that moment I felt an utter longing to be in the dance world, as I loved the musicality, the emotion, and the power of movement. I had always 'danced' in my imagination, but this reality was life-changing, making me into a total 'dance tragic.' The whole magic of the ballet and the theatre stole my heart, and from then on, I longed to be on the stage. I was in love. It was beautiful, elating. It was sensual (although not sexual). It was dance.

After seeing this performance, dancing continually occupied my daydreams. The movement and music created feelings of ecstasy; the kind that existed in the virtual world of the stage. In the final act, where the Prince kissed Sleeping Beauty, I saw him as a savior who had rescued her from death and thought the wedding represented 'The End.' Living happily ever after meant they were best friends forever, and that was that! I did not imagine him ever kissing her again, and I never considered what happened after they floated off the stage into the sunset. I am sure the normal sexual emotional, energy, and desire felt by other people was, for me, channelled into balletic dreams. Instead of sexual desire, I had a yearning to dance that gave me an inner glow and unique sense of being alive – even if it was just in my imagination.

Teenage Career Ideas

I desperately wanted to fulfil this deep passion for dance, as it held far more interest than contemplating marriage. The idea of dancing as a career was most compelling. But, having been an asthmatic child with a mild spinal scoliosis, being a ballet dancer was not a practical pursuit. Therefore, I thought I should formulate a more sensible plan. So, I decided a realistic pathway could be to care for young children by training as a preschool teacher.

Being culturally aware, I thought that *one day* I might fulfil the social norm by marrying and having children, and thus I would match the ambitions of my school girlfriends. In the 1950s, most teenage girls returned home after finishing school. Their aim was usually to refine their domestic skills and socialise within their community in search of a suitable boy to marry by the time they were twenty-one. Some young women did work, though mainly as secretaries or shop assistants, until they married or became pregnant with their first child. Despite not wanting to be different to my school friends, I craved a career path and think I wanted to 'stand out' from the crowd.

In the meantime, being a teacher would fulfil an ideal to give children opportunities for the early socialisation and confidence I had lacked as a child. Keeping in mind the events of war had limited social interactions beyond the family circle, and governments had not set up preschools. Therefore, I warmed to the idea that children of the future could have early education and social interactions, so unlike me, they would not need to invent imaginary friends.

The preschool teaching goal and being in the workforce meant coping with further training in the city. Although I missed my parents and home terribly during the boarding-school years, I knew I was not interested in home-domestics and preparations for marriage. For me, the stirrings of personal ambition far outweighed looking for the right young man. However, despite feeling satisfied about my teaching idea, I still harboured that desperate desire to be a dancer or somehow be engaged in the theatre.

Objection to the Theatre

To my regret, in a career-interview I told the school chaplain about my professional ambitions, including the possibility of becoming either a ballet dancer or a preschool teacher. Being a conservative Methodist, religious man, he was aghast by my dance/theatre aspirations and stressed I should *only* aim for childcare. In fact, he even insisted on a second interview to enforce that I should disband any ideas of dance or the theatre as a career. He said something like... '*There are not very nice types of people in the theatre world.*' Whether he had visions of sexy, high-kicking girls in fishnet stockings I will never know. But, I was annoyed by his attitude, and I could not understand his thinking. This incident stood out, as it was the first time I rejected an opinion of a person who held authority. Fortunately, my parents were sympathetic, stressing that he was a '*fuddy-duddy,*' meaning he was conservative and old-fashioned. Nevertheless, I did not have the physical attributes for becoming a dancer – especially without any early physical training to prepare my body – so preschool teaching appeared to be the most sensible choice.

Social Belonging

With hindsight, I can understand how lack of any sexual desire helped my development towards a career rather than marriage. At the time, I also wanted to be popular and felt the need to belong to my social peer group. Nevertheless, I also wanted to follow my own artistic dreams, and this inner tension was to lead me into similar decision-making struggles throughout life. Therefore, it was always going to be an effort to remain true to my unique self.

The internal dilemma about my future was a mixture of how to be in accord with my teenage friends and how to become a dancer or a teacher, while sensing that I still wanted to somehow become a star or hero. By being a star, I do not mean the type that would be constantly in the media, but rather one who was admired by the public or colleagues. I also fantasised about being a special agent spying against the enemy, or a superwoman character who solved mysteries and rescued people. At the time, my favourite radio drama series, *The Blackburn Adventurers*, featured a husband-and-wife detective team. In the story, Jeffrey and Elizabeth Blackburn never had time for love, and they were always climbing through darkened windows or crawling under hedges in pursuit of the bad guys.[10]

A Summary of My 16-Year-Old Self

On the surface, I was an outwardly quiet, not very fit young girl, who dreamed of dancing and imagined being a strong leader of something. I think there has always been that streak of 'maleness' causing me to want to show courage, resilience, or be a rescuer who could solve mysteries. Categorically, I was not interested in boys in a sexual way, but I did want to emulate the aspirations of my friends. Most importantly, I wanted to be loved – because deep down I could not believe I was intelligent or attractive enough to anyone other than my parents. At this stage, embarking on a career was uppermost in

---

[10] With no television in the 1950s, radio plays were addictive listening for most people. The *Blackburn* plays were based on the novels of Adelaide writer, Max Afford, and featured excellent radio actors.

my mind. In my case, *'sweet sixteen and never been kissed'* was quite true.

First 'Life Crisis'

Although I did not dismiss marriage, as even at sixteen, arriving at the marriageable age of twenty-one seemed to be far away in the distance. Besides, when I was in the last term of school, I experienced a health disaster that was to reshape my career goals. It only took one unexpected viral infection for me to totally reassess the future. Despite being shy and timid, after becoming quite sick, I was to eventually find a new strength to follow a pathway towards my more artistic leanings.

My final months at school were quite dramatic, as what began as a mild sore throat, developed into a prolonged illness. It was just four weeks before my final exams when the illness morphed into fever with a dreadful hacking cough. Indeed, it was upsetting to feel so bronchially sick again, as in that year, I had enjoyed reasonably good health. Therefore, it was depressing to be wheezing and coughing – yet again! Also, I was frustrated to be ill during this vital final examination time, so I tried to pretend to be okay. Eventually, I found myself admitted to isolation in the 'sickroom' although the school doctor insisted I would quickly recover. This did not happen as the fevers and severe coughing continued.

The day before my English public exam, the school principal visited my 'sickroom,' telling me I needed to *'pull myself together'* and get to the appointed venue to sit for this all-important assessment. She also suggested my nerves were causing me to *'malinger,'* meaning I was using illness to avoid exam stress. I realised the English exam was critical, because obtaining the final school certificate relied on a pass in this subject. Also, in those days, examiners used assessments that depended on *only* final examination results, and marks gained throughout the year were not counted. Indeed, I needed this *'leaving certificate'* for entry into the preschool training college, so I was anxious to qualify. Naturally, I made every effort to obey the school principal and was ashamed by her insinuation that I was shirking or malingering.

The exam was a disaster. In those days, public examinations conducted by the state education department were held in huge public venues, such as in the cavernous city Showground Pavilions. Here, examination authorities assembled students from all schools in one place. As there were over a thousand students, searching for your given student allocation number on the tiny folding desks was a nightmare. It was here my coughing echoed throughout the huge examination hall, and after vomiting over the exam paper, the adjudicators removed me from the venue and called a taxi to return me to school. The taxi driver only reluctantly agreed to take me in case I threw up in his vehicle. At the time, this whole episode felt like a shameful catastrophe.

Meanwhile, my parents had been blissfully unaware I was ill, as they were not told because the doctor continually stated that I would soon recover. Because I was ashamed and thought I had somehow brought the illness on myself, I did not tell them either. After my fellow students secretly alerted my parents about my condition, they promptly removed me from school. These days, I think they might have litigated against the school's lack of care. What followed was six miserable months of slow recovery after other doctors diagnosed me with whooping cough and double pneumonia. Although I had received immunisation against basic diseases, in the 1950s, health authorities did not consider extra booster injections were necessary.

I was pleased to leave the institutionalised environment of boarding school where lack of medical attention meant I had left under negative circumstances. Despite being ill, I still felt an academic failure by not passing the required exams. Also, I was depressed by not being able to plan for the future until my health became stabilised. In retrospect, I am sure this dramatic episode inspired a more resilient side of my personality. Also, coping with this calamity eventually led me to follow my true ambitions, and so it became the first lesson in learning how to find meaning in the darker episodes of life.

Reflection

The Decisive Moments in Life

Recalling my school illness made me think about pivotal moments in life. Being sick at a crucial time created my first life crisis that was to lead me to make a serious life decision; one which had not come through any persuasion from teachers or parents.

During a long recovery, I had the opportunity for some soul-searching, and so I developed the courage to step into a risky unknown career path of classical ballet. In the process, I gathered support from parents and family, whose '*why not have a go*' attitudes were positive and encouraging. Fortunately, it was not the desperate kind of crisis that needed help from a psychologist, so the situation was not beyond my ability to cope.

I like the concept of the 1998 romantic/drama movie *Sliding Doors*, where the doors of a train slide open, creating the possibility for two stories to unfold.[11] In the first, the main character enters the train, and her life takes a certain direction with the events that follow. The second storyline recounts the *other* life she would have experienced by *not* going through those sliding doors at that

---

[11] *Sliding Doors*: a 1998 movie starring Gwyneth Paltrow, written and directed by Peter Howitt.

moment. This movie plot now reminds me of my own life, with specific decisions made at those 'crossroads' instances where I faced an alternative life-pathway. The school health disaster was to create one of those occasions when I found the willpower to make one of those 'sliding doors' type of choices.

Years later, when I came across the 'crisis counselling' topic in one of my university courses, the first thing I learned was that a crisis presents both danger and opportunity. I can well remember the cover of my textbook depicting two Chinese symbols which meant just that – *'danger and hope.'* It is like the often-quoted idea of *'a crack is where the light comes in,'* as found in the poetry of the Persian poet, Rumi, or the song lyrics of Leonard Cohen.

In my situation, I had two choices. The first choice was to wallow in the disappointment of a failed exam and consider *not* following through with any career ideas. The second choice was to take a risk and follow the almost impossible option of entering the dance world. It seemed to be an exciting idea, despite knowing that some people would question my wisdom. Even then, I instinctively knew the riskiest path might bring far more opportunity for personal satisfaction.

With hindsight, I can analyse now why even a mini crisis can occur for quite complex reasons. In my case, life decisions after finishing school created a dilemma on three levels.[12]

1. It was *developmental* – occurring just after the school years, which is the normal teenage time for change and when there are dramatic shifts in life.
2. It was *situational* – meaning that it happened as the result of sudden illness that was unexpected and out of the normal.

---

[12] Website about types of crises – https://www.verywellmind.com/what-is-a-crisis.

3. It was *existential* by creating an inner conflict – meaning, if I wanted to seriously consider a career in dance, then I had only a small window of opportunity to train my body while I was still young, so it seemed to be a 'now or never' kind of decision.

I knew when making life decisions that answers are not easy to find. Hence, I was lucky in having a sabbatical healing time to gather my thoughts. Then, as new plans took shape, the future began to look exciting, and I even began to feel adventurous. In retrospect, I am amazed by my 16-year-old ability to design a blueprint and make bold decisions. On the other hand, it is a part of normal teenage development to undertake challenging risks. I was also emotionally moving away from my parents and immediate peer group, with a sense of growing independence.

Therefore, I became resolute in joining the unknown world of dance, instead of continuing the more sensible approach into early-childhood education. Naturally, these career proposals fed the teenage ego of wanting to be a competent adult, but it was a gamble considering I had little stamina to undertake strenuous balletic type of training. However, with this urging passion, I was prepared to face grueling dance courses and move away from home once again. Besides, I reasoned that such intensive physical exercise would at least restore my health.

With the craving to dance and a defiance to show others I could do something exceptional, I was able to muster some spirit of courage. Although I wished to emulate the marital happiness of my parents, I also wanted to model their 'can do' attitudes and endeavor to fulfil my own ambitions. It was my mother who reminded me of her expressed goals to be a businessperson, author, or dancer, while never giving herself permission to follow any of those aspirations.

Besides, in her era, few women dared to put other interests before wifely duties, but she wanted me to be different.

Later in life, similar crossroad situations would occur. For example, when I started my own dance school, dealt with two divorces, and moved to live in different cities. Or again, when I left my beloved teaching to become a full-time carer for my elderly parents. Therefore, this first crisis became an important teacher for my forthcoming journeys that would have all those elements of angst, risk, and confidence of hope.

The Positivity of a Crisis

Throughout life, I have been surprised how a critical turning-point situation can clear the way for a better future. At the time, it can feel devastating, then years later, seen as a blessing. Mind you, I have always tended to go into the *'eye of the storm'* – meaning I try to get to the core of a problem to move myself out of pain into a new direction. This may sound brave, but it is only self-preservation in the knowledge that self-medicating or hiding can only prolong the suffering. I also like *action*, as doing something has always felt better than doing nothing. As they say, *'go through fire and water'* to face danger, or in yoga where you *'breathe through the pain.'*

Global Crisis

I digress, to mention that currently, the whole planet is in crisis where everyone is coping with an unknown dangerous virus, climate change, and results of war. But it is an opportunity for the world to unite in a co-operative way to create a positive 'new normality.'

In my country, it was a change to see our politicians try to work in a more bipartisan way when dealing with Covid. They began to consult experts, amend plans, and strove to communicate honestly. Despite this temporary improvement, there is still the fight to balance the dictates of public health, the economy, social inequality, and freedom of choice.

Consequently, in the face of a global situation, I can only adjust my activities to deal with the health and environmental challenges with thoughtful care and hope everyone else does the same. I now am getting used to dealing with uncertainties and crises both large and small.

As a summary of this reflection, I am grateful I was presented with a life dilemma at an early age. I had to listen to the dictates of both my head and heart to find new and unconventional pathways towards what felt like an exciting future. It also gave me the courage to enter my dancing days, which I explore in the next journal.

JOURNAL 4

Dancing Days

Dear Journal,

Recording the following era relating to my latter teenage years will revive many good memories; despite it being a time when I did *not* advance any understanding about my sexual self. It was a period when I grew in confidence, and even now, I still wonder at my audacity in taking a career direction with absolutely no blueprint for success. However, I thought if I could not become a dancer, then maybe I could be a teacher. (The old idea if you 'can't do it, then teach it' applied here.) Indeed, I was desperate to appear adult by fulfilling a daring ambition and not to be the sickly little schoolchild anymore.

During the pneumonia episode, I remember deciding I wanted to get control of my physical health. I did not want doctors to examine me anymore or be a continual problem for my parents. The slow recovery gave me valuable space to think and formulate my own personal report card and career goals. It went something like this...

Body report:
Bad: No strength, curved spine, slightly deformed toe on left foot, not flexible, and breathing a bit shallow.
Good: Not overweight, flat-chested, well-shaped legs, feet with high arches – all being good attributes for dance.
Goals: Ballet lessons fortnightly in the city to improve health and which would be 'therapeutic' after chronic illness.
Visit podiatrist for feet and minor toe deformity.
Career ideas:

Enroll in a correspondence course in English, sit again for a public exam, then reapply for the preschool-teacher training course.

Try to train in dance/drama full-time by enrolling in a city dance studio, then aim to teach dance to little children. (Teaching in a country region where children did not have access to this kind of dance instruction.)

Conclusion:

Aim for the second career idea, as it would fulfil both the dance and teaching desires. Despite an imperfect body and late start in training, if I were not good enough to be a dancer at least I could teach!

Dance/Drama Education Begins

My understanding parents went along with the dance plan, as they were happy to see their physically weakened daughter show new eagerness for life. I selected a reputable city dance teacher, and to my delight she was willing to take me on, even when my only visible attribute was abundant enthusiasm. I was most fortunate in my choice of a professional dance instructor. She had dedicated much of her work in using creative movement to promote health in disabled children and was renowned for her dance therapy with recovering poliomyelitis patients. I believed her when she said that under her tuition, '*You will have a healthy, strong body in two years*' – and she was right! This woman with the ramrod straight back became my first dance guide and mentor. In the meantime, I did not bother to try to repeat the failed English exam.

The philosophy of the dance studio was to acquaint students with all aspects of art, music, drama, and theatre. There were also a variety of teachers, directors, and artists who visited and worked in what was a combination of a teaching studio and performance theatre; so my education was not just in dance alone. This time, it was emotionally easier to be away from home to live with a kindly elderly couple and begin intensive full-time dance tuition.

In the meantime, I gained certain attention in my hometown by pursuing this kind of creative career. When the parents in the local community found I was training to become a dance teacher, they begged me to instruct their daughters. This encouraged me to propose a future idea of opening a private school to teach dance and drama in my hometown country area, and where I knew children were eager to have access to these theatrical art forms.

Fortunately, my teachers were supportive and recognised I was enthusiastic in achieving such a goal. They decided I should also work as an assistant in the theatre/dance school to gain extra teaching and business/administrative experience. Therefore, my education included theatre management, stage makeup, costuming, stage direction, lighting/set design, dance history, choreography, and working in the studio administration office. Now, with a true sense of purpose, I began to train with utter dedication to be the best teacher possible.

Dear Journal, although the dance/theatre school did not lead to romance with any males, it took me into a world that fully engaged emotions and demanded strict attention to the physicality of the body. The dancing training suited my asexuality, where any idea of searching to be loved dissolved into the delight of using my body in a new and creative way. Moving to the music generated an emotional outlet that was both rewarding and uplifting.

Then again, the training also strengthened personal resilience and acceptance of my own body. In all, this career move created a total physical and mental make-over – although it did not advance any conscious sexual enlightenment. Indeed, it was a unique female world where the girls dominated the stage and were not subjected to male competition. In those days, other young men often called other boys who danced '*sissies*' (girls), or worse still, '*poofters*' (homosexuals); both terms meant to be derisory and unflattering.

Female Dance World and Marriage

The dance-training aspect was my favourite part of the studies. As indicated, the earlier proponents in this art form did not fully appreciate the physical beauty of male dancers. Consequently, men were not encouraged to let their natural strength shine, except to do the heavy lifting in partnered 'pas de deux' balletic sequences. Therefore, males did not feature in the main spotlight, and I almost felt sorry for their roles as props to lift, hold, and present the female as the main star. Fortunately, this changed once the Russian dancer Rudolph Nureyev appeared on our stages with his strong technique and almost sexual presence.

I noted both my fellow male and female students spoke more about dance than serious dating. Marriage was only a vague dream at the end of their dancing lives; particularly if they expected to have children. Most teachers were unmarried women and socially accepted because of their dedicated artistic calling. My teacher openly declared that marriage and dance were never a good mix, and that for a dancer, it would be giving up her soul! Also, there was a false idea that your body could never physically return to dancing form after having a baby.

At this time, dance almost felt like a religion, and I felt spiritually dedicated to the ritual of training. Once, I remember having a dream where I was exercising at the ballet barre in the presence of a woman dressed in a nun's black habit. Her expression was telling me that dance was now demanding my utter devotion. Hence, with this image in mind, I exercised every day with convent-style discipline and felt this dream was a sign of the serious spiritual commitment required to be an achiever in the artistic world.

Dance not only promoted the attitude of acceptance of my own body, but also the self-assurance to perform in front of an audience. The other fun aspect was putting myself into acting roles, where I inhabited virtual characters and portrayed their imaginary lives. In fact, I was more comfortable becoming another person in the pretend world of the stage than being my real self. In turn, I developed a curiosity about other people and how they culturally behaved, or how they expressed themselves through their unique personalities. So, I became a discreet people-watcher, and I confess to still having this habit of observation today.

Physical Body Image

At first, my body was nowhere near the kind of instrument to use for dance demonstration as a teacher. It took weeks of practice for my back to straighten, arms to soften, the core muscles to strengthen, and for correct foot placement to occur. Drama also helped my vocal development, after years of shallow breathing and speaking in short, breathy sentences. Gradually, I began to develop greater physical balance, strength, flexibility, and stamina. My other advantages for dance were my naturally high instep, suitable body weight (although I lost about three kilos in the first six months), and fortunately, I did *not* have a well-endowed curvy female form.

Androgyny

It was a bonus to have a genderless body, as heavy-chested girls found problems with balance, costume fitting, or dancing closely with a male partner. Besides, the big-busted girls bounced in a way that was visually distracting! I still smile at Sir Robert Helpmann's unfavourable comment on nude dancing, where he declared he did not like any bits of a body moving after the music stopped! So, having an androgynous body was ideal, and that is how I wanted it to remain. I also began to enjoy the high moments when I mastered a step or achieved a new physical feat – those instances were gold. Again, this training and body ideal suited my asexual soul; not that I recognised it at the time, knowing only that I was comfortable belonging in the dancing world.

Study of Androgyny

Years later, a lecturer presented an academic paper on the topic of androgyny, expressing that it could somehow affect gendered behaviour. I found this interesting, as it reminded me of those early teen years where I always hoped to keep my 'sexless' physique. The authors wrote from the view that certain people had integrated both elements of the feminine and masculine, making them flexible in sexual expression. Thus, they had risen above the need to behave or look as either masculine or feminine. While I recognised I had an androgynous body, with a degree of male elements in my personality, I still considered myself as female in gender. The article did not refer to asexuality, but it was interesting to consider whether androgyny was a factor in defining gender expression.[13]

Nudity and Art

It is interesting to note how gender is treated in different art forms. I was fortunate that balletic art accepted the female form, compared with the women who aspired to be portrait artists. Reasons as to why women were not known or inspired to be leading artists are clearly articulated by the art historian Linda Nochlin.[14] She highlighted how social institutions and cultural education created the rules of

---

[13] This paper is from the book *Our Sexuality* (6th ed.), by R. Crooks & K. Baur (1996, Brooks/Cole Publishing), and is currently available online.
[14] See Wikipedia – American art historian Linda Nochlin (1931-2017).

feminine behaviour, including the odd idea that a woman was not capable of genius. Coupled with this thinking was the social ideal that a lady should be moderately accomplished in a wide range of domestic and artistic endeavours, rather than be brilliant in just one. Also, it was amusing to note the old attitudes to women and life-painting of the nude. In my grandmother's day, a woman could be an object of this form of art, but she could not be a creator – especially by painting a nude man.

Physical Aesthetic Appreciation

After further reading, I came across the idea that a person could be attracted *'aesthetically'* to physical bodies. Even though I feel contented with my own shapeless body, I often admire the form and features of both men and women. With men, I particularly appreciate those who have a dancer's physique. Therefore, I would call myself a *'bi-aesthetic'* when it comes to physical attraction. I also do not mind looking at aesthetically filmed sex scenes, particularly where the performance has emotional feeling and is artistically choreographed similar to partnered dance.

Even now aged over eighty, I have the same basic body shape of my teenage years, except for the natural gravitational sag in my upper arms and jawline. Also, in my early dance training, we had to eat healthy foods, which succeeded in taking away any desire for fat or sweets or any need to follow an additional diet. This means I have always been slim but never anorexic, as I aspire to have a good degree of muscle definition and strength. Recently, this has caused me to wonder if my asexuality meant food never became a substitute for lack of sex or companionship.

Touch and Nakedness

In the dance/drama world, there is naturally a lot of physical touching. Our teachers constantly put a hand on us to correct body alignment, and we dressed in tights and leotards to reveal the clear demarcation of our figures. Dressing and undressing in front of male or female fellow dancers was always for the purpose of performance. Consequently, we did not express ideas of sex or feelings of embarrassment in this kind of environment. In fact, the philosophy was to view our bodies objectively as the *'instruments'* of our art. Only once, I remember when a dance teacher muttered to a male student, *'For goodness sake, get decent underwear and dress yourself to the centre!'* thus causing him to slink out of class.

Choice of Clothing and Gender

Speaking of everyday dressing, I realise my choice of clothes has always followed a certain practical norm relating to those early dancing days. Since then, I have always liked clothing to be comfortable for movement, with small-heeled shoes for both walking and running. Also, I preferred clothes that showed my boyish shape and did not accentuate any female curves – not that I had hips or cleavage to display anyway!

At the dance studio, it was quite modern to wear black slacks as a dance-teaching uniform, despite few women ever choosing pants in the 1950s. The trouser uniform was practical for movement and gave me a certain sense of authority. The style at the time for girls included starched petticoats under full gathered skirts, with flat shoes and hair worn in a ponytail – so our long dark 'male' pants were quite a contrast. In performance on the stage, and when stepping into an imaginary role, I did not mind what costume I wore. Although my size made me suitable for feminine roles, choreographers often asked me to perform the stronger, sometimes male, dramatic parts. Somehow, I had the emotional flexibility to portray either strength or gentleness – so many of my costumes were not always the pretty balletic tutus!

Thinking back, I never dressed to be sexy, and I have never chosen clothes for the purpose of attracting a man. Yet, I have always wanted to suitably dress for the occasion and blend with the fashion of the day – *if* the style was acceptably comfortable. For example, a tight-fitting pencil skirt and high heels would never be my wardrobe choice. However, I did wear shorter skirts with high boots in the late 1960s, and in the 1970s, I wore the loose caftan dresses, while avoiding the horrible cork platform shoes.

Social Life During the Dance/Theatre Training Era

Because of training demands at ballet school, I had little social time other than attending orchestral concerts or ballet, opera, and drama performances. However, there was an element of social interaction with male members of the city orchestra. A couple of my dance colleagues always insisted we sat in the front row of the concert hall, so they could have eye contact with the younger musicians. Eventually, after becoming known as regular fans, we received invitations to join the young oboe and viola players after the performance.

The girls and I took delight in joining these young men for late-night coffee at a roadhouse (a petrol service station). In 1955, these newly opened service stations were one of the few places still open after 11:30 p.m. I thought it was most sophisticated to meet with professional musicians and loved the conversations which focused on their devotion to music, just as mine was to dance. To me, it was all very brotherly, and I was in awe of the level of musicianship that had enabled them to join a renowned orchestra. No way did I see them as boyfriends, but I am sure my dancing colleagues did harbour such fantasies.

On one occasion, I stayed for the weekend with one of my fellow dancers. She had a brother who invited me to join him to search for mushrooms in a nearby wood. At one point, much to my astonishment, he made a clumsy attempt to kiss me. My reaction was to jerk away and ask what he was doing. I could not see what had instigated this emotional move, and I certainly did not read the signs of his attraction. He was my friend's brother, so I treated him as if he were my brother too. The incident bothered me, as I reacted in a prudish manner and wondered why I did not feel flattered as other girls might have been.

Whenever I went back to my hometown for holidays, I attended local dances, and only to please my parents, I was a reluctant debutant at an Old Scholar's Ball. On this occasion, I did not have a boyfriend to partner me, so I selected a cousin to fill the role. Although I liked ballroom dancing and found it quite easy, I did not like dancing with the young male partners. It was always an uneasy experience, as I was not excited by their close physical proximity, and I could tell they were not comfortable dancing with me. Most young lads appeared embarrassed by their lack of technique, and it seemed by their constant apologies, my known dance training was intimidating for them. Therefore, I desperately tried to make my partners feel at ease by adjusting to their awkward moves to make them look proficient. Despite my valiant efforts, making progress around the ballroom floor was always an agonising effort. On these occasions I preferred to be a 'wall flower' to escape the boredom of pretending to enjoy myself with self-conscious male partners.

Even with the discomfort of social life, my main delight was being involved in the theatre. During this era, I began to feel more at ease with myself, as the only things that mattered were improving my dance technique and teaching young children to the best of my ability. I was certain this was an excellent career choice, and I knew it was the beginning of a good working life.

To summarise, my time training at the dance studio in the 1950s was a comfortable place for an asexual person like me. Why? Because it was all about the physical body and dance – not sex. Conversely, there was a part of dance technique that did have a natural sexual element I recognised as pleasurable without realising it was a type of masturbation. I will explain my thought on this natural phenomenon in the following reflection.

Reflection

Masturbation

When journal writing about my dance-training days, I realised a unique physical sensation often occurred during the exercise regimes. Years later, I realised this muscular reaction was sex-related and a form of masturbation.

'Core-Orgasm'

During dance classes, I found certain abdominal exercises could create a type of orgasmic reaction. For years, I did not know this experience had a name, but I was aware of the feeling and knew when it occurred. With the use of strong core stomach muscles, I could induce a vague 'good' physical feeling through a downward contraction of the abdomen. It was pleasant, and I interpreted the sensation as stemming from the emotional thrill of performing dance movements to music. It was much later I learned this phenomenon had something to do with a natural physical sexual response.

The 'Core-gasm' Discovery

It was only a couple of years ago I came across the word *'core-gasm'* when thumbing through a women's health magazine. The main article was about exercise and sex, with the heading *'How to Core-gasm.'* Immediately, I became curious and wondered what the word 'core-gasm' really meant. I read on with amazement, as it described the exact sensation I experienced when contracting my core pelvic floor muscles. I understood it was a normal physical and neurological reaction and not just emotional. Naturally, I had not formerly equated this type of physical occurrence with sexual arousal; only that it was a nice feeling. On the other hand, research has suggested that regular exercise kindles those good brain-boosting chemicals, which is why dance and stimulating exercise could be a probable substitute for sex.

Internet research also confirmed the existence of this kind of orgasm. Here it explained that a 'core-gasm' can cause a deep muscular sensation resulting in a noticeably pleasant physical reaction. It reported that women with sensitive nerve endings and strong core muscles can often achieve this kind of physical buzz. To me, it is not the dramatic orgasm as portrayed in movies, but nevertheless a quite satisfyingly nice experience. Further reading on the topic of masturbation showed that women can even achieve self-stimulation by crossing their legs, clenching their muscles, and causing pressure on the genital region. A brilliant advantage of this type of orgasm is that it is achievable in public without anyone noticing – just as women can practice their pelvic-floor exercises while waiting at a bus stop. Again, some women can reach an orgasm spontaneously by the power of their thoughts alone, although this may not qualify as masturbation without any physical stimulation. However, to me, orgasms achieved by any means (with or without sexual intercourse) could be defined as a type of masturbation.

In these days of acronyms, a core-gasm is known as an E.I.O. (exercise-induced orgasm), or as E.I.S.P. (exercise-induced sexual pleasure). However, for an asexual like me, a core-gasm is just a good physical sensation rather than anything to do with sexual desire. Interestingly, the 1953 Kingsley report also included women mentioning a type of sexual feeling in relation to muscle movement contraction. Medical sources also reveal that increased blood flow caused by exercise can create a vaginal orgasm, along with an increase of the feel-good endorphins. The Kegel contraction exercises recommended to strengthen the pelvic floor can also have the same effect.[15]

Childhood Masturbation

Even as a child, another strange type of masturbation occurred without any sexual connotation. Because I had trouble breathing properly at night, I used to place clenched hands between crossed legs, squeezing my leg and stomach muscles – a sensation resulting in my breath becoming more even. ('Breathing out' or exhalation was always the main difficulty when experiencing bronchial asthmatic spasms.) Somehow, the practice helped me hold my breath longer than normal, thus enabling me to exhale more easily. Therefore, I treated this activity as a way of relieving physical discomfort, and now I suspect this ritual was also a form of masturbation. When my health improved during puberty, this behaviour just faded away. Even throughout my teenage years at boarding school, where girls talked about boys and sex, I do not remember any mention of masturbation.

In childhood, no adult ever openly mentioned masturbation to me. Only once my aunt declared children should not lie around in bed, as it could encourage them 'to play with themselves'. I did not have a clue what she meant, and I thought it referred to being lazy and reading in bed as was my custom. Later, I came to realise that touching yourself in private places, even to satisfy an itch, was not preferable behaviour. Certainly, I never equated masturbation with love or sex, and I considered it just as a vaguely pleasant bodily

---

[15] Step-by-step guide to performing Kegel exercises – www.health.harvard.edu

function. I have also both despaired and laughed at the ridiculous myths that abounded around masturbation, including that it could cause infertility, hair loss, mental illness, physical weakness, and blindness.

Masturbation and Asexuality

I found it interesting to read what other asexuals expressed about masturbation. A few asexual folks do engage in and enjoy masturbation, and yet they still do not want partnered sex. Like all human diversity, some asexuals will do it, while others do not. The human body has obviously developed to have sexually aroused reactions, so it is only normal that the body behaves in a sexual way whether you want it to or not. I read, too, that a few asexuals treat masturbation as just an annoying physical thing and become irritated by having to waste time to deal with it. They often used phrases such as '*an itch you had to scratch*,' or they claimed that masturbation was '*like a good sneeze*.' Some referred to the practice as '*using the restroom*' or '*cleaning out the plumbing*,' with the latter being specifically for males. For others, it was an oddly satisfying physical function, while some thought it was a nuisance. In most cases, this practice never inspires sexual fantasies and does not seem to awaken any desire for actual sex with a partner. If asexuals do masturbate, then I believe it is for physical satisfaction and without imagining being with another person.

Study on Gender Attitudes Towards Masturbation

In a university course, I read a discourse on the topic of masturbation relating to the different attitudes of men and women. It reported that men were comfortable about masturbation and could talk openly about it in a variety of colourful terms. Women, on the other hand, were not always accustomed to discussing what they did with their hands for private pleasure. The author suggested that women held a strong 'love bond' with their mothers in a way that did *not* equate with sexual independence. However, men were able to love their mothers but still masturbate without guilt, thus being able to more easily separate sex from love. In marriage, it suggested that if a man breaks unconditional trust and looks at another woman, the wife can feel enraged because she expected the same 'love deal' she had with her mother. This analysis seemed complicated, but it raised the notion that love and sex could be separate.[16]

Masturbation and Sex

After reading more about how to induce one's sexuality, I felt guilty about not exploring masturbation properly as a gateway to sexual experience. I questioned myself as to why I had not used this practice to develop my own sexual appetite. Sex, according to the literature, was the fuel and energy of life, with masturbation being a practice that could help towards becoming a fulfilled sexual being. Besides, it was supposed to be good for tension relief, an aid to sleep, and could help in creating a calmer mood.

At one stage, I even hoped masturbation would awaken the sexual appetite I obviously lacked. Once, as part of a study assignment, we had to purchase something from a sex shop, so I bought a boring plastic vibrator. Such experimentation with this aid was short-lived, as sadly, I would just fall asleep on the job or forget it was in the drawer. Eventually I decided this electric toy made a great foot massager, so it was repurposed until the batteries ran out and then discarded in the rubbish bin.

Sexual Satisfaction and Dance

I delighted in having physical control over my body and the ability to move with energy and stamina. In the process, there were some

---

[16] Reading from *Women on Top* by Nancy Friday (1991, Hutchinson).

pleasant emotional states in addition to the previously described 'core-gasm.' As runners get a high, I used to get the same feeling after a good dance class or successful theatre performance. In fact, I can clearly remember one male dancer declaring that *'dance was better than sex.'*

During the act of an exhilarating dance performance, I like to think chemical reactions occur which relate to the emotional states experienced in the body. When dancing, one is totally 'in the moment,' so nothing else seems to exist other than the all-embracing feeling of emotion and physical musicality. Therefore, I believe dance can create a special kind of euphoria, where there is a sense of surrendering and 'giving' your body to the art. It is certainly something I have experienced, and what I interpret as a 'virtual libido-love' sensation. For me, dance always created elements of the spiritual/sexual, along with physical sensations that elevate feelings of being joyously alive.

JOURNAL 5

Socialising and a Boyfriend

Dear Journal,

I began my working life with a profound sense of achievement having completed three years of rigorous dance training. It was also when I began to feel socially more self-confident and, after a time, even managed to have a boyfriend!

Returning to my regional hometown had been challenging with the excitement of opening my own dance school. Plus, I felt proud of my efforts to organise a business venture at the youthful age of eighteen. Meanwhile, I regularly travelled to the city so I could continue to further advance my theatre and ballet education. The local arts community and my parents were most supportive, and it was rewarding to have a career that brought an extra artistic focus into my home district. Certainly, I was no longer the sickly girl who felt she had been a failure in so many ways.

Indeed, my theatrical training had given me a real sense of self-esteem and having a unique place in the world. Also, I was full of youthful passion about fostering the love of dance in young children. It was gratifying to give students an opportunity for this type of tuition at an early age, as in the past, country children had no access to professional dance or drama instruction. My students were enthusiastic, and I delighted in their progress, so it was easy to dedicate myself to this work. However, from the beginning, I was *not* comfortable in negotiating the local social life with people of my own age.

Social Acceptance

Although I had the respect of the community, I did not feel fully at ease with other young women. All the girls I knew were talented in the kitchen, highly domesticated, had boyfriends, and enjoyed the local sporting activities. I did not mind being a bit artistically atypical, but I also wanted friends and to feel socially acceptable. Therefore, I attended local dances, tried to play tennis (badly), and joined youth groups. In a great effort, I even tried to learn to bake 'good' country food such as sponge cakes, scones, and pastries, despite my savoury tooth not relishing the idea of eating them.

Part of me had a desire to behave like other girls, which meant engaging in the subtle search for a husband. In the fifties, an unmarried lady was often known as an '*old maid*' or '*spinster*' who had been unable to attract a husband. I noted that all the other young women my age had a prospective husband in sight and were soon wearing engagement rings. All their excitement and conversations cantered on weddings and buying linen or kitchen items for their future homes. They did not discuss sexual matters, as sex was not supposed to happen until after the wedding. (I guess this was why we wore virginal white wedding gowns and had honeymoons.) The other motivation for couples to marry was probably so their sex lives could begin!

Any pregnancy before marriage was a social transgression. Even if a couple conceived during the honeymoon, there were always people counting the months to check if they had 'done it' (intercourse) before the wedding. Unexpected pregnancies before marriage caused great distress, and I know such occurrences often sadly resulted in attempted suicides and abortions. Girls sometimes disappeared for a 'long holiday' to visit a distant relative, only to return after a couple of months looking very pale and unrefreshed by their 'holiday.'

Although I was not interested in any sexual interactions, part of me worried about being a single young woman in a country town. Also, I had the vague dream of marriage, along with a husband and children who all adored me. Meanwhile, I felt an awkwardness with boys, and I just wished I could have fun conversations with them rather than the usual exchange of stilted sentences. Up till now, I had been living closely with my mother, attended a girls' boarding school, and engaged in a female theatre/dance world. Therefore, I had existed in a mostly feminine environment, and I was curious to know what boys thought about their lives. I wanted real friendships with them, and to experience something akin to genuine male affection.

My brother was four years younger, and we were apart for six years with separate boarding-school experiences that did not coincide. Therefore, we did not share the same friends or interests. Although boys were a mystery to me, I saw enough of my father to know he was the most important male in my life. I imagined that if I married, it would be to someone who could make me laugh like my dad.

The First Boyfriend and Courtship

Dear Journal, relating this part of my life now seems quite bizarre, as it highlights my considerable lack of self-understanding and my concern with wanting to conform to prevailing attitudes of the time. But, after attending local dances, one young man seemed quite confident to dance with me.

He was friendly, with a seemingly jovial disposition, and could manage to hold a reasonable conversation. It was flattering to have someone other than my family members treat me as being interesting and loveable. He had come from another state to work on a local development project, and being seven years older than me, I saw him as a sophisticated man of the world. So, I allowed him to become my regular boyfriend and liked the fact that I felt more socially acceptable with a man on my arm. This desire to fit in was at odds with my wanting to be an arty singular type of person, rather than a domestic stay-at-home spouse. At this time, belonging to my peer group was just as important, and I harboured the idea that I could somehow continue dance teaching into the future; not that it was normal for wives to work in those days.

After fourteen months, I vaguely thought that an engagement would follow as he hinted about marriage. I knew a former broken relationship had hurt him, and I hoped a future with me would bring him new happiness. I liked him in an affectionate way, and we always held hands and kissed good night after an outing. On odd occasions, I tried to imagine having sex with him but thought it was something that would miraculously 'sort out' if we ever married.

When he did propose marriage, I decided to accept, thinking no one else would ever find an androgynous dance teacher to be attractive. Besides, we had a comfortable friendship, and being engaged to be married meant I could belong in the happy world of young couples. I also believed that married life would somehow create the fortunate state I saw my parents enjoy. Then there was the 'rescuer' part of my personality, and I was pleased to think our relationship had mended his formerly broken heart. In fact, I enjoyed this engagement era, as it was all about social outings with other couples, and sex was still not a serious consideration.

Choice of Wife in the 1950s

After our engagement announcement, I was dumbfounded by the number of young men who told me they were disappointed, because they had secretly viewed me as a prospective wife. I asked why they had not revealed their real interest towards me on past social occasions. Their answer amazed me, saying they wanted to have fun before approaching a girl they highly admired. It was a matter of being in a state of 'readiness' before they chose a prospective wife to be the future mother of their children. So, without knowing, I had been on the potential wife list!

Since, I have wondered how many marriage proposals have come from this pragmatic view of who would make a good wife, mother, and supporter of the husband's work. In the 1950s, some young men must have explored relationships, not just because of sexual attraction (as my grandfather often said, *'sowing their wild oats'*), but also for status and social respectability. Despite being asexual, I feel marriage choices made from this kind of rational point of view without any real passion could be in danger of becoming boring, lacklustre partnerships.

The Marriage Decision

I believe my lack of confidence about male/female relationships contributed to me accepting a marriage proposal from my first boyfriend. There was also the idea that marriage would surely dissolve my lack of sexual interest, and it would give me someone to love who, in turn, would love me. I also harboured the fear that he would feel hurt if I said, 'No,' or hesitated. Then again, perhaps I accepted this proposal because I believed no one else would ever ask me. Anyway, for whatever reason, I said, '*Yes*'!

With an engagement ring on my finger, I did begin to think about sex, but I still thought the honeymoon would miraculously stimulate and 'turn on' sexual excitement. I was sure it would be like learning to swim or ride a bike, so that once you had experienced intercourse, all would be well. Nevertheless, I believed prior sexual research would be necessary, and so I decided to look for a book about marital sex and birth control.

In the meantime, I was pleased to be lining up for the altar at the 'right' age of twenty-one. My future husband also seemed pleased by reassuring me that I was a 'good catch'! I cannot believe why I thought my decision to marry was a sensible idea. At the time, I was not sure whether having a close friendship and being in love were the same thing. Besides, I obviously had little relevant knowledge or understanding about sex. In addition, I did not like cooking and was unsure if I was suited to the role of being a domesticated wife. Nevertheless, I decided to seriously practice culinary skills, and I was determined to tackle all future housework with the same care and attention I gave to a theatrical production.

Above all, I knew it felt important to obey the cultural/social norms of the day. Consequently, reviewing this marriage decision has made me think about the power of these norms and effects of the prevailing culture.

♥

Reflection

The Power of Culture

Sociology

As a mature-aged university student, I can still remember my first sociology lecture. I knew nothing about the subject, nor had I ever given a thought as to the societal or cultural influences on our everyday lives. After a term of lectures, I soon realised how systems of social norms and hierarchical structures continually guided our decisions and behaviour. The unspoken expectations of my family, the influence of single-sex schooling, peer groups, dance training, and ideals of my local home community had all exerted far more sway on my life than I realised. Most importantly, social transmission of how to behave as a female happened without much awareness on my behalf.

Culture of the 1950s

Cultural and social factors in the fifties had its own unique effect on how people conducted their lives. Girls tended to live in the parental home until marriage in their early twenties. After marriage, it was normal for children to arrive within a couple of years, making childcare and housework a main part of the woman's role. Men were the financial providers and head of the family, with married women living under the formal title of taking the husband's surname. Even postal letters would be addressed as Mrs. John Smith, rather than using her given first name. If women did work, choices were to become a nurse, teacher, shop-assistant, telephonist, or secretary. After marriage, our government mandated that women were to leave the public workforce, and if female teachers wanted to marry, they had to resign according to the rules of the state Education Department.

At the time, Australian society tended to follow the UK in approach to patriotism, education, and style of government. It was after the Second World War, the advent of the contraceptive pill, European immigration, television, youth music, and the culture of the USA that Australian views began to change. Also, society viewed the family unit of mother, father, and at least two children as an almost sacred ideal. In addition, sex was a conservative topic, gender differences not tolerated, and homosexuality was illegal. Therefore, it is not surprising these social and cultural factors had an impact on how I thought I should conduct my own life.

Social and Cultural Influences

Through study of sociology, I began to learn basic definitions about the social/cultural elements and what is meant by beliefs and values.

- o Social impacts – meaning the effects of influences from sources such as family, religion, current economics, media, and artistic expression.
- o Cultural influences – being the basic beliefs, attitudes, and values that guide personal decisions and conduct.
- o Beliefs – referring to *ideas* held as true that give rise to one's *attitudes* and opinions.
- o Values – were defined as the important *behavioural ideals* that govern the way one acts and communicates.

It took some serious thinking to understand what *ideas, attitudes,* and *values* really meant, as I had previously used them interchangeably without much thought. Through sociological research, I came to see how the social/cultural climate shaped my beliefs, defined how I saw myself, and informed my sense of belonging in the community.[17] It also confirmed why I had needed acceptance and to feel equal with other people. Therefore, it was my beliefs and outlook on the world that guided my actions and behaviour. In turn, this related to my approach to child rearing, relationships, artistic tastes, and dress fashion in everyday life. But it took me awhile to understand that strong cultural influences did not change my core sexual orientation.

Cultural Effects on Sexuality

As an asexual, how did cultural/social influences affect me? I am pleased my fellow young asexuals did not experience the limitations imposed by the mentality of the 1950s. No wonder in 1959, I

---

[17] Since 1974, I have found sociology enlightening, and I often dip into the readable books of sociologist Hugh MacKay, who so clearly describes our Australian way of life. His book *Generations* reiterates much of my experience of growing up in the 1940s. (*Generations: Baby Boomers, Their Parents & Their Children* by H. MacKay (1997, Pan Macmillan)).

thought I should strive to get married and have children according to social expectations. At the time, sexual ignorance and lack of self-knowledge did not alert me to any alternatives. As asexuality was unrecognised and did not have any representations in the arts or media, how was I to know or see that aspect in myself? So, I felt obliged to obey the compelling prominent social/cultural norms, along with seriously wanting to fulfil the aspirations of my family and peers. The deep need for acceptance and feeling equal to other people was incredibly powerful. Despite my artistic individuality, it was going to be a long time before I found my asexual orientation, so I stubbornly clung to the idea that I should be heterosexual.

Culture and Asexuality

Since asexuality has become named in the twenty-first century, how has this affected the younger generations of today? In my own youth, if I had obeyed my deepest inner instincts, then perhaps I would not have married at all. Ignorance led me into pathways where I suffered from unwise decisions that I can never completely regret. For example, I am grateful to have undergone the joy of raising my own child, delighted in grandchildren, and now, even great-grandchildren. Then, there would be other rewarding experiences, such as when a second marriage led me into the adventure of living in another city. Finally, I learned valuable lessons from my failed relationships and attempted marriages. How? All attempts to share life closely with someone else has helped to redefine my values and gradually taught me about myself. In particular, I learnt that I could engineer change when parts of my life became intolerable.

But, what of today where culture is more willing to promote sexual differences? Would I fear loneliness or isolation, and would I be sad in the knowledge that I did not fit into a sexual majority? For young asexual people these days, I suspect they can feel dejected about belonging to a small sexual minority and be anxious in their search for satisfying relationships.

As social and cultural understandings have changed, it is now permissible for me to have a different sexual orientation and to have an atypical lifestyle. Such changes of acceptance in the social climate offer some relief, as these days, I would *not* feel obliged to be married or feel pressure to have sex. At last, I know there are other ways to be loved and to experience a fulfilled life. That is why I live happily alone, still take dance classes, write, take courses in various subjects, care for people in need, and avoid baking cakes. In fact, I often think the present ideals of marriage should be re-examined along with a redefinition of what constitutes a family. Here, I mean a family as created with loving parental-type relationships and not just biological parents.

In Australia, I like to think we have reaped the rewards of social benefits – including a greater acceptance of sexual orientations. I have grown to be more flexible in my thinking in matters of gender and sexuality, and now I feel resilient to any criticisms of my own beliefs. This also means I am not worried about the appearance of being odd or queer. At least in present our Australian society, one is free to carve out a unique way of living if you are creative and have the courage to be different.

It was better to become my authentic self rather than pretend to be something I was not by trying to be socially acceptable. What do I mean by authentic self? I think the true self where my *outer* behaviour is in harmony with the authentic *inner* me. That means having candid thoughts, feelings, and behaviour that does not bring fear of shame or criticism. So, for the younger asexuals, I hope they can find their own unique path and harmonious place in the world. As Carl Jung said, '*The privilege of a lifetime is to become who you truly are.*'

Asexual Recognition in Society

Asexual orientation belongs to the brilliant myriad of variances that make our animal kingdom so successful. As humans, I like to believe we have evolved so well on this planet due to human diversity – including the positive role that minority gender identities can bring. However, society has not always understood or applauded diverse sexual orientations for the contribution they can make to the lives of others. Let us hope our culture will not just recognise asexuality but see how a degree of asexuality in a society is both acceptable and beneficial. I am sure asexuals can devote extra valuable time and ability to their professions and community groups, enabling them to advocate for many people beyond their immediate family and friends.

Just as the feminist sociology is still addressing the lack of power and inequality experienced by women, I hope more public awareness will aid basic human equalities lacking in the LGBTIQA+ world. Also, I wish the present ideal of lifelong marriage could become more flexible as the notions of *'till death us do part'* and *'for better or for worse'* are often so unrealistic. That a person can fulfil the promise to be an intimate friend and sexual partner over the course of a lifetime is a huge task, considering how life events can make lifelong partnerships such a difficult minefield of intercommunications and personal adjustments. Couples express such hopeful dreams of mutual love by their beautiful and often expensive weddings, but often with different outcomes as shown by the number of divorces and broken partnerships.

My next journal will tackle one such sad marriage dream that began with so many hopes that I wanted but never fully realised.

JOURNAL 6

Wedding and Honeymoon

Dear Journal,

I believe this entry will surely bring back uncomfortable memories about my original marriage expectations along with the later disappointments.

Engagement

With a ring on my finger, I thoroughly enjoyed the social acceptance of being engaged along with the public congratulations that followed. The two-year engagement was a busy time, as I still taught dance, had my twenty-first birthday, prepared for the wedding, and enjoyed the social outings with other engaged couples. As far as physical intimacy was concerned, my fiancé and I indulged in loving embraces, with only a few giggled references about the future honeymoon, as keeping chaste was the accepted rule of the day. So, it was easy for me not to worry about intercourse because we followed the strict social rule of no sex before marriage.

As the wedding date drew closer, I began to consider what it would be like to experience sex after we were married. I asked other young women whether there was a book to give more information about contraception; this was before the Pill was introduced. I also wanted to know more about the sexual act itself, and what emotions to expect. Here, I presumed it created exulted feelings of a kind of love euphoria.

Sex Preparation Before Marriage

The only ancient textbook I could get was titled Married Love by Dr. Stopes.[18] At first, many churches did not accept the book, because of its open discussion of female sexual desire and birth control. Despite this, publishers sold many copies in the first week, and it was translated into over twenty languages. Despite its limitations, the book had more data than in my old school science book, and I wanted to uncover two things:

1. Being a dancer, I was interested in the physical part of intercourse.
2. I wanted to know what emotions could occur during the act.

In other words, I wanted to know how the body behaved physically during sex, and how it would feel from a being-in-love psychological point of view. Reading this book now would be interesting, as the only main technique described for having sex was the missionary position. That is, where the man lies on top of the woman during intercourse; the term coming from Christian missionaries who encouraged this position to converts in the new colonies. In all, the sexual ritual seemed manageable to me, because after all, couples had been doing it for thousands of years.

There was also a mention of the broken hymen plus the shedding of a few drops of blood during the first intercourse, where in novels, I read it was proof of the female's former virginity. This seemed a touch messy, so I presumed it was a minor thing as married people only made light-hearted joking references to spots on the 'first-night' sheet. Then, I wondered whether the 'few drops of blood' was correct, after remembering my original introduction to menstrual bleeding had been a little misleading in this regard.

---

[18] *Married Love* by Dr. Marie Stopes (1918, Fifield & Co.).

However, I was more interested in the emotional states that were supposed to occur. Here Dr. Stopes waxed lyrical. She described in poetic words the *'sensory intoxication'* of how a man could arouse a *'woman's body and soul'* to reach a *'mutual crisis of love,'* which I think referred to an ecstatic state of orgasm. I therefore visualised sunsets and swimming in seas of heavenly passion, and I wanted to know how her stated *'a thrilling longing for the uttermost union'* really felt. Although I suspected this kind of description was romantically exaggerated, I thought perhaps only poetic words could describe such a wonderful feeling.

There was a chapter on birth control methods, with the main ones being *'coitus interruptus'* (a weird phrase for the man withdrawing before he reaches orgasm) and spermicides. Dr. Stopes was a pioneer in birth control, particularly as she did not approve of abortion. 'Coitus interruptus' sounded unreliable to me, so I decided that spermicide creams would be the way to go.

Spermicide creams came in a toothpaste-type tube with an applicator to insert said creams into the vagina just before intercourse was about to happen. The technique was messy, and the enclosed instructions suggested it was wise to perform the 'love act' on a bath towel. This sounded to be a most unromantic and clumsy practice, which I later found to be true. Also then, condoms were not always dependable or considered comfortable for the male, and it was the female who seemed responsible to manage birth control. Certainly, I did not want to get pregnant straight away, although I imagined having one or two children in the future.

Despite my industrious sexual research efforts, I was not prepared for marriage in any way. Besides, I can see it was more about fulfilling a storybook idea of life. Now, I know that nothing would have educated me properly, and I had no idea that normal sexuality may not have been a part of my natural self.

Wedding Night and Honeymoon

As for the wedding night and honeymoon, it was a bit of a disappointment from a sexual point of view. Let us say no blissful heavens opened – only nervousness and pain. Plus, Dr. Marie's mention of a 'few' drops of blood on the sheet was wrong! My husband did not know what to do or how to comfort me, so his way of coping was to put his head on the pillow and quickly fall asleep. Meanwhile, I washed the hotel sheet, laboriously picked bits of confetti out of our luggage, and tried desperately not to feel too disillusioned. At this point, I was still determined to be the happy bride in the hope that things would improve. On the positive side, I did feel a sense of new adulthood now that I was no longer a virgin.

Despite the awkward initiation, I decided the first night was only a rehearsal, and with practice it would develop into a beautiful dance. I was vague about how this fantastic performance was going to happen, as the only idea of foreplay was tongue kissing; a practice which for me was not always pleasant. In reality I had no education in the art of seduction. Even in American movie love scenes, one only ever saw single beds with the man (usually wearing ugly striped pyjamas) sitting on the bed obeying the then-famous Hollywood moral rule of having one foot on the floor. As for experiencing a man in sexual action, I was surprised by the physical effort of huffing and puffing, and I wondered why his enjoyment looked so painful. The part I certainly liked was the male face after intercourse, where his features softened into an expression of relaxed serenity. In fact, this was my favourite part of the whole act – just watching him fall asleep after making love. This was also the moment when I would congratulate myself on having 'done my bit' to create his sexual satisfaction. Somehow, I believed I would eventually feel the same sort of gratification, but in the meantime, I developed the ability to disappear out of my body during intercourse. This was a weird sensation of distractedly watching myself from above, or as if a part of me had temporally ceased to exist.

The rest of the honeymoon did not improve, and after a week, we returned early from the seaside town. This was necessary so I could visit a city doctor after developing a bad case of cystitis. Despite the discomfort, I somehow remained positive and held onto the hope that once I became adjusted to the physical act, then sexual rapture would surely follow. In the meantime, I welcomed the need to avoid sex for a short time, but I worried about not fulfilling my husband's expectations. As we had never tried anything sexual during the engagement, I presumed the honeymoon could have been a great disappointment for him. To put it mildly, I thought it was a bad start on the sexual front. However, he did not show concern, but he may have been at a loss to know what to say, or perhaps he was actually satisfied. Of course, I held the belief that his sexual needs were much greater than mine, and it was my duty to give him gratification.

Unfortunately, with no communication between us about our first sexual efforts, sexual activity became something I grappled with silently. Today, one would surely talk to their partner, use humour, give loving assurances, or explore ideas for mutual pleasure. Back then, there was a reticence to discuss sexual concerns, and even today, such crucial conversations are not always easy. Humans can discuss a variety of topics with ease, but for odd reasons, the subject of sex can still be awkward and layered with hidden anxieties. In this case, I ignored any need for discussion and felt sure things would be fine if I just worked on being a devoted wife. Besides, I was always a glass-half-full person, and so I believed that devoutness to my husband would create marital happiness.

Reflection

Sex Education in the 1950s

The previously mentioned Dr. Marie Charlotte Carmichael Stopes, who wrote the first popular book about married sex, was an interesting character. She was a botanist, who was interested in the rights of women, and the subject of eugenics – that is, the now unpalatable idea of improving the human species by selective mating. Born in the UK in 1880, she was one of the rare female academics of the time, so her life story does make an interesting read. She was also a poet, which could explain her flowery prose when describing orgasmic climaxes.

In relation to the first sexual experiences on the wedding night, a doctor once told me how he despaired of dealing with so many uneasy post-honeymoon consultations. These concerned new brides with bad cases of cystitis who were highly embarrassed about their introduction to sex where both partners had been nervous and inexperienced. This type of infection was probably caused by internal irritation, making it easier for bacteria to enter the urethra. Also, it can evidently be caused by spermicides, although in 1950 no information was provided as to possible causes. Naturally, doctors were relieved when the contraceptive pill arrived, so couples began to have premarital sex and live together before marriage.

Introduction to sex education was wanting in the 1940s and 1950s, plus people had other problems coping with World War II and the post-war recovery. Therefore, in my youth, sexual knowledge was only gained from parents and shared information with teenage friends. It was not until the early 1960s that I became aware of the Pill, and in 1970s, I began to absorb the new attitudes towards sex and the ideals of feminism.

Much later, in the 1980s, a program discussing sexual orientation was introduced into a school where I was teaching. This was promoted by the AIDS epidemic and well received by the students. However, I can still remember some young girls repeating very derogatory remarks about homosexuals which they had gleaned from their parents. Also, the student who stated, 'I understand about homosexuality, but who and what are heterosexuals?' Thus, I believe education is vital for a more fully public understanding of sexual diversity.

JOURNAL 7

Marriage and Pregnancy

Dear Journal,
This entry will not be easy to write as I endeavour to recall the disheartening realities of what happened after the honeymoon – although I know there were positive highlights too.

For the first twelve months, marriage created an interesting challenge of adjustments. I was learning to manage all the domestics in running a household, searching for acceptable part-time work to buy needed domestic appliances, and coping with living in a new city area. I expected these daily changes, so they did not upset me, but my husband's gradual change in demeanour certainly did. Although our sexual life was not overly enjoyable for me, I am sure it was not the source of the growing angst between us. I never refused my husband's advances or made any excuses to avoid intercourse, and I strongly believed sex was an important ingredient for a happy marriage. In fact, I was the one who usually initiated any loving gesture towards physical closeness. There seemed to be something else going on, as he was beginning to be secretive and related differing stories about progress in his work. Therefore, I began to sense the former trusting basis of our partnership was gradually fading.

I surmised my husband's changing attitudes and behaviour revealed deeper problems. He now avoided any discussion about money, often procrastinated about achieving any of his self-proclaimed goals, and showed anxiety in unfamiliar social situations. His original happy, self-assured manner disappeared in this new city environment, and I wondered whether his original outward confidence had served to hide insecurities. This led me to question whether his original confident mask was hard to sustain within the new responsibilities of married life.

Despite my efforts to communicate, he resisted talking about any personal problems, saying there was nothing wrong. In my attempts to rekindle his former positive spirit, I put all my energies into showing loving care and made sure I put his daily needs first. Of course, I was aiming for the kind of supportive partnership I had always witnessed between my own father and mother. At the same time, I missed my home community and my parents, but it was for other reasons I gradually began to feel a lonely dread as I faced each day. This was not about a touch of homesickness, but the feeling of sad frustration that I was somehow failing my husband by not meeting his expectations.

The other disquieting aspect was a deep sense of loss of my former dancing life.[19] It was painful not to be teaching, and my only dance activity was ballroom waltzing with my husband on rare social occasions. We had also begun married life in a part of the city where it was impossible to travel to my old theatre school. It became clear that my expected 'career' was now one of being a good wife, as very few wives engaged in professional work after marriage. Here, I tried to forget about the warning from my ballet teacher that marriage and the desire for a dance career were not a good mix.

Isolation and Anxiety

Gradually sex began to add to my feelings of emotional isolation – still I never refused, feigned a headache, or made any protest. It was not easy for me, as intercourse became a duty; one that often involved suddenly having to respond to my husband's needs without much

---

[19] I had transferred my country ballet school to young dancer, who I had trained as a teaching assistant.

foreplay. In fact, the act felt more like a release of repressed anxiety rather than affection, and I sensed his inner disquiet. In addition, I still coped with the chore of birth control creams, followed by the cold bathroom washing after intercourse. Then, I began to note some minor physical discomfort, which I now know was partly due to an undiagnosed slight pelvic deformity. Nevertheless, I still hoped 'true love' (whatever that was) would develop to make both of us happy, or at least lovingly content with each other's company. It also became clear that my husband's finances were not as healthy as he had given me to suppose, and I wondered whether this was the main cause of his growing angst. Also, I knew he passionately believed in the prevailing idea that men should be the main financial providers. Therefore, I deliberated whether he lacked the confidence in being the main breadwinner.

A Working Wife

To solve the problem, I decided to search for a suitable nine-to-five sales-assistant job in a city department store. I thought this would be socially acceptable as I could be home in time to cook the evening meal, and married women without children did work in these jobs. Besides, I figured it would bring in extra money, as it was now clear that my husband's financial situation was not in a healthy shape. He was often late in paying the weekly rent and could offer a bare minimum amount to buy food. Fortunately, I did obtain work in a city department store, and it was a relief to meet people and bring home an extra salary. My husband was not overjoyed about his wife working, probably because he was ashamed of not being able to support us both, so he only grudgingly agreed.

Gender and Finance

Being a woman, I did not have a say in the management of personal finances. Once, after I deposited my salary into our joint bank account, I was keen to enquire as to the balance. I was embarrassed after the male bank teller rudely refused to tell me, saying that only my husband had permission to make such enquiries. In those days, even legal documents referred to wives as material possessions (chattels). At the time, I also noted my work salary as a female shop-assistant was different to the male assistants who did the same kind of work. This situation meant I was delighted if asked to work in the male-controlled 'Manchester' (linen) department or in men's clothing, as then I received a slightly higher wage. Serving in male departments brought another bonus, as it was physically easier than working in the female-run crockery department where one dealt with heavy piles of pottery. It was these kinds of issues the feminists of the 1970s began to address, and today, inequalities for women are still under question.

1950s Work Culture

Life behind the sales counter in a department store revealed the social standing of women who worked there. Most were unmarried women, resembling fussy old ladies with narrow lives, who lacked humour, and were most possessive of 'their' department within the store. They appeared fearful of the male-dominated store managers and never spoke of male/female relationships. (Although once an anxious middle-aged saleswoman asked me how babies were born and whether they came out of your navel!) Overall, these single women found themselves socially alienated by their unmarried status, so work was their focus in life, and many only went home to their cats. In fact, it was a microcosm of the fifties culture, where I noted only men were in management with women delegated to selling feminine articles, plus typing, filing, or cleaning. In fact, throughout the whole store there was a definite tiered pecking order of managerial control.

My department store work took place before television, so I had not seen the show *Are You Being Served?* Years later, when I did finally view this comedy series, at once I recognised it as portraying a work scene identical to my past shop-sales experience. It was the same cultural world of the store hierarchy, with characters displaying their obedience to strict work rules and manners of urbane servility – not to mention the ridiculous rivalry between staff and other departments.[20]

Pregnancy

Once realising I was pregnant, married life took an interesting turn. It was after the wedding of a friend, where a late night and two rare glasses of champagne meant I must have been careless with birth control creams. It only took two weeks to realise I was pregnant, as I began a strange hankering for black tea, green apples, and apricots – all of which convinced me I was entering the state of motherhood. I was ecstatic!

In the beginning, my husband seemed pleased and enjoyed sharing the news with my parents and his old drinking mates in the local home hotel. He also enthusiastically wanted to return to my hometown with the idea of starting his own business. This pleased me, as I was delighted to be closer to my parents, and to have them nearby for the birth of their first grandchild. At the time, I did not know my husband had been sacked from his city job, as he led me to believe he had resigned. Here, I am sure he was only salvaging his pride by not telling the truth.

---

[20] *Are You Being Served?* was a British sitcom parodying the class system in a department store, including funny interactions with customers, other sales staff, and management. The London BBC broadcasted sixty-nine episodes from 1972-1985 and was popular in Australia and many other countries. (https://en.m.wikipedia.org/wiki/Are_You_Being_Served?)

The first four months of pregnancy were busy, along with moving back to the country and preparing for the baby. Fortunately, I was feeling well and only experienced minor morning sickness. With all the change happening in our lives, I do not remember much about our sex life at that time, only that I was delighted that my husband appeared happier with the prospect of a change in his working life. However, after seven months into the pregnancy, I noticed he reverted to noncommunication at home, and his original enthusiasm about the baby seemed to have waned. Although I was not a large pregnant lady, it now was physically obvious that a baby was on the way, thus making parenthood more of a visual reality. I thought he might have been concerned about money again, as he now faced the added stress of supporting his wife and coming baby. I tried to enquire about our financial situation, but as usual, he did not want to discuss how much money we had in the bank. Meanwhile, I was in a rapt state about the baby, so I tried not to worry and just concentrated on the excitement of the coming birth.

Reflection

'Red Flags' in Relationships

When rereading this journal section about those first two years of marriage, I can see how I ignored the *'red flag'* signals of looming relationship problems. Those inner warning signals are hard to recognise in close friendships, let alone address with effective communication and action. For me, these emerging doubts were disturbing, because they questioned my own values and boundaries of what I thought should be normal marital behaviour, and they challenged some of the original impressions I held about my husband's personality.

Early in the marriage there were no obvious clashes or arguments, but it was the more subtle changes in attitudes or odd incidences of negative behaviour that became noticeable. Now I could honestly see there were differences in our emotional needs, plus how we differed in approaches to work and finances. With work, he struggled to stay on schedule, often deferred starting a task, and wanted to make sudden career changes without forethought or planning. His handling of money was more optimistically vague compared to mine, and there was no realistic budgeting for the future, other than my own attempts with limited information. There was also his secrecy about bank balances, including the 'supposed' ownership of a car still garaged at his original home location.

In fact, when he mournfully confessed, he did not truly own a car, I arranged to sell some antique possessions to buy a vehicle and put it in his name. The motivation to do this was probably to buy his admiration, help him to save face, and to be a rescuer. His reaction? I remember he just simply said, '*Good idea*,' and accepted the gift, while telling other people he had bought the vehicle himself. There were red flags here, but I did not address this behaviour or even want to think about any underlying problems. Of course, the biggest red flag came later with his growing lack of enthusiasm about us having a baby as the pregnancy progressed.

I cannot remember any instances of receiving gifts or unexpected loving gestures. No flowers, special proposals for shared outings, or those caring offers to help with domestic chores. I was always the one who tried to instigate any actions of loving support to make him feel wanted and to get his affection. This was sad, particularly as I thought it was the little kind-hearted acts that deepened devotion between couples as well as sexual intimacy.

Then there were the odd instances where his original outward show of self-confidence would wane in any new social situations.

Here, he would feign tiredness or suddenly refuse to attend a planned occasion. Strangely, he *did* want to visit my parents when he could, because I think my father could bolster his confidence. At this early stage, I also noted he did not easily make close friends, and he never developed new relationships during the time we lived in the city. It was only in a familiar social scene accompanied by a few bottles of beer that his original outgoing personality would return.

Did I voice these differences? Not really. If I did tentatively try, he would deny anything was wrong, and in turn, I would push doubts away. My original attraction to his outgoing nature as a mature, independent, worldly person was slowly beginning to change. I also felt that his first attraction to me cantered on the idea that I was a suitable 'catch.' On reflection, I do not believe either of us held a deep mutual loving attraction, and I think we both engaged in a 'window-dressing' display of a marriage.

Therefore, I ignored red flags, as I did not want to listen to inner doubts or to face the possibility that our relationship did not reflect a genuine, mutual love. Even during our engagement period, I had avoided hard conversations or confrontation of any questionable behaviour. One example was when he mysteriously disappeared from my twenty-first birthday celebration without explanation, only to later say, '*he felt tired.*' No way could I face the shame of breaking an engagement or a wedding vow, plus I felt I should accept a degree of sacrifice and put the 'hard work' into a relationship. Again, both of us are to blame by not communicating to uncover the hidden truths about our insecurities.

Now, I believe the '*for better or for worse*' phrase in the marriage vows is questionable, as there is a personal limit as to how '*worse*' things should be! But back then, I could not face the fear of rejection and possible public shame to act on these hints of disunity in our marriage. This would have meant dealing with painful truths, testing difficult compromises, or facing the humiliation of separation. Sadly, we had trapped ourselves in a relationship without the personal skills or emotional intelligence to act on any signs of discord.

There are internet sites that outline the early warning signs of problems that could develop in relationships. Psychologists point out subtle red flags, including occasions where one partner tests the boundaries of what the other considers to be acceptable behaviour. Also, when one has a 'gut' feeling that they need to *fundamentally* change who they are and adapt to their partner's expectations. In other words, reshape themselves to fit with another person that is *not* in harmony with their own beliefs and values.

These days, with the wisdom of age and hindsight, I have more confidence in facing unpleasant relationship situations, as I know the consequences of nonaction. Not paying attention or not facing up to relationship problems usually caused my past break-ups to be even more complex and hurtful for everyone involved.

To anyone beginning long-term friendships or partnerships, I would say ignore those early *'red flag'* warning signs at your peril and be brave in having those difficult discussions to achieve necessary compromises. My own mantra is that life is too short to waste by trying to cope in painful relationships that one can bravely change, avoid, or sadly end in a manner of gracious uncoupling. By 'gracious uncoupling', I refer to where couples choose to end a union with the utmost respect and consequently, with minimal emotional damage.

JOURNAL 8

The Birth Experience

Dear Journal,

I know this entry will endeavour to cover my greatest joy and deepest despair! To begin, the birth of my son was both wonderful and concerning at the same time. The baby was captivatingly beautiful, but the father's reaction was concerning. Dear Journal, I do not want to sit in harsh judgement of my husband, as he may have been deeply apprehensive about becoming a father. Here, he could have been fearful about the responsibility to financially support both a wife and child. If so, it is possible he could not even voice this to himself, and therefore was unable to recognise or share his innermost anxieties.

The evening I was due to give birth, he visited a mate to share a few beers. When he did come home late into the night, I was having regular back pains, but his immediate reaction was to get to sleep, in case I had to wake him later during the night. By 3:00 a.m. I knew it was time to get to the hospital but could not understand why he was strangely reluctant to take me. I stayed calm, timed the pains, and then insisted action was necessary! He finally obliged, although I sensed his fear and disinclination to face the reality of the situation. Now the birth was imminent, he behaved as if he did not want it to happen, but thankfully drove me to the hospital door and then left without a word. Of course, in those days, fathers were absent at the birth, so it was only the mother and medical staff involved. At this point, I only hoped he would become more excited after the baby arrived.

For me, birth hormones were happening – so my focus was getting the baby into the world as safely as possible. Being narrow hipped with small internal measurements, managing a natural birth was questionable. Fortunately, my dance training meant I could control muscle relaxation between contractions and therefore did not need anaesthetics. Giving birth was like a rehearsed performance that took all my attention, so I was not thinking about anyone else during the process. The baby arrived quickly, and my main comforting thought was... *if so many women in the world had given birth without medical aid, then surely, I could do this in a hospital situation!*

Being a natural birth, my son did not appear crying with half-closed eyes. Instead, he was wide awake with curiosity and squirming in an energetic display of agility. Unfortunately, that energy caused a last-minute birthing problem, where he decided to virtually slide sideways into the world. This did cause a stab of real pain, as up until then, I had not been in unbearable agony and nothing like the childbirth pain contortions I expected. The nurses whisked him away and fussed over this energetic, thumb-sucking, wide-eyed little boy. Meanwhile, the doctor remained to stitch the tear injuries, saying he hoped it would be 'neat' as stitching was not his best skill! Still full of adrenaline, I did not worry about physical injuries, even if they were to become a minor problem in the future. Then, I remember just laying alone in the cold delivery room shivering from my efforts while patiently waiting for a chance to see my beautiful newborn. Finally, a nurse appeared with a warm blanket and a cup of hot Milo, which to me, was the highlight of the actual delivering process! Thank goodness birthing practices have now improved to become more of a bonding and exciting family ritual.

Reaction After Giving Birth

Here, I want to acknowledge that like with most women, the birth experience proved to be an exhilarating performance. Even if sex had been a bit problematic, at least it had been worthwhile to produce a wonderful new life, and it was undoubtedly to be my most creative endeavour. Therefore, I never regretted this marriage, as it gave me the opportunity to bring a special new human being into the world.

During this magical event, I was conscious of doing everything for the baby's safe delivery, so I was able to put my husband's inattentive behaviour to one side. Now it was all over, I thought his reaction would be one of pride in seeing a child that he had also created. Sadly, this positive hope was to only evaporate in the coming weeks.

Immediately after the birth, the nursing staff tried to contact the new father. However, they could not find him, nor had he phoned to enquire as to whether the birth had taken place. Finally, when the doctor was able to tell him of his son's arrival, he did not instantly come to the hospital, waiting until visiting hours instead. I did not see his reaction when he saw our baby in the hospital nursery, as I was in a nearby ward with slight haemorrhaging. Later, he came to visit me, only to put his head on the bed and say he was tired and overworked. For the next seven days in hospital, the same pattern occurred, I was sore, he was tired, and the baby was happy!

I was anxious to get home to become the 'model' family, in the hope that my husband would become more relaxed into his new family life. I surmised that he needed special attention just to avoid feeling 'displaced' by the baby. So, I insisted on managing at home without any extra help, even though the baby and I were still recovering from a hospital staphylococcus infection. My mother suggested she could visit me daily to help, but I decided to manage on my own.

Here events get more depressing. My efforts to cook, clean, and care for the baby to present a beautiful daily homecoming for my husband did not seem to work. His behaviour was strange, as he could not express what was worrying him and seemed to be depressingly anxious. He naturally believed it was a mother's job to look after the child, and a crying baby at night obviously troubled him. Because of this, the baby slept in another room, and I certainly never felt comfortable to ask him to attend the baby or help me. However, he still bitterly complained of having his sleep interrupted.

Sadly, I did not see any real bonding with his child despite all my encouragement. Except, of course, in the presence of family or strangers when he would suddenly pick him up for a brief time and appear to take an interest. Unfortunately, this often resulted in tears from the baby who was unaccustomed to receiving attention from his father. *'Bit of a Mummy's boy,'* he would say and promptly hand him back to me.

Then there was the matter of resuming the sexual intimacy of married life. The doctor warned that the first six weeks would be problematic for sex, as recovery was needed for wound healing along with concerns about infection. I did communicate this to my husband who chose to ignore the doctor's advice. However, I did not want to refuse any sexual advances and desperately wanted to make efforts to show affection for his sake. Here, I assumed he had forgotten I was still healing from postnatal injuries, and there was often bleeding during and after sex. But I did not complain or alert him to any of my discomfort, as I thought his needs were more important than mine. I knew he must have had an inner conflict of emotions which he was unable to communicate, and so I did not protest or say, *'No.'*

One might think this unfeeling demand for sex would have led to my asexuality, but at the time, my aim was all about creating a loving family and pleasant my husband. I still hoped that after healing, sexual pleasure might be a possibility, and in the meantime, I thought it was my responsibility to cater for his desires. I also continued to be concerned that arrival of the baby could have caused him to feel emotionally exiled, so despite any pain, I hoped sex might help him become more optimistic about family life.

Difficult Memories

Dear Journal, even after sixty years, writing about this period of my son's birth still feels disturbing. Although events have been disquieting to recall, I was surprised by the depth of emotional detail I could remember. In re-evaluating this piece of the past, I still believe my intention to create a loving family was sincere. Obviously, I clung to the hope of a miraculous improvement in this anxious post-birth atmosphere, but hope alone could not heal the situation without any real communication.

At the time, I wondered whether I could have accepted marital sex with more eagerness if I had received genuine affection from my husband. However, I do not believe this early sex life caused my asexuality, and the challenges during this time only served to make my real orientation even more 'invisible.' On the other hand, I am sure this difficult experience caused me to become resilient and to always be self-reflective about my behaviour. These attributes of strength and self-analysis were to eventually help me understand why the sexual side of marriage would *never* be easy for me.

The Pill

I had another postnatal worry. With the unexpected occurrences of marital sex and with my husband's plain unhappiness, I feared becoming pregnant again. So, I asked the doctor to give me a prescription for a new kind of contraception they called the Pill.[21] He could not hide a bit of a smirk, obviously thinking that we could not keep our hands off each other! How wrong! At least the Pill brought on the first menstrual period after six months, for which I was enormously relieved. The doctor also mentioned that having sex so soon after the birth had not helped after-birth healing. In his words, *'You are a bit untidy down there'.*

Being the Perfect Wife

After months of silence, I felt helpless in the wake of my husband's refusal to admit anything was wrong other than he was unexplainably tired. As a result, I felt sad, rejected, and alienated. In fact, I tried to deal with the situation like a 1950s wife in the *Good Housewife's Guide* that stated how a wife should treat a husband. The origin of this Guide is not precisely known, but it said...

- o *Have dinner ready. Plan, even the night before, to have a delicious meal ready on time for his return. This is a way of letting him know that you have been thinking about him and are concerned about his needs.*
- o *Most men are hungry when they come home, and the prospect of a good meal (especially his favourite dish) is part of the warm welcome needed.*
- o *Prepare yourself. Take fifteen minutes to rest so you can look refreshed when he arrives. Touch up your makeup, put a ribbon in your hair, and be fresh-looking. He has just been with a lot of work-weary people.*

---

[21] The history of the first oral contraceptive introduced into Australia in 1961 as noted on the website of the National Australian Museum. (https://www.nma.gov.au/defining-moments)

- *Be a little gay (that is, appear happy) and a little more interesting for him. After his boring day, he may need a lift, and one of your duties is to provide it.*
- *Clear away the clutter. Make one last trip through the house just before your husband arrives. Gather up schoolbooks, toys, paper, and then dust the tables.*
- *Over the cooler months you should prepare and light a fire for him to unwind by. Your husband will feel he has reached a haven of rest and order, and it will give you a lift, too, as catering for his comfort will provide you with immense satisfaction.*

So, I cooked the nice dinner, cleaned the house, looked to my appearance, and made sure the baby was fed and organised. Also, I lit a woodfire in our older-style house that still had a chimney. Sadly, none of these efforts worked.

During the months following his birth, I did not want my baby son to detect my growing unhappiness, and I made sure that bath-time and any interactions with him were always full of joy and smiles. In truth, I wanted to cry into the bath water, but even at that early stage, I wished for him to see parents who loved life. At the time, I made every effort to hide my anxieties about what might be the cause of my husband's obvious discontent. Of course, I kept on trying to communicate, but I only faced a continual wall of silence.

Refection

Communication Problems

When writing about marriage and motherhood, I remember the lack of communication between us as husband and wife. Any conversation efforts to uncover causes for his obvious unhappiness resulted in only silence or denial. This kind of stalemate has led me to reflect about a specific type of interaction difficulty – namely, *'stonewalling.'*

'Stonewalling'

In any relationship, conflicts are normal, although I found trying to understand and resolve such conflicts was a challenge. When my husband 'shut down' towards me, it was the first time I came up against this type of stonewalling or silent treatment. Silence was a huge barrier as it prevented me from uncovering any real problems. In this situation there was no incident that could reveal an underlying cause for his disquiet.

This kind of silence was foreign to me, as in my own family life there had always been fun debates, stimulating conversation, and philosophical searchings covering any manner of topics. In this way, problems relating to emotions, relationships, religion, politics, or financial concerns were all aired and debated. Therefore, family members resolved any differences of opinion through friendly, spirited discussion rather than the tension of silence or sulking. I now realise stonewalling is a behavioural pattern often used by people who want to avoid delving into an issue or problem.[22]

Gaslighting

Along with stonewalling, there is the other diminishing behaviour called gaslighting. This term refers to someone who plants doubts into the mind of another person, making them feel less intelligent. It is done in a way that the victim believes problems are their fault, and consequently, they begin to question their own intuition and beliefs. This manipulation of putting another person down is a way to regain

---

[22] For information on stonewalling, see https://www.verywellmind.com > stonewalling.

emotional power and to effectively avoid tough questions. In my case, efforts to enquire about the cause of my husband's unhappiness were often met with silence or gaslighting responses – both verbal and non-verbal, such as:

- Glaring at me as if I were being an idiot or too stupid to answer.
- Inferring I was not caring for the baby if he ever cried.
- Scraping the roast dinner into the bin and then eating bread and jam.
- Turning away if I showed casual affection – indicating it was the wrong time.
- Inferring that he worked longer hours and had less sleep than I did.
- Saying I was trying to be 'too perfect' by keeping the house clean.

I often thought about the last point where he would say, '*You are always being too perfect and trying too hard.*' But instinctively, I knew if I had done less for him, I would have been berated. At one stage, I wondered whether I should have confronted my husband rather than let myself become a victim of silence. Uneasily, I was afraid that angry reproaches on my behalf may have ignited a more physical type of violence – such was the atmosphere of pressurised tension. Although I had no evidence that this would happen, the fear was there anyway. As a result, I did not respond aggressively, because I sensed that having a row would have only made things worse.

There is also the term '*breadcrumbing*,' meaning to 'lead someone on without being emotionally truthful.' These behaviours are more common these days through impersonal dating sites where people can easily stop communicating without explanation or can manipulate personal facts. I did experience this on social occasions when my husband would show some interest in me and the baby in front of others and then resort to distant behaviour when we returned home.

On reflection, I realise these behaviours meant my husband could avoid confrontation and not face questions as to why his life had ceased to be rewarding. I do not believe he meant to be emotionally cruel, but he certainly showed a lack of emotional insight. I am sure he felt trapped and did not measure up to his own idea of success. Whatever his intentions, stonewalling and gaslighting were effective ways to cause our relationship to shut down.[23]

---

[23] Further information can be found online about 'gaslighting' – https://www.healthline.com-gaslighting.

JOURNAL 9

Divorce

Dear Journal,

This will be a difficult entry about how the marriage quickly dissolved and ended in divorce. Even with a child involved, distressing events continued to unfold leading to the strange dissolution of our marriage. From the beginning, my husband and I were trying to fulfil the social expectations of marriage, so sadly we both suffered through a partnership that was not built on any feelings of true passion.

Events Leading to Separation and Divorce

Even now, I do not want to blame my husband, as I like to think he had good intentions, and that he did not understand the source of his own hidden fears. But, for whatever reason, he kept a grim silence after our baby was born, and try as I may, I could not unearth the reasons for his depressing demeanour. At the point of becoming a father, he did not seem fully prepared for the responsibility – either emotionally or financially.

I became aware lack of money was still a concern, and on one occasion there was a surprise home visit from the local bank manager to tell me our bank account was in overdraft. (Why he decided to speak to me and not my husband I do not know, except he was one of my father's good friends.) This event prompted a rare moment of communication with my husband, and he admitted that attempts to start his own business had not been successful. I suggested that with my mother's help, I could resume part-time teaching by reopening the dance school. (At this time, the former teacher had just left to be married in another town.) Although he hated the idea that his wife *'had to go to work,'* he must have known there was no alternative.

My efforts to be a working mother were successful, and our financial situation improved. Nevertheless, this did not please my husband as he continued to be uncommunicative, and I feared he was not attracting enough clients for his business. Somehow, I started to feel that real love was not the foundation of our marriage, and my hope for a happy future together gradually began to fade. Besides, I did not have the skills to break through the barriers of noncommunication, nor were there any suitable counselling services available.

Departure Without Explanation

Despite my efforts to provide economic help, he suddenly announced he was returning to his parents' home in another state. He left with no explanation as to his reasons or future intentions. He only gave a vague statement about leaving *'to work things out.'* This was my first experience of *'ghosting,'* where someone close to me left without any apparent reason. My reactions were to feel a weird mixture of relief, fear, and confusion. Relief, that I was not facing the daily atmosphere of tension; fear, because I did not know what the future held; and confusion, since I was unsure why he had left so unexpectedly. I did not know whether the baby and I were meant to follow, if he was looking for work, or if he was getting financial support from his parents. What I did know was that he left behind debts for me to address, which related to money being owed to many local businesses.

Desertion or Adultery

When I tried to communicate with my husband, his reaction was to send a letter featuring only one main written sentence that said, *'Give up the dance teaching – there is a house here if you will come.'* There were no expressions of affection and no details about whether the mentioned house was supposed to be our new marital home. Nor did it express any added persuasive sentiments or information, so I was sure he did not want me to agree. I surmised the lone sentence was to cover his legal position – so if I refused, I would be the *'deserter'* in the case of an eventual divorce. This was before *'no fault'* divorce where the legal grounds were either *'desertion'* or *'adultery.'*[24] Being in the role of a deserter meant I would not qualify for any personal financial support. After making a special visit to talk to him in person, I left convinced by his remote behaviour that he did not want a family life.

I then made a serious life-assessment about my future with the aid of professional advice. I went to my family doctor, a psychiatrist, a lawyer, and a minister of religion. They were all helpful – except for the minister of religion who just inappropriately put his hand on my knee and wanted to talk about my sex life! The psychiatrist and lawyer both recommended that I make life decisions based on what I could guarantee would be best for my son and myself.

As the future of my child was the most crucial factor, I decided with my parents' help to stay in my hometown and continue teaching dance on a part-time basis. Here I had family support, could earn a living, and my father could be the dominant male figure in my son's life. So I made the decision to end the marriage, and I became the first divorced woman I had ever known outside Hollywood. In the meantime, the state newspaper published in the court listings that I was the *'deserter,'* and despite many friends and acquaintances asking for explanations, I was reticent to discuss the matter.

---

[24] The 1975 Family Law Act ushered in 'no fault' divorce where the reason for parting was that the relationship had irreconcilably broken down, meaning it was no longer necessary to prove that either partner had offended.

The painful end to the marriage still raises disquieting memories today – but I have never regretted that difficult decision. As there were other troubling occurrences relating to my husband's behaviour, I had become quite resolved to be a single parent. At times, tension in the marriage was such that I feared real harm to either myself or the baby. However, there is no purpose in digging up negative recollections, particularly where I have an almost deliberate memory-loss of details.

Divorce and Guilt

For years I knew the local community gossiped about what might have happened in the marriage. Knowing how important it had been for me to 'belong' to the social scene, I was painfully aware of local community reactions. However, I had absolutely no regrets in choosing a life where I could ensure an atmosphere of security for my son and myself. At the time, I received the best advice available, but I never did find the explanation for our relationship breakdown. So many factors are still unknown as to whether my husband suffered a form of depression or had circumstances in his earlier life that could have emotionally impacted him.

All I could do was search for a sense of self-forgiveness and accept that I would never know all the deep emotional causes for the breakdown. However, I do not think my asexuality was a huge factor, as I was prepared to be fully co-operative to do anything to break the awful silence between us; silence that I found quite frightening. Before my final decision, I had been willing to accommodate sex in our relationship for the sake of preserving any hope of love and family life, only to finally accept that such compromises seemed impossible.

♥

Reflection

'Ghosting' Behaviour

There are many things to reflect on from my marriage break-up, but one concept was quite intriguing – that is, the strange, disturbing experience of when my husband '*ghosted*' me and left without any obvious reason.

I understand the term '*ghosting*' refers to the circumstances when a friend, partner, or spouse disappears and leaves your life without explanation.[25] In this situation it is hard to pinpoint a valid reason for their departure, and you agonise as to why your efforts did not keep the relationship alive. In my case, it led to an ongoing fear of dealing with these types of passive-aggressive people, who use silence to block any communication thus making compromises and reunions impossible.

When '*ghosted*' by a close partner, there is no closure, particularly without an obvious altercation to give reasons for the departure. I can still remember feeling totally at fault, as if I had somehow deserved the unspoken resentment. As much as I hated big 'break-up' scenes, at least it would have proved I was *worth* the struggle and fight towards a mutual reconciliation.

This kind of disregard can cause not just the pain of rejection, but it also creates the dreadful uncertainty of not knowing why. In my case, I played out various scenarios in my head searching for answers. There were questions such as – *Did I cause this? Why did I not see this outcome? How can I avoid this ever happening again? What am I going to say to other people?* Worst of all, it denied me the knowledge

---

[25] There are many online sites that can further explain 'ghosting' in relationships. Just search for 'ghosting behaviour psychology.'

to rationally process the experience and thus learn from any of my mistakes.

Regarding the person doing the ghosting, they seem to walk away without facing any heavy discussions or drama. I can only assume it is a quick and effortless way to avoid giving any answers or justification for their behaviour. Also, there is no need to deal with responsibility for anyone else's feelings. Despite this, I do believe people express the *'best'* behaviour they can in any situation to protect their egos. This behaviour may not be right, just, or kind – but it is usually the best strategic emotional reaction they can muster at the time. I learned this fact later when studying educational psychology for my teaching degree. In the same way, I came to understand why children and students who misbehaved were selecting the only action they instinctively knew to *'save'* themselves. By *'save,'* I mean to support their feelings of not getting their immediate needs satisfied, and to cover the fears of inadequacy that lay beneath. When this happened to me in my first marriage, I could only guess my husband's behaviour came from a place of shame and inability to face the complexities and burdens of family life. Still, I worried as to how I might have contributed after being left alone without explanation.

Recovery from ghosting *can* happen. Over the coming years, I studied many aspects of communication. I read and practiced assertive training techniques, reflective listening, communication styles, conflict resolution, and how to have 'crucial' conversations. I noted all these approaches could be successful if there was dialogue, but with an impenetrable wall of passive-aggressive silence, nothing can work.

After such an emotional rejection, it was a matter of realising my intentions were good, but it took an effort to believe I was still worthy of any love. I eventually had to call on a special kind of resilience in the knowledge that not all situations in life bring closures or clear answers.

Therefore, some happenings are still just one of life's mysteries, and it could reveal more about the insecurities of the other person who did the ghosting. He or she obviously could not deal with the discomfort of their emotions, nor did they fully understand the hurt caused by their method of departure. In the end, one has to say, '*go in peace*,' and move on, as life is too short to do otherwise.

JOURNAL 10

Single Life

Social Life After Divorce

Although I was sensitive about what people thought of me, I was prepared to face single life with my head held high and determined to ignore the opinions of others outside my family. I decided on this approach after one of my father's friends asked whether he could speak with me, as he prided himself on solving other people's relationship problems. I was both annoyed and faintly amused by his self-righteous attempts to persuade me to continue my marriage. I chose to politely inform him that he had not lived my experience, so any life judgements had to be mine. After that incident, I refused to discuss the outcomes of my marriage other than with trusted family members, medical doctors, or legal practitioners. So outwardly, I put the marriage disaster behind me and got on with life.

Deep down, I wondered if I would be a suitable candidate for leading a nun-like life and just dedicate myself to doing virtuous deeds. Of course, I felt deep disappointment in losing the illusion of creating my own family, but for the sake of my son, hiding away was not an option. As a result, I concentrated on my son's needs, my students, community work, and just enjoyed the freedom to be myself. I certainly did *not* give a thought about looking for sex or another partner, and in the meantime, I managed to develop a satisfying social life.

Single Life

Through my son's interest in sport and being actively engaged in his school, I was able to have social contact with a wide variety of people in local organisations. I worked on the school committees, aided in local theatrical productions, and organised dance/drama performances. This way, I resisted the temptation to '*hide away in shame*' because of the broken marriage vows. I knew people were curious as to why I became a divorcée, but my positive demeanour did not inspire the need for explanations; not that I could have given a satisfactory answer anyway. In the beginning, when I met local people, I would note their glazed eyes and could almost see their minds whirling with questions. Conversely, it did not take long for other local dramas to displace any gossip or curiosity about my personal life.

How did I manage as a single working mother? Undoubtedly, my parents sustained me with their substantial support, enabling me to achieve a fulfilling life. It was a blessing to have my child surrounded with the same jovial family atmosphere that I had experienced in my childhood. Also, he did not experience divided loyalties, considering his biological father chose not to visit or communicate, and so consequently, he did not exist in his life. I delighted in being a mother, because I am sure it made me a better teacher, since I could see every child from a mother's point of view. It was also rewarding to resume work and have the satisfaction of control over my own money, as there was no real child-support from my former husband or the government. Fortunately, life became balanced with teaching, sharing home domestic work with my mother, and not forgetting the daily delight of raising a fun-loving child. At the time, I took some comfort in seeing blended families on American TV shows such as *The Brady Bunch*.[26]

Things changed again when my son started school, creating a situation where I had more time to take on extra secretarial work. This meant broadening my contacts, and it was through this work that I came to meet more single people. These included young men who had moved into the district to accept professional positions or were sales representatives of local firms. Together with some single females, and a few married couples, I became part of a fun social group. We enjoyed many beach barbeques and gatherings at a rented farmhouse where the latest music and spontaneous free-style disco dancing abounded.

The Social Friendship Group

I just loved this kind of casual social life as these friendships were all platonic. Being single with a young child put me in a unique position of being out of the marriage market, as it was not common in those days for a young man to marry a divorcée and bring up stepchildren. Therefore, I did not detect jealousy from other women, but I instinctively knew not to pay their husbands any special attention. Overall, I appreciated this period because good friendships based on entertainment and respect were all I socially needed. The group covered a wide age range, and they were always happy to have my young son included in events. However, there was one significant male friendship (I will refer to him as R.J.) who still remains in my constant memories.

---

[26] These 1970s USA television shows portrayed a diversity of family groupings including: *My Three Sons*, *The Partridge Family*, and *The Brady Bunch*.

A Special Platonic Friendship

At first, I knew R.J. as a shy man who was serious, intelligent, and had a highly responsible career. I enjoyed his company and conversation on topics covering politics, social justice, and religion. Over time we became firm friends often sharing social occasions together, so I am sure the locals saw us as *'an item.'* He came from a conservative background, and I sensed his friendship with me did not please his family, as I was a divorcée and therefore not viewed as a suitable prospective wife.

The interesting factor of our relationship was that we did not seek any form of physical affection, and in ten years I can only remember him hugging me once. The one exception was when we were engaged in ballroom dancing, where I would subtly steer him around the dance floor as he was not confident with either the steps or tempo. However, despite the non-physical show of any affection, he was happy to hint to others that one day we might marry. This suggestion of marriage was not in keeping with his private behaviour, and I did not take these vague insinuations at all seriously. Deep down, we were both playing a role, undoubtedly motivated by social expectations.[27] He knew I was not keen to marry, and I recognised that he, like me, would not have been comfortable with the sexual expectations of married life. Nevertheless, he became my mentor and lovingly devoted friend, who always challenged me to become a truer version of myself. He was also accepted by my son, who seemed to sense that this man was not going to take me away from him. My son therefore enjoyed his visits, particularly when extra money would magically appear in his money savings-box!

---

[27] The American slang term for this sort of coupling is known as being a 'beard' – that is, knowingly or unknowingly using someone to conceal identity or sexual orientation.

The Benefits of Platonic Friendship

Of course, I wondered about R.J.'s sexual orientation, although I did not bother about it as the friendship was so comfortable for both of us. On refection, his deep concern with moral principles could have been an influence on his behaviour. The genuine answer is that I will never know because we never ventured to discuss anything to do with our lack of physical expression of affection. Again, he may have been asexual like me – but naturally, the concept of asexuality was then non-existent in public thinking. Although I will never know if we could have created an interesting partnership as an asexual couple, I do know we were able to sustain each other in a confirming way. I gave him support both socially and professionally when his work became stressful, and he gave me a sense of social respectability along with the confidence to extend my horizons.

Inspiration to Study

As well as dance, I was intellectually curious with an interest in philosophy, history, and literature. R.J. recognised my thirst for knowledge and suggested that I should seriously pursue tertiary study. I thought this was an impossible idea, as my sad school days of ill health meant that I did not have the necessary certificates for tertiary application. Nevertheless, he planted the idea, and eventually such a possibility formed into a plan that was to cause another major change in my life. It meant contemplating a move to the city where I could explore new challenges – academically, artistically, and with opportunities for broader life experiences.

There were a couple of other incidents that reinforced the feeling that I was ready for change. On one occasion, when I was giving special ballroom lessons at the local school, a visiting Education Department Inspector viewed my teaching. He was full of praise about my interaction with the students and suggested I should aim to become a qualified teacher in the Education Department. I found his interest very flattering! Another similar incident inspired me to think about extending my knowledge in theatre dramatic arts. A visiting drama lecturer conducted a workshop and made a positive comment about my acting ability. It only took this one encouraging remark for me to want to pursue training and further education in this field.

These interactions only confirmed the urge to explore the possibility of moving into a new tertiary learning environment. I also thought such a move could achieve a more flexible artistic career, as I now wanted to extend my knowledge in dance, drama, and education. Although my present teaching was satisfying to a high degree, I still desired to learn more modern dance techniques, further explore the realms of theatrical drama, and widen my access to new teaching possibilities.

This plan entered my mind at a time when my son had finished year-six schooling and was nearing his high-school education. Although I knew he had been quite contented with the local primary school, a city high school could offer a wider range of subjects compared to our country school. Until now, I instinctively knew a drastic change of home or relationships would cause him some insecurity; however, at this point, the time seemed right to also expand his horizons. Besides, I could tell he had an adventurous soul and was ready to explore a new home environment. The other factor related to my parents, who I believed would benefit by having their own lives less cluttered without an adult child and grandchild permanently living in the same household.

I am forever grateful to those kind men who challenged and inspired me to engage in such new ventures. Thus, I will not forget the people who truly brought out the best in me, and so I still remember R.J.'s friendship, the school inspector, the visiting drama lecturer, and my parents – as they all gave me the courage to take another leap into the unknown.

Reflection

Platonic Friendships

The inspiration I have gained from friends such as R.J. has caused me to value such relationships, even if they were only transitory. So often I hear the phrase '*Oh, we are only friends*' – inferring that friendship is a lower form of relationship compared with the higher intensity of sexual love.[28]

Nonetheless, I feel society should give the ideal of friendship more status in the realm of human relationships. In my parents' marriage, I am sure it was the strong element of comradeship that sustained their long partnership. Since the time of the ancient Greeks and Plato, philosophers recognised that a friendship could exist without sexual involvement. However, in modern times sexual love has certainly become a central focus. So, I asked myself, *what is there to admire and value about platonic relationships?*

To me, there are the following wonderful mutual elements of...

- o common interests
- o shared values, attitudes, and world views
- o a sense of spiritual/emotional connection.

I think there can be expressions of...

- o shared humour
- o loving understanding
- o mutual joys, fears, sorrows, and joint endeavours

---

[28] In Journal 20, I have talked more about the importance of friendship as it relates to asexuality.

- o   an equal sense of 'give and take'.

The care and support I have received from this type of friendship has usually felt non-biased and unconditional – meaning that platonic friends are willing to accept each other's flaws and mistakes. For me, these friends have been…

- o   an anchor or safety net
- o   a mentor or therapist
- o   a person who was ready to defend or protect.

When in communication with a close loyal friend, time can pass with astonishing speed. I knew one woman who bought an hourglass so she could estimate the length of phone calls with her best friend. For her, the passing of an hour felt like fifteen minutes, particularly if their communication felt 'in tune' with each other. When interacting with a friend, I also enjoy those times when we seem closely emotionally connected and there is a real sense of mutual understanding.

Attachment Theory

Recently, I read comments on *'attachment theory'* in adult relationships. It said that *'securely attached'* adults are usually self-assured with intimacy, are independent, and feel positive about themselves. *'Anxious-preoccupied'* adults are less positive about themselves, struggle with independence, and have the likelihood of self-sabotaging their relationships.

This theory illuminated understanding about my healthy attachment to family and friends. But in the past, I was also *'anxious-preoccupied'* while trying to be heterosexual. I felt inadequate in my efforts to be a good sexual lover and was in danger of trapping myself in unsatisfactory relationships. In the process, I tried so hard to please any partners in a way that was not healthy – so overall, my attempts to 'attach' in a sexual way were not successful.

Then, there were other times when I had the tendency to overly rescue a needy person, and where I was in danger of becoming co-dependent or bonded in a way that detrimentally affected my own well-being. On the other hand, I realise the sense of needing to attach to people and please them sexually occurred because I did not understand my asexuality. Therefore, I can see why I felt a degree of entrapment and self-doubt in those relationships where I tried to be physically intimate. Fortunately, I now consider myself as having 'secure attachments' in platonic relationships, as I am happy in my asexual orientation, plus understand my style of intimacy – even if it is not physically sexual in the usual way.[29]

A Summing up of Platonic Friendships

My platonic friendships are devoid of the highlighted emotions of sexual tension, and they develop without any need for physical closeness. Of course, friendship does have a certain physicality that relies on body language, words, and tone of voice. Also, I have always been aware of my urge to attach with other people through a desire to seek affection. Indeed, I was desperate to find the satisfying *'like minds coming together'* type of intimacy. To me, there is nothing better than sensing that you are *'on the same page'* in the caring interactions with another person.

I know these friendships can last a lifetime or only exist for a short span, depending on the complex happening of life events. I have known a couple of friend-relationships to fade when distance, marriage, or children intervened. Or again, where beliefs or attitudes change, causing a drifting away from one another.

---

[29] Further information on 'attachment theory' in children and adults can be found through websites such as at www.simplypsychology.org/attachment.html

Being an asexual, I naturally have always found platonic friendships to be beautiful and able to cross age, race, or gender. Therefore, my best past and present memories arise from those precious times shared with people who were not '*just friends*' but 'walked with me' as a genuine partner in life – even if it was only for a brief period.

JOURNAL 11

University Life

Dear Journal,

This entry will recount my challenging era of re-education and where the move to city living was a big undertaking. At the time, I was ready to take risks, particularly within the climate of the feminist movement and politics in Australian society. There were changing attitudes to sex and an atmosphere of revolution in the 1970s younger culture. I had read a book called *The Greening of America*, revealing how younger people were ready for social transformation, and in turn, this further inspired me to explore new horizons.[30] Although my dance teaching was a creative endeavour, it was beginning to become routine, and I was desperate to investigate innovative ideas. In other words, I was experiencing some degree of creative *'burn out.'*

In what was a bold move, I decided to take a sabbatical of twelve months to undertake extra modern dance training, with the help of a small educational arts grant. At the same time, I explored what avenues were available for tertiary study in literature and drama. Luckily, share-house accommodation became available in a suburb near the dance studio and a school where my son could undertake his final primary school year. With encouragement from my parents, we started to engage in this city-life experiment not knowing whether it would be temporary or permanent. At first, I did not know how to

---

[30] *The Greening of America* by Charles Reich – originally published by Random House in 1960. The 25th anniversary edition was published by The Three Rivers Press in 1995.

qualify for enrolment or financially afford tertiary study, so the future was most uncertain.

The Experimental Year of City Life

This opportunity to explore city life once again, and to live in a house with other tertiary students, was both challenging and stimulating. I knew my son and I would need to save every dollar if we were going to survive twelve months. Therefore, I planned a tight budget using my savings along with a small government single-mother's pension that had recently become available. In addition, I was able to teach a couple of dance classes each week at my former dance school. At this point, I had no idea how long we would survive. In an effort not to overspend, we bought groceries by the armful rather than use a shopping trolley, as that was the physical gauge of what we could afford.

I must admit during the first two weeks there were moments of thinking, '*Oh, what have I done?*' and wondering if I had made a huge mistake. Fortunately, things began to feel much better once my son began school and I started a typing course. I also made enquiries as to how I could gain high-school subjects needed for tertiary study. An interview with a career advisor led me to understand that if I passed a university adult entry exam, I would not need to have a high-school certificate to qualify for university. This was good news.

Fortunately, it was a political era where mature-aged women could more easily enter tertiary institutions. Within the growing feminist environment of the times, I felt encouraged to study for the tertiary adult entrance exam, which would allow me to enrol in a suitable teaching degree majoring in drama.

I remember frantically studying for this exam by teaching myself basic math, delving into general knowledge topics, and making myself write three or four essays every week. At least my formerly disrupted schooling had not killed off my desire for learning along with thanks to my parents who inspired the ideal of lifelong education.[31]

Meanwhile, my son settled into his new school where I regularly undertook voluntary work in the school library. During this first year, other than enjoying the company of the young people in our share house, I did not engage in any social life. As for men, I only communicated with the male teachers at my son's school. Here, I was impressed with the school principal (S.D.). He was a creative teacher who took an interest in my dance teaching, and having been a professional athlete, he was also an inspiration to my son.

In fact, it was S.D. who was the next person to motivate me towards extending my academic horizons. He was happily married, so without any fear of awakening his romantic interest, I had the confidence to trust him in helping me to fulfil any new scholastic goals. I also admired his genuine regard towards the students, and they adored his fun and enthusiastic teaching approach in the classroom. Together, we held the same educational values and mutual passion towards the creative arts. In the meantime, my old mentor-friend, R.J., was busy with his work back in my hometown, plus travelling overseas, so sadly I did not see him often.

Fear of Academia

I was fearful about my lack of education and wondered if my academic skills would measure up to the other, younger 'A' level university students. To assure myself, I visited a psychologist for an educational assessment. After testing, he convinced me I would be able to cope well with tertiary-level study. During the session, he stressed that academic success was as much about time management,

---

[31] Further reading – https://www.researchgate.net > The Emergence of Lifelong Learning.

organisation, and arduous work as having a high score in any intelligence test. This later proved to be excellent advice. The psychologist also said that my lower math score showed more fear of the subject rather than lack of capability. Remembering how so many of my primary-school days had been lost to illness, this was understandable. Also, in year three at the age of seven, I had experienced a scary teacher, who had not helped my confidence – particularly in arithmetic.

This first year culminated in the success of passing the adult entrance exam, and I found myself accepted into the realm of tertiary study. I was ecstatic and can still remember the excitement of relating the news to my parents from a public phone box. So began the four-year Bachelor of Education degree, where my son and I were both students together; me at a university, and my son now at high school. Therefore, this 'gap' year heralded a major life change. The only downside was having to inform my former hometown community that I would be away for an indefinite period.

In facing four years of study, my son and I knew we would continue to be financially poor – along with the other students living in our rental house. However, I believed it would be a rich experience, as we had an opportunity to gain further education, take advantage of the city art scene and explore new relationships. Certainly, I felt in tune with the political *'time for change'* era that embraced the new feminist movement ideology. For regular income, I could just survive with a women's retraining grant and study payment as the State Education Department were then contracting trainee teachers.

Being a Mature-Aged Student

Despite passing the university entrance exam, I still had real doubts as to my academic abilities. My young fellow students had mostly achieved 'A' final exam results at their former schools, compared with my ancient school certificate from twenty years earlier. For this tertiary entry, I had only taken a university entrance exam that consisted of multiple-choice questions – so what I did not know, I guessed! The exam only needed a couple of paragraphs of creative writing which was manageable, but I had never completed an essay longer than five hundred words. Therefore, I decided to work painstakingly hard to achieve an acceptable tertiary standard. Because I was a lone older woman, I did not think I would be directly involved in the lives of my fellow students – but then, I found this assumption to be entirely wrong.

Student Relationships

Being the only mature-aged woman in my courses, I quickly decided it would be wise to develop collaborative relationships with the student community. To my surprise, I found a warm acceptance from these young people, who were equally stressed in this educational environment, where they no longer had class teachers to guide their learning. Also, many were exploring their first sexual relationships along with developing the self-discipline necessary for university study.

Having enrolled in drama meant it was necessary for all students to work, discuss, and perform together – so friendly cooperation and communication were essential to pass our practical stage-acting exams. Because of this, it was crucial to behave as a team member of the student population. So, I dressed like they did in corded jeans and regularly met with these new young friends in the student café areas. Here, I shared all their daily joys, sorrows, and stresses of our assignment workloads.

On the other hand, the lecturers were the same age as me, and they obviously found it a novelty to have an older female student in their tutorials and lectures. As it happened, in this new era of access for women into the tertiary domain, I was one of the first mature-aged females in my university institution. In the beginning, I had invitations to join the lecturers on informal occasions in their staff quarters, and they went out of their way to give me special attention. Yes, I remember there were sexual innuendos underlying some of these interactions, but I had no sexual interest in these men. Besides, I was completely intimidated by their obvious high academic intelligence, so it was easy to politely ignore their overtures.

For this first year of tertiary study, I detached socially from my own age group – a fact that did not bother me. Of course, I was curious about the changing attitudes towards women, gay/queer people, and the current questioning of sexual behaviour. But for me, it was coping with the challenge of study assignments, assessments, and exams. I also enjoyed the popular music of the day and now think it became the 'adolescent' era I had never experienced – as my earlier teenage years were all about obeying the strict daily routines of classical dance training.

Sexual Study

Naturally, at times I did vaguely wonder where I fitted in the sexual realm, particularly after a couple of lesbians and young homosexual students approached me with questions as to my sexual orientation. By the second year, I began to research on all matters sexual to try and understand the kind of 'lust love' that my young student friends were eagerly looking for. I did not want to develop sexual relationships, and my interest was only one of ambiguous curiosity. Thus, I began haphazardly researching in the extensive university library and always had 'sex' or feminist books to dip into as a break from my set study readings. I somehow hoped the modern writers on the topics of sex and feminism would lead me to understand and define my own place in the heterosexual world. These kinds of authors were refreshing, as they widened my perspective about the role of women in society.

Feminist Readings

The four authors who impressed me can still be found on websites – were Simone de Beauvoir, Betty Friedan, Germaine Greer, and Marilyn French. (See bibliography.)

One of the first books I delved into was *The Second Sex* by Simone de Beauvoir. She highlighted the role of women in history and how they had become trapped in *'reproductive slavery.'* For her, marriage was a *'perverted institution,'* and she drew attention as to how organised religion had played a part in the subordination of women. With my brief experience of marriage and my growing religious doubts, her views made a strong impact.

The Feminine Mystique by Betty Friedan also made an impression. Her idea was that society had cast women into their roles because of their biology. I had never questioned why the expected destiny of a woman was to be a stay-at-home spouse and mother. Through her writing, I could see the wisdom of women having economic freedom and wider professional choices. She spoke of women not experiencing the same *'self-actualisation'* as men; that is, not being able to have or use opportunities to reach a greater personal potential. This book affirmed I had been right to extend my career prospects.

The other thing I gleaned from the Friedan writings was a certain sympathy towards males. She was sorry for their roles of having to be strong men who should not readily show feelings or tenderness. She saw people as being equal human beings (both men and women), who could help and complement one another. This was a likeable idea, as I loved the notion of being a team-player and a leader *with* men. In fact, I used to fantasise about being a Joan of Arc – but one who fought alongside a man in battles. At one stage, I even wore a Joan of Arc medallion with my 1970s caftan dress. However, I did not go along with Friedan's idea of homosexuality as being a result of gender-confusion in childhood.

Of course, I tried to read Germaine Greer's *The Female Eunuch*. I say tried, as I only read the parts I thought related to me. It was certainly a scholarly book, and at time, it was not an easy read. That said, I clearly understood her questioning of the myths of marriage and motherhood, in that these roles mainly '*served*' the man. I also agreed with Greer's notion about social conditioning playing a big part in gender behaviour. In addition, she made me feel guilt free if I decided not to have any more children, and confirmed my choice in taking up tertiary study at this stage in life.

On the topic of books, one that caused the most reaction from me was *The Women's Room* by Marilyn French. Here, the main character was a divorced woman who went on to study literature, which sounded a bit like me. The book presented many feminist issues, including the lack of women's identity, being subordinate to men, and the need to constantly check the mirror to be glamorous for the other sex. French's story also presented the notion that men had to see themselves as being superior to women, which was quite odd, as they were superior in terms of holding the economic, political, and social power.

I had grown up believing men were not just physically stronger but more intelligent – so therefore they held the main positions of influence. It was French's book that highlighted how male power permeated in relationships, family, education, business, science, law, government, and the media. Again, I was reminded how many women cooked and sewed, yet with few exceptions, it was the man who was the chef or fashion designer in the public domain.

My reaction to this book was visceral. It clearly awoke that feeling of validation in having faced and survived the social stigma of divorce, where I had experienced the same underlying concerns. After putting the book down, I can still remember feeling a righteous angry response in the knowledge that by being born female, you could expect unjustified treatment. It was also a relief to feel less guilty about wanting a career and wishing to have the same status men received in public life.

Sexual Performance

Naturally, I looked at books relating to the sexual performance itself, including the Kama Sutra, which was surprisingly complex despite its artistic images and writings.[32] I found reading and talking about sex academically fascinating, although there were still the elements of mystery, secrecy, and a sense of the risqué. Being aware of this, I hid my sex books from the younger students, as I noted they became quite giggly and nervous when discussing such texts like the Kama Sutra – besides, they treated me as an older, non-sexual, sisterly type of friend.

The other book I remember was one showing sexual intercourse positions, but instead of using nude drawings of people, the author had used teddy bears! It was full of illustrations with teddies coupled in many sexual postures – all with the same bland, contented 'Teddy' expressions on their faces. The idea was to make the book less confronting, and I was delighted the conclusion included an apology for any emotional harm to teddy bears!

---

[32] The Kama Sutra is the ancient Indian Hindu Sanskrit text on sexuality and emotional fulfilment in life. The texts outline four life goals: morality, prosperity, spirituality, and 'Kama' which is related to pleasure and love.

Of course, there were other subjects that decidedly changed my world view and attitudes towards society, human behaviour, and religion.

Academic Topics That Changed Me

There were a group of topics under the label of '*Theory and Practice of Education.*' These included viewing education through the academic lenses of sociology, psychology, philosophy/religion, and history. In truth, they did much more and taught me to question many preconceived ideas.

To summarise...

- *Sociology* confirmed how the current social norms had influenced my behaviour.
- *Psychology* highlighted the complexities of human behaviour – including my own.
- *Philosophy* raised the deeper questions of life relating to moral behaviour and religion. There were also questions around the understandings of creativity and imagination, plus what words such as love, attitude, belief, and faith really meant.
- *Religious study* used a non-judgmental examination of different doctrines, and I realised just how much religion instruction was interpreted from a male perspective. I also came to understand that moral behaviour could be separate from religion.
- *History* taught me how historians can distort facts and present bias in the 'creative' retelling of past stories.

Student Feminist Groups

There were feminist groups on campus who were determined to spearhead change. Overall, they aimed to *not* present themselves as sexual beings who dressed to please men. In protest, they did not wear bras, wore shapeless long dresses, grew hair everywhere, and embraced freedom from female domesticity. For them, men did not *help* with the dishes, they *did* the dishes on a normal regular basis. On the other hand, they did not reject sex but did not want the patriarchal society to control their sexuality.

Somehow, I did baulk at the idea of learning to love and understand our own bodies by bringing mirrors to inspect our sexual nether regions! This was practical for some young women who had no idea of their own anatomy 'down there.' In this regard, I knew my body quite well, so I did not bother to take part. Then again, it reminded me that my own anatomy did not look 'tidy,' with some scarring because of old birthing injuries. Subsequently, it did make me aware that I may need some medical attention if I were ever to consider sleeping with a man again.

The other feminist group on campus was militant and aimed to get laws and social practices changed. I admired these women for their strength of purpose in keeping involved in their political door knocking on many government doors. At least they were able to achieve some changes – such as better access for women in economic work and no-blame divorce laws. Then there was the introduction of the pronoun of Ms for divorced women who were neither a Miss nor a Mrs.[33]

Summary of Study Years

Overall, I felt inspired during this academic era with the introduction to so many new aspects of learning. I worked hard, dreaded failure,

---

[33] In Australia, feminist supporters formed The Women's Electoral Lobby (WEL) in 1972 to bring women's issues to the political forefront. (www.womenaustralia.info/biogs/AWE0021b.htm)

and overcame inner fears to explore contemporary ideas – including those relating to sexuality.

One of the other main pieces of learning related to an examination of religion and how this changed my beliefs. Consequently, new religious understanding gave clarity about the old attitudes to sex and moral beliefs that had been prevalent in my high-school years. Therefore, I will summarise what I learned about sex and religion in the following reflective essay that grew out of the 1970s study experience.

♥

Reflection

Religion and Sexuality

One of the unexpected outcomes of my four intensive study years was the introduction to religious studies and philosophy. These subjects became a major reason as to why I began to question my beliefs and attitudes to sex and religious hypotheses. Since then, I have continued to adjust my ideas on spiritual matters and exam the big questions, like '*What am I doing here?*'

Although these days I do not follow a particular religious doctrine, up to about the age of thirty, I tried to follow Protestant beliefs and rituals. Even then, many religious notions did not sit comfortably, and I always felt some disquiet in hearing the constant refrain of being born a sinner. Also, with the undercurrent about sex being sinful, I had trouble understanding the biblical interpretations – particularly relating to '*original sin.*'

Original Sin

What if we were viewed as being born basically 'good' rather than bad and sinful? Would we then have had a more positive outlook on human nature? In Christian churches, infant baptism serves to wash away '*original sin*' so the child can be '*reborn*' and renamed as a child of God. The first biblical sin in the 'Fall of Adam and Eve' story included bodily shame as a result of Eve being a disobedient woman. Somehow, sex, the physical body, and sin seem intertwined in terms of religious morality.

Therefore, it is understandable that the early church gave explanation that the godly Jesus was born of a virginal mother – so no sex or sin involved! In my youth, society upheld the belief in virginal purity of no sex before marriage, along with the strange leap to fully embrace sex after you left the altar. Unwritten rules dictated that sex should only take place within marriage, meaning that single people had to restrain all physical desires. So, as sex could be sinful, church leaders wanted any physical and psychological temptations removed.

Control of Desire

One section of my family were Methodists at a time when their church was completely against ballroom dancing – in case the physical closeness could induce a sexual desire. In this matter, my mother's family openly defied their parish churches, to the point they deliberately built large dancing 'ballrooms' in their houses. Therefore, I was grateful for their dancing genes, along with their strength to stand up for their own beliefs. I was amused by other local churches who allowed ballroom dancing – but with the proviso that instead of holding a partner close for waltzing, partners had to connect with extended arms and whizz around on the spot.

Because there existed a sense of fear about certain bodily functions, natural physical functions needed to be either hidden or controlled. Some people also considered masturbation as physically harmful, plus female menstruation and menopause were not topics for open discussion. Still, during my travels I have come across religious venues warning women who are menstruating to not enter. When pregnant, I wore loose clothing to conceal the signs of pending motherhood, where today fashion applauds a life-growing belly. As I write, I am pleased with the news of Woolworths stores openly acknowledging female menstruation by listing *'Period Care'* in their larger aisle signage. Although the female body's ability to produce life is truly remarkable, I admit that menstruation, childbirth, and menopause are not easy processes for women, but I think tainting these functions with shame is quite offensive.

In my mother's teen years, her parents did not encourage basic pleasurable activities engaging the body on Sundays. This included no ballroom dancing, no playing of sports, and no music other than hymns. The church promoted the seventh day to concentrate the mind on religious thoughts and certainly not moving the body or engaging in any fun activities. Once when my mother was playing modern jazz tunes on a Sunday, my grandmother did not openly complain but just quietly replaced her music book with a musical hymn sheet. Mother's reaction was not to protest but to play the hymns in a jazzed-up swing style. What did Grandma do then? She quietly returned the modern music to the stand – so it was a case of a graceful back-down to let the music be a freedom of choice!

In church, I noted one could gaze at artistic statues, stare at beautiful stained-glass windows, and sing anthem-like hymns, but there was *no* dance and little body movement other than standing, sitting, and kneeling. Years later, I was delighted when church authorities invited me to dance in an inaugural service to celebrate the union of Presbyterian, Congregation, and Methodist churches in becoming The Uniting Church. How times had changed; although at the time, we danced in long skirts and used mainly expressive arm movements.

In fact, I rather like the old pagan idea where the body was a sacred vessel of the gods and where sex was a creative and artistic force of nature. The old pagan religions often had more equal regard towards the masculine and feminine, with procreation celebrated rather than feared.

Christian Love

As a child, I understood that I should love Jesus and God to have my sins forgiven if I wanted to get to heaven. Secretly, I knew I *did not* love these unseen people – so back then, I thought pretence was my only choice for salvation. Later in life, I could not understand St Paul of The New Testament, who wrote the beautiful Corinthian letter about the sincerity of love, but who also saw marriage to being inferior to chastity and celibacy. Not that I realised at the time there existed a belief about the end of the world being nigh, so perhaps marriage and having children was not a priority. Some present-day biblical students have suggested that St Paul could have been an asexual, or he was only suggesting that a single life created more time for Godly deeds. The other vague suggested reference to asexuality was when Jesus referred to eunuchs, *'who were born this way'* (Matthew 19:12). However, these vague bible quotes do not really provide any positive justification or acceptance for an asexual way of being.

Before, I had looked to the Church for guidance in career choices and marriage problems without much success. But, I can remember the shame of breaking the public vow made in a church about remaining with my husband *'until death do us part.'* Like asexuality, finding my own spirituality has been yet another journey. In fact, I am sure the religious influence was a detrimental factor in trying to uncover my true sexual orientation. Other than a heterosexual marriage between a man and a woman, and with sex only allowed in marriage, there were no alternatives as presented in 1950s moral climate.

Subsequently, sexual behaviour from a Christian point of view was originally confusing and did not provide me with any comfort. For years, with the social/cultural pressure, I felt I had failed or sinned from a moral/religious point of view by being divorced. Although sex did not matter to me as a single person, it did matter if I ever wanted to be in a loving marriage. I also began to feel that love and sex could be separate, as for me, any attraction towards having a partner was all about wanting love and not sex.

Academic Religious Studies

At university I enrolled in topics on religion to explore the historical origins of theatre and music, which formed in the expressions of many ancient spiritual practices. Also, studying other religions was a wonderful adjunct to the study of drama. Being an actor meant you constantly had to put yourself in the shoes of other characters, with their distinctive ways of thinking and believing. The other motivation was the 1970s, modern approaches to study in our university religious department. Here, the broadminded lecturers presented religion without judgement and approved if nonreligious people followed their own moral practices and personal rituals. So, I also felt encouraged to develop my own beliefs and to accept others' beliefs. The religious study gave me new perspectives in three ways...

1. I realised how much religious doctrine came from the interpretation of ancient scripts by men who held conservative social beliefs. They had 'faith' but were men of their time, who held narrow views of women, did not understand gender diversity, and had a fear-based idea about original sin.

2. Sex was related to the evils of the flesh with the Christian emphasis being on the blessed state of being a virgin. This odd thinking could have come from an early misinterpretation of the Hebrew word for an unmarried woman of childbearing age. Somehow, it came to mean a woman who was not yet sexually active.

3. To me, Christianity was a patriarchal religion, which yielded to a mystical 'Father' where rules and rituals were for the forgiveness of sins and to create hope of an 'eternal' life after death. (Noting the term 'Father' created an image of a male-gendered, patriarchal god.) As a child I knew you had to obey your parents, teachers, and an unseen god. As an adult, I thought I should follow this mystical godlike father with the same almost childlike obedience.

After I completed my studies, I felt brave enough to formulate my own beliefs, and it felt more adult to take self-responsibility in making moral decisions – by weighing up priorities, examining intentions, and undertaking kindly behaviour. I came to see such self-regulation needed moral effort in both thought and outward behaviour. Here I remember my own father, who believed more in action than just prayer. For example, when a local farmer broke his leg just before crop-planting, other men asked Father to pray for his recovery. Father's response was *'I will do better than that. I haven't time to get to church, because I will be organising all the farmers to sow Pete's crops next weekend.'* This was an act of true moral responsibility, and it proved how kindly thought could be translated into a real outcome.

My Moral/Spiritual Beliefs

I make no apology about 'cherry-picking' moral ideas for good living from several religious and philosophical sources. Although I still lack conviction about organised religion, I believe in the emotional need to express an inner spiritual life and to celebrate the miraculous wonder of my own birth. Also, to marvel at the little blue orb of our earthly planet-home.

On the other hand, I do not dismiss all the kindly human values as expressed in the teachings of various wise prophets, including Jesus. There is much to admire in the creativity inspired by the religious spirit, although my motivation to visit churches is usually for historical/artistic reasons or personal reflection rather than religious ritual. Of course, I do attend weddings, christenings, and funerals out of respect for other people. I also acknowledge the charity work of churches and do not decry anyone's version of who they perceive as being their God(s).

It must be hard for some atheists, humanists, or agnostics who ask the deep moral questions of themselves. In fact, it would be easier to obey 'given' commandments and totally accept a dominant male God than search for the moral truth within myself. It is the 'Agape' universal and all-embracing love I would like to feel towards people and the world. To nurture this type of love through my own thought and behaviour is easier said than done.

Although I no longer entertain the idea of a patriarchal superhuman God who has a plan for everyone, I acknowledge an inner spiritual life that inspires care of self, fellow humans, and the world. If I have any 'faith' at all, it is in the human capacity to demonstrate loving compassion to other human beings and all living things. Also if I ever used an idea of God – it would be a collective name for the positive *spirit* of creativity, and feeling of love towards living things.

Therefore, my spirituality is now based in a humanist idea where I constantly need to consult my 'best self' for guidance, plus listen to the wise prophets of today and yesterday. In fact, I acknowledge my '*wise self*' with whom I have internal dialogue to sort out life-priorities. This 'self' shows I should aim for caring, loving, and celebrating life with gratitude. I am sure all good souls look for something bigger and wiser beyond their normal everyday lives – so, even an atheist like me adopts rituals and philosophies to fulfil those deeper human spiritual needs. In fact, I love the Sufi idea where there is a sense of a 'divine awe' the second before you laugh – that being the pure delight of recognising a truth.

But what has religion got to do with my asexuality? In my own constructed cosmology, I celebrate the creative wonder of diversity and emotional intensity that exists in sexuality and artistic experiences in life. As an asexual, I do not like for religious belief to diminish my human sexuality. The powerful drive of sex is one of the wonders of our human existence, and as an asexual, I celebrate the creative life-force that resulted in my own birth.

JOURNAL 12

Planning for Relationships

Dear Journal,
This entry describes the stage when I engaged in spasmodic efforts to self-evaluate my life and recommenced looking for loving heterosexual partnerships.

During my final study years, I gained the confidence to again question my lack of close physical relationships. It was also the hippie era of '*free love*,' and everyone was examining sexuality from a more flexible point of view; so I decided to use the newly acquired psychological knowledge to seriously analyse my own life.

Maslow's Hierarchy

I liked the psychology of 'Maslow's Hierarchy' – the chart of human needs as defined by Abraham Maslow in 1943.

The chart seen as a five-tiered pyramid of human 'needs' covered the following aspects...

1. physical/safety
2. love/belonging
3. self-esteem/achievement
4. self-actualisation/self-worth
5. transcendence and spirituality

In contrast, instead of a pyramid, I used another diagram presenting a simple rectangle to construct my own life-evaluation schema. Below, the first diagram shows the almost impossible ideal of a balanced life, and the second lopsided shape represented my life as I saw it at the time.[34]

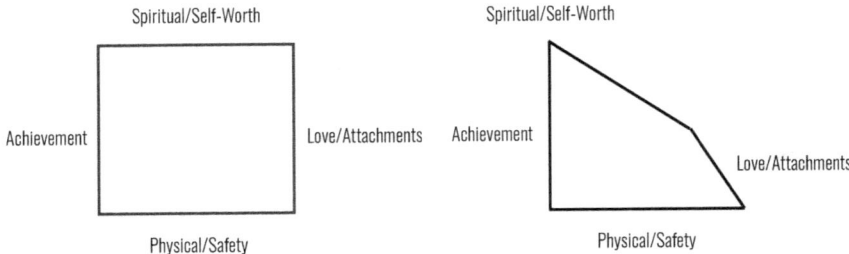

From my diagram, I could see my areas about love and self-worth were unfulfilled. Consequently, I did not feel comfortable with myself as being worthy of love. I did not know the missing element preventing a more balanced life lay in the lack of knowledge about my asexuality. Although I could never say I was unhappy, I assumed my lack of sexual relationships meant that I was missing an important part of life's love experience. Therefore, I decided I should put more effort into overcoming my basic disinterest in sex, and it was time to make a serious rational plan to remedy myself.

A Plan to Find 'Heterosexual Love'

With hindsight, I still marvel at my continual efforts to become a 'normal' woman who could fully want a man. Despite all my newly acquired learning about contemporary choices for women, the strong example of my happily married parents still had me believing I could find 'sexual love' in a heterosexual relationship. I knew I was not a lesbian and I liked male friendships, so I vaguely wondered if my lack of sexual desire might have resulted from the shame of being divorced – coupled with the responsibility of being a single parent.

---

[34] This version of Maslow is from the motivational speaker, Bert Weir, and his book *You Were Born Special and Wonderful – What Happened?* (1993, Weir Knightsbridge).

PLANNING FOR RELATIONSHIPS

Then again, I doubted that it was anything to do with my former marriage, and I was sure my divorce had occurred for other reasons. In fact, I *still* do not believe the sexual side of my first marriage was a major cause of the breakdown. However, at this stage I liked my life and did not mind living alone, but believed I might be happier within a caring relationship. Being loved by someone was certainly an attractive idea.

I thought if I tackled the sexual problem like an ongoing academic project, then there might be a way of achieving this elusive loving partnership. With hindsight, I can see that taking a heterosexual path in the search for love was not realistic. But, in my late-thirties, I still believed in the marriage ideal and so formulated the following plan based on Maslow's chart of human needs to guide me in the quest.

It looked something like this...

1. *Physical*: Arrange a medical appointment to fix scar tissue and deformity resulting from giving birth and get adhesions removed so intercourse could be more achievable. Decide on a method of birth control; either the Pill or have fallopian tubes tied, as I had ceased birth control since my divorce.
2. *Social/psychological*: Accept invitations to social functions and practice connecting or engaging with men. Talk to males about sex if the connection reaches a comfortable level. Finally, allow sexual contact to happen if it seems safe and respectful.
3. *Philosophical*: Do some deeper research into the concepts of love and romance with the aim to develop clearer definitions and meaning.

The university environment created a good space to examine these other personal elements in addition to my studies. Now I felt was a suitable time to take charge of my social life to become that intangible sexual me. So, it was near the age of forty, I put my plan into action.

Attention to the Physical

Firstly, I went to a nearby older GP doctor to discuss my concerns about labia scarring and birth control options. I came away feeling both annoyed and frustrated by his examination and comments. Yes, I had scarring, but he also declared that my internal muscles had '*atrophied*' due to lack of sexual activity for the past twelve years. *What?* He tentatively hinted about problems with 'my husband' but when informed I had been divorced for many years, he said, '*That explains the situation.*'

I then suggested that in the future I might rectify the 'atrophy' condition and asked if I could have a script for the contraceptive pill. He gave me a most disapproving look and told me that he could not, as it would be against his moral practice. *Really?* It was then I spied an icon of the Virgin Mary on his desk and realised I was speaking with a religious old doctor who did not want me exploring 'immoral' pathways. He warned me against listening to any new permissive ideas that did not take marriage seriously. So, being a divorcée seeking sex was clearly putting me in the sinful, naughty corner. The doctor suggested I should make another appointment for a longer talk, but I was too annoyed to ever go back. I then found a woman who was a competent GP and far more understanding. Therefore, she gave me a prescription for contraception without any qualms. Although I was still at childbearing age, I saw myself as a devoted teacher of dance and drama with my students taking the place of any more children. My own son was a teenager, and although I enjoyed being a mother, I did not want to start the whole childbearing process again.

Later, when I found I did not like the side-effects of oral contraception, I decided to see a gynaecologist about a more permanent prevention of pregnancy and to deal with my 'untidy state' after the childbirth stitching. A small surgical procedure fixed adhesions so sexual intercourse would be more possible, and the use of tampons made easier. *Yay!* At the same time, I had my fallopian tubes tied, so now I was physically ready for intimate relationships. I was pleased to have completed the 'physical' part of my plan, but I was still not fully committed to dating someone.

Social Life and My Son

At university, it was difficult to meet suitable heterosexual men my own age, considering I was mainly with young students who had just left school. Despite this, their youthful enthusiasm to explore relationships inspired me to investigate the social/emotional side of my own life – besides, I was conscious that my son was also entering a stage of sexual awareness. Being only a couple of years younger than my fellow students, he displayed a normal heterosexual interest in girls. At the time, I was grateful he could get a wider variety of information from my student friends and professional places such as the Family Planning clinic. His interactions with my fellow young students also gave him more general knowledge and a healthy approach to relationships with the other sex. I still feel relief that he grew into being a happily adjusted young person who was always comfortable with his heterosexual orientation.

Meeting Men

As for me, with my newly acquired drama skills, I found it easier to engage in meeting men at disco dances or social events. Just catching eye glances seemed to create a connection, and at least I had the satisfaction of males taking some notice of me. These interactions were socially rewarding, as I had previously deliberately avoided attracting this kind of interest. However, there was tension, as I could not tell how such exchanges would develop, and I was still ambivalent about even seeking intimate closeness with a man. Nevertheless, curiosity along with a desire to be normal and to be loved were the main motivators.

On the downside, many of these hetero guys were a bit needy. Often, they were between marriages, recently divorced, married – but ready to have a fling – widowed, or lost and lonely. They were fundamentally respectful, friendly, and more than ready to develop a connection. On the other hand, I quickly became the shoulder to cry on, or the sisterly supporter for their problematic life situations. For my part, I did not mind being the sympathetic friend, as I was comfortable in this type of caring role. So, I often found myself being the 'supporter and helper' while these men were mending their hearts or trying to escape a 'tired' marriage.

However, there were times when I became the object of male desire. Uncomfortable situations arose when a male companion would make a sudden reach for my hand or grab my shoulders for an unexpected kiss. These moves usually took me by surprise and seemed to occur without warning. Sometimes during an evening farewell, my date would lunge towards me, and with my head pinned against the car window, my free hand would be frantically reaching to open the door. This was often my fault, as I could not always 'read' the emotional moves.

Of course, one would expect the kindly hug motivated by friendly affection, but not the sudden dramatic actions that probably emanated from a natural, lust-inspired emotion. I could never foresee or understand the lust-driven element of sex, as opposed to the kind of physical gestures that resulted from loving feelings. I could only just tolerate a sexual approach that I believed came from a place of honest affection. But sex for fun or pleasure was something I rationally understood, although deep down, I could not feel in the same way. For me, I preferred the idea that sexual expression resulted from feelings of genuine love, but I realised that not even a sincere bit of affection awoke any passionate desire in me.

After a couple of dates, my male companions could obviously feel my boundaries were too narrow for them. Often, they kindly expressed I was not ready for a committed relationship and assumed I was too involved in being a mother, or too dedicated to study and dance. Then again, men often detected from my conversation that I was only *'putting my toe in the water'* where relationships were concerned, and not a serious candidate for intimate liaisons. Even in situations after a long night of dancing and dining, where I managed to sleep with a date on a bed or sofa for the remaining hours – it would usually end with a dawn departure that was disappointing for the poor man.

I even tried to be academic about dating – so I looked for men from a variety of professions, who were younger, older, or with a different world view. Through this kind of investigation I found any man, regardless of race or culture, did not have me imagining any desire to sleep with him. Dancing, socialising, going to restaurants and events together was a *'yes'* for me. An invitation to kiss and cuddle was a *'maybe yes.'* Bed together, was still a *'no'* – though I persuaded myself to be brave enough to try. So, on occasions, try I did, but there was always an after-feeling of sad disappointment. With hindsight, I feel regret that I wasted the time of these hapless men. I could have unwittingly toyed with their emotions or promoted sexual arousal that was never to be satisfied. In those days, I think the term for women like that was *'a prick teaser'*! In my defence, it was never my intention to be dishonest, and I always held the vague hope that my sincere friendly efforts would awaken some sort of latent sexual appetite.

I can now see it was a fruitless struggle that would take many more years to resolve, mainly because my problem was invisible.

Sometimes, I still wonder why I put in all the thought and effort. Probably, it was because I wanted to share the same exciting sexual conversations my female friends seemed to enjoy, along with the desire to be loved by someone.

The other positive spin-off was that I could transfer my relationship experiences into the realms of dance and drama. This meant I could use any emotional adventures to improve my stage performances. In drama, this technique is called *'emotional memory,'* where feelings experienced in real life can help to create a more authentic portrayal of characters on stage. Therefore, even my failed sexual misadventures could serve in giving me valuable lessons in human behaviour that could be of use in other ways.

Coping with Intercourse

After the exploratory study years, dating straight men continued in a spasmodic fashion - albeit still problematically. On the positive side, I was better at engaging, connecting, and at times, even coping with the odd sexual encounter. How did I cope? It developed into a technique – a bit like surviving an unpleasant task and doing it as well as possible. The procedure entailed...

- o Drinking alcohol prior (sometimes two glasses to slightly numb the senses).
- o Secretly apply KY jelly beforehand (to prevent physical discomfort if I could not control my own 'core-gasmic' timing).
- o Physically controlling my own orgasm (core-gasm) to ease friction by using the correct type of abdominal contraction.
- o Engage in prolonged conversational chatting during foreplay (thus making the actual intercourse much shorter).
- o Use of music (to aid emotional mood and relieve stress).

- Watching my positioning and breathing (to keep a degree of calm and control).
- Relax mentally as much as possible, and so induce the ability to float out of my own body (which was a way of removing myself from the situation).

There was always a sense of relief when intercourse was over, along with the satisfaction that I had 'performed' and willingly given the man what he wanted.

I also avoided oral sex as it was not to my taste. But I did encourage the 'L/R' (leg release) technique – referring to when intimate interactions had aroused the man, I would encourage him to come (that is, ejaculate) on my leg. I did not mind a man doing this, as it made me feel less guilty about not giving him the satisfaction I felt he deserved. The 'leg release' ritual became standard practice, after which I would be lovingly kind and grateful for his show of affection.

If sex did ever occur normally, my dance/drama skills also helped. Having a supple body, I used dance to prolong foreplay, and I used my drama experience to enact vocalisations of rapture, thus drawing on my performance techniques.[35] I was often pleased with my simulated sexual routines, particularly if I received approving feedback from my partner. Meanwhile, I was always desperately hoping I had disguised the fact that the sex was a job and not an act of passion. Sadly, after 'making love' I usually felt waves of depressive emptiness, and there was no contented afterglow. However, I liked sleeping or 'spooning' next to the firmness of a male body.

Then, there was always the problem of where such encounters took place. I could never cope with having sex in my own home, so

---

[35] I am reminded of the American romantic comedy movie *When Harry Met Sally* (1989, Columbia Pictures), where the actor, Meg Ryan, gave a memorable vocal performance of an orgasm.

they occurred in hotel rooms, the man's home, or while away on conferences. Fortunately, they were with men I trusted; except they were more acquaintances than close friends. Because of this, I now cannot even remember their names or professions. If a close male friend did stay after a night of dancing, it usually only entailed long philosophical talks and cuddling with the occasional 'leg release' ritual. Fortunately, I never experienced a partner who was disrespectful or forced me in any way.

In all, having sex was like visiting the dentist, where uncomfortable procedures take place but where one bravely does not protest. At least the dentist knows he or she might be causing discomfort, while I would hope my partner was imagining our equal enjoyment. Dance also helped here, as dancers always endeavour to conceal the physical effort – unlike sport, where one can show the labour of exertion. The sexual intercourse situation often reminded me of my grandmother who once jokingly said, '*We were told to just do your duty and think of England.*' This meant sex was a duty to produce children for the then-existing Victorian British Empire. As for me, it was my 'duty' to do what my partner sexually expected.

Pornography

Back to my sex challenge. The other course of action was to go to the cinema to view a pornographic film and see if that would give me inspiration. Certainly, the sex scenes in televised films did nothing for me; I often lost concentration and used those segments as time for a coffee break. In this case, I just wished the film had a decent story plot and believable drama. Years ago, I had seen sex portrayed in the 1950s films that consisted of one ardent kiss in the final camera shot, usually with 'THE END' scrolled across their faces. Now, more recent movies show frantic scenes where couples mutually rip off clothes after only experiencing ardent eye contact. Here just an exchange of meaningful glances seems to give rise to a rapid exchange of lustful pheromones.

As for a pornographic film, the one I saw was virtually funny. One scene opened with a girl riding a horse in a see-through negligée, which seem to be a huge turn on for the other male actor watching nearby. *Why* she was on a horse wearing flimsy night attire without a saddle did not matter to the plotless movie. Sex scenes evolved without any believable storylines and usually occurred in inappropriate places such as schoolrooms, doctors' surgeries, office broom-cupboards, or behind library shelves. They also happened without any clear psychological reason, and the characters seemed so magically primed for sex that it would have me thinking, '*What on earth brought that on?*'

Sadomasochism

As for cruelty or bondage – it is beyond my imagination to see how that could ever be pleasurable. I intellectually understand the pleasure/pain experience principle but would not want to engage in it myself. If someone restrained me to cause a denial of physical freedom, then this would create feelings of apprehension, not delight! Even mild harm to the body would bother me, as I have profound respect and desire to protect my own precious physical anatomy. I am sure such attitudes come from my dance experience, where we had to give our bodies prime care for performance. Besides, I do not like the idea of relinquishing any of my personal power or control.

Tantric Sex

I even remembered academically exploring the idea of Tantric sex.[36] It certainly sounded good in written text, where it described gentle, slow, sensual practices and rituals with a partner that could result in heightened sexual feelings. In such rituals, it was not necessary to make intercourse the major goal. Pleasuring your partner seemed to be a generous and kind thing to do, and as it was like 'a sexual dance,' I wondered whether this would help in creating sexual desire, but it never happened for many reasons. Whenever I raised the topic, the reactions were either, *'That's weird stuff'* or *'I couldn't be bothered taking all that time to get satisfaction.'* Then again, despite my vague interest, I was unable to trust that such a practice would not lead to more unwanted intercourse. Anyway, this short-lived Tantric idea faded into the ether.

To summarise, my social relationship experiments during this stage were not successful, but I was still prepared to keep on trying. Why? I assumed it must have been the desire for affection and not wanting to face the prospect of being alone for the rest of my life. But now to the final part of my plan, which was to research the topic of 'love' and how it differed from other feelings.

The 'Love' Question

My philosophical research into the complex notion of *'what is love'* was not that successful either. I understood some kinds of love, such as parental love for a child, the caring affection towards one's staff or students, the love of a platonic friend, sexual love, and the 'Agape'

---

[36] Tantric sex comes from the ancient Hindu concept of *'tantra,'* referring to rituals that 'weave' the physical and spiritual together. In Tantric sex, an orgasm is not the goal. Rather, the goal is a slow exploration of the sexual/physical sensations of the body. Today, partners use the practice to become sexually 'in tune' with their bodies.

form of universal/unconditional love. However, at this time, I did not discover a definition that encompassed the basic dynamic of such a wonderful feeling. People liberally use this one little word 'love,' yet, it was frustrating not to find an adequate description of this most beautiful emotion of human experience. With all the diverse types of desires creating so many intensities of the love-emotion, it is going to take further thought to get a grip on this 'love stuff.' Love has undoubtedly been the hardest issue to unravel and express – so I will return to this topic later.

Meanwhile, my best sexual discussions took place with my special gay/queer friends who had also explored love and sexuality in their own way. Out of all the explorations to achieve an intimate relationship with a man, it was my dear gay/queer friends who engaged in kindly discourse and gave me the most comforting support. They made me feel safe despite my sexual confusion and insecurities – so I wish to salute them all.

Reflection

The Gay/Queer Community

During and following the midlife study era, my greatest source of affection and care came from supportive friendships with gay/queer men. Fortunately, dance and the arts attract these remarkably creative males who have an enhanced eye for the visual and sensitive abilities to 'read' people. There was one such male in my academic course who was ten years younger, and being a single, divorced mother, he could see I, too, was 'atypical' within our student community. Through him, I gained introduction to a gay/queer nightclub where improvised social dancing abounded, and I was in my element.

As a single female, I feel blessed having gay/queer male friends. Why? Because this kind of friendship is unbiased, trustworthy, honest, and without the tension of ulterior sexual motives. Therefore, I was comfortable in the knowledge that these men did not want to sleep with me. They clearly liked my company, loved to have someone to join them on the dance floor, plus they gave me a male companionship that was both rewarding and empathetic.

With the gay/queer men I could discuss anything – whether it be my reticence relating to sexual intercourse, talking about feelings of alienation, or sharing our likeminded interests in the arts or literature. They offered friendship with the kind of intimacy that comes with genuine communication; plus, we shared the mutual endeavour of wanting social acceptance as well as a meaningful career.

There was always a sense of real companionship, and I appreciated how gay/queer men could express a sensitive understanding of male behaviour. Besides, as they often have a sense of fashion, I respected their advice on dress, hair style, and home décor. I also loved their humour, and how they could laugh in a world where isolation, rejection, lack of social justice, and fear of persecution had been ever present. Therefore, I instinctively understood their struggle to be themselves, and I felt empathy towards their anxious experiences of *'coming out'* about their sexuality to family and friends.

The gay/queer community was a perfect place for people like me who did not socially fit in, as it created a space where I could feel accepted. Here I truly relaxed and did not feel I had to act in a heterosexual way. In any sexual discussion, neither they or I could explain my lack of heterosexual or homosexual desire. Although one gay/queer friend did say, *'You are above love, darling – so just enjoy being you.'* He was the first person to sense that I was fundamentally happy in my default state of not needing a sexualised kind of love. The *'being above love'* comment I am sure did not mean I was somehow spiritually pure by *not* wanting sex. He meant I had a different, more remote way of loving and suggested that I was a slightly weird social butterfly. I liked this idea that I could spread myself around to be affectionate towards many people in a generalised way.

Once, I went with a gay/queer friend to a counselling meeting for young homosexual people. At one point, the leader asked what I had in common with the other attendees, considering I was not a lesbian. It was then I examined why I connected so closely with my gay/queer friends. At the time, I gave the following reasons: I was a divorcée, a single parent, a feminist, a mature-aged student, and a teacher of dance – all of which alienated me from other women in my age group. Therefore, I liked being with people who were socially alienated in some way, as I knew I was too, albeit for slightly dissimilar reasons. Of course, my comfort with gay/queer friendships had to do with my lack of sexual interest – not that I even acknowledged such a thought at the time. I just loved being with them as I shared the same sense of being different.

I also considered my gay/queer friendships had a beneficial effect on my son, and he was able to accept and understand the gay/queer world without prejudice. On the other hand, these men never propositioned him for a same-gender relationship, and they accepted him as a heterosexual young male. In fact, my gay/queer friends were more like brothers who looked out for his welfare.

Not a Lesbian

After communicating with gay/queer men and women about their life journeys, I constantly thought about my own efforts to connect with heterosexual men and wondered whether I was on the right track. Once a well-spoken lesbian woman approached me and asked whether I had ever thought about a sexual relationship with a woman. This was easy to reject as I did not like the thought of physically embracing women. Also, I preferred the social banter and more direct type of male conversations, which meant I inclined towards men's company – even if I did not want to sleep with them. Frankly, it would have been easier to be a lesbian than be on the fruitless hunt for a heterosexual man. Sadly, I did not feel sexually attracted to females either, and so I continued to seek friendships in the gay/queer world while haphazardly searching for a partner in the hetero world.

Asexual Acceptance in the Gay/Queer Community

Relationships with the LGBTIQA+ community gave me something else to consider. Although my experience with the gay/queer community has never presented such a problem, I understand that some asexuals have reported nonacceptance from the gay/queer community. Since knowing about asexuality, people have asked whether I ever received or sensed rejection from the gay/queer people. Only once a gay/queer guy laughingly called me a '*fag hag*,' meaning a straight girl who hangs around gay/queer guys. Then, the term was slightly derogatory, inferring that a woman was either a closet lesbian or lacked the confidence to form intimate relationships with straight men. These days the term is '*fruit fly*,' and it can be trendy to have gay/queer as well as straight friends. However, I dislike the idea that such friendships could be abused by those females who want a virtual 'gay/queer husband,' or someone they use only for shopping advice. I also like to believe that female friendships with gay men can be mutually valuable. If I were a gay man, I think it would be advantageous to have a sisterly female friend to support and advocate for my welfare. Besides, if sexually diverse people have experienced family rejection, then finding friendships that create a virtual family would also be beneficial.

Unlike many asexuals, gay/queer people know what it is to receive overt unacceptance and be socially persecuted. They have been physically attacked (even murdered), imprisoned, and experienced continual derision of their sexual expression. Gay/queer people have not had a choice other than to challenge and educate against such negative public reactions. Naturally, an asexual person does not have this degree of attack or quite the same history of abuse. This is because asexuality is more invisible, and without overt sexual behaviour, it does not bring the same kind of scrutiny.

Asexual Social Suffering

As an asexual, I do feel akin to that same sense of hidden oppression and fear of nonacceptance if I reveal my sexual identity. This means asexuals *can and do* feel alienation, harbour a need for secrecy, suffer fear of loneliness, and feel a challenge to their sense of identity or self-worth. If asexuals reveal themselves, they can expect criticism, opposition, judgement, and omission from certain groups in society. They, too, will hear negative questions, disbelief, suggested cures, and weird ideas about potential causes. Asexuals will continue to feel emotional pain if they remain silent but face negative reactions if they speak out about their orientation. 'Dammed if they do and dammed if they don't!' Either way, asexuals can suffer; so for me, it feels better to reveal the truth and hope that members of the gay/queer community will be my greatest allies.

An asexual can also expect to meet doubts in the medical world and where sometimes doctors and psychologists are ill-informed and still hold old-fashioned ideas about sex and gender. Therefore, I am grateful for the acceptance I have found in the gay/queer community and hope other asexuals feel the same inclusion. It is my hope to stand with my gay/queer friends as we struggle for acceptance and work against any injustices for the acknowledgment that gender diversity is both normal and desirable.

JOURNAL 13

♥

Marriage and Divorce No. 2

Dear Journal,

This was certainly another era of new explorations and risky decisions! At this point, I took part in various teaching ventures as well as enjoyed seeing my son begin his career path in education. When he began to explore his own relationships with girls, I realised that soon he would not be so emotionally reliant on me. With his growing independence, I knew I would experience the 'empty-nest syndrome,' which made me again think about searching for a long-term partner to fill this void.

Motivation to Move Interstate:

The motivations for my next big life decisions were twofold. One, the aspiration to seek new career experiences, and two, my son leaving home to live with his girlfriend. Naturally, he was planning his life without needing my daily closeness, a fact that as a mother and teacher I applauded. On the other hand, I knew our parting would create an element of personal loss. Therefore, when the opportunity to study in another city came my way, I accepted a place into a tertiary creative/therapeutic dance course. I thought this was a good move to leave my son with the freedom to be himself and at the same time give me a challenge to explore life in another city. There was a 'twin' desire to have him close but more importantly, to see him embrace his own independence. Besides, I knew we had the ability to stay emotionally bonded despite any physical distance.

Another factor was a desire to extend my dance education with a focus on creative and therapeutic movement for a wider range of people. I sensed my dance/drama work needed another creative boost. At this stage, I was teaching in various venues, and being a freelance educator, I was working like a travelling performer. This meant I seldom saw the ongoing development of students while heavily engaged in part-time contract teaching in schools, tertiary institutions, and dance studios. Acceptance into a tertiary dance course and an opportunity to work in new city artistic environment seemed to be an exciting move. So once again I arrived at the crossroads, where I felt compelled to investigate new horizons. I also thought this might be a suitable time to look for a partner to replace my son, and besides, there was still that hidden social pressure to be married.

Husband No. 2 and Moving Interstate

Before I left my home state, I had met a man (A.T.) who was a decade younger. He was sociable and highly intelligent, with a self-deprecating sense of humour. Having worked in the media, A.T. was a skilled journalist and had a good speaking 'radio/TV' actor's voice. He displayed an attraction towards me, which was flattering, except I presumed the friendship would not develop, as I was intending to move interstate. As fate would have it, he, too, gained an excellent position in the same interstate city where I was to study, and it was only natural to keep contact after we moved. Because we were both carefully watching finances, it seemed sensible to combine our resources, so we decided to rent a flat together. The next event brought forth that other aspect of my personality – that is, being a 'rescuer.'

The Tendency to Rescue

A.T. had constant pain in his joints that did not seem to relate to an ordinary injury. After extensive tests, he received the diagnosis of a chronic muscular disease that was not curable. Naturally, I felt sorry for him and did all I could to encourage varied forms of therapy to help his condition. Meanwhile, at this early stage in our relationship, I felt emotionally closer to him and did not mind that his disease caused a reduced display of physical affection. In other words, he was often too tired for sex.

During the first twelve busy months, I gained teaching work, threw myself into dance study, and became the almost indispensable carer to my new friend. I replaced the care of my son with another man to support. Somehow, this relationship was different, as care for my son was all about making him independent, and care of A.T. was doing the opposite. In fact, I was well on my way to becoming a co-dependent, where I was becoming stressed by doing all the worrying and being overly involved in treatments to help his illness.[37]

The Marriage Proposal

At a wedding reception for mutual friends, A.T. was slightly intoxicated and made the big announcement to all assembled that we were to be married. This declaration took me by surprise, as although he previously said that we made a good team and hinted that he could not live without me, he had not seriously discussed anything about having a long-term relationship. Even now, I cannot fathom how I just sat there, smiled dumbly, and nodded in vague agreement. Somehow in that moment, I thought having an amusing friend for life would not be such a bad idea. A.T. was fun, obviously adored me, did not want children, and utterly supported the idea of me having a career. Of course, there was the sex thing, but I thought I could manage, as his muscular disease confirmed that our sex life would not be all that vibrant! Within six months, we were married, and my

---

[37] Co-dependency occurs when caring for others creates physical or emotional damage to oneself. I came to recognise my co-dependent tendencies after reading *Co-dependent No More* by Melody Beattie (1989, Collins Dove).

parents were delighted, believing I could now have the same emotional warmth of marriage they still enjoyed.

What I ignored were the deeper motivations at play. The social pressure to have a partner, the rebound of parting with my son, the tendency to be a rescuer, and my need for affection. After a twenty-year gap between marriages, I considered myself to be older and wiser, so I thought it was time to give this partnership a 100 percent try. Of course, I also managed to ignore other 'red flags' by not paying attention to the fact that A.T. liked long alcoholic lunches, was overly generous in spending his money, and did not suffer fools gladly. This translated into him often drinking too much, not being a good money-manager, and becoming quite angry if people did not agree with his point of view. But, at the time, I was sure this marriage would work, and besides, I considered I was now a more intelligent woman of the world. How wrong I was!

Trying to be the Good Wife

Because I was so determined to be a good wife, I secretly attended small courses in sexuality and later enrolled to study a graduate diploma in human relationships that included topics on gender. These short courses created a good environment for talking about sex with other women. During the sessions, I found the sexual discussions did not cause me any unease; only curiosity to find the 'key' that would give me a pleasurable, or at least, more desirable sexual experience within marriage.

The other women participants were unhappy with their sex lives and current relationships. Most had inattentive husbands and wanted more sex, or they doubted their attractiveness and desired more loving sex. I felt sad for all of them, but I did not share quite the same problems. They liked and wished for a better sex life, and I just wished I could like sex.

To explain myself to the group, I just said, '*I found trouble in enjoying intercourse.*' I did not admit to myself I had never felt inspired by the idea and could not truthfully answer the question of '*Why don't you tell him what you want?*' What I surely wanted was a hug, kind words, and sleep.

Compared to me, the other women were in much more psychological pain, so I just melted into the background and hoped the sessions would help them. Most all left the course with plans of action which included seeing a GP for physical problems, having meaningful conversations with husbands, and doing everything to improve their general well-being.

My take-away notes only consisted of two main points:

1. Although sometimes I felt physical discomfort, being ballet-flexible, I could adjust myself without too much problem, so I did not think doctors could help.
2. I did resolve to talk to my husband about my 'take it or leave it' attitude to sex.

However, trying to discuss anything with A.T. was tricky. There was never the right moment when he was in the mood to listen seriously. He would turn any comment into a joke, was often a little too inebriated to talk sensibly, or was too tired from arthritic pain. As verbalising anything about sex was just too awkward and problematic, I tried to please him in other ways.

On one occasion, he suggested buying a waterbed, which he said could be 'sexy'! He went ahead to purchase a second-hand one and was delighted when his body felt more comfortable sleeping on a sloppy mobile surface. However, when he fell into bed, I was in danger of being catapulted out of the other side, which really did happen a few times! As for improving our sex life, it was impossible to control movements or balance on this slushy mattress. I finally decided it was a relief that he slept better on this wobbly bed, and besides, I could be most forgiving about the lack of sex.

There was one positive sign when I accidentally found that A.T. had awarded me a reasonable sex score! When tidying the bookcase, I unearthed a sheet of paper that listed about twenty female names with sex scores next to them. At the top of the sex list was *'Slut'* with 20/20, then *'First Girlfriend'* with 19/20, *'First wife'* 15/20, and then me *'Second wife'* rating 17/20. I was quite pleased that I had managed a reasonable B+. At least my occasional sexual performances were acceptable and A.T. was apparently more or less satisfied. I even surpassed his ex-wife and a few other attractive women I recognised from his old photo album!

Meanwhile, my son became engaged to be married, and we were both optimistic about this stage where we had chosen partners to share the challenges of life. To be honest, the first year of the marriage was manageable, as A.T. was pleased with his work and I was also doing well with my teaching and studying. We both worked long hours without a lot of spare time together, so it was easy not to recognise any underlying problems. Besides, I was enjoying exploring what this vibrant, new city had to offer in relation to arts, study, and teaching opportunities. After twelve months, the honeymoon period ended with a combination of health and work problems.

Health Problems

I woke one morning with severe sciatic back pain that left me almost unable to walk. To my surprise, A.T. showed little or no sympathy and told me to get myself to a doctor via a taxi. I presumed he had a vital early work commitment, and after persuading a reluctant taxi driver to take me (who wanted to call an ambulance), I managed to get treatment and extensive X-rays.

MARRIAGE AND DIVORCE NO. 2

The X-rays were interesting as they explained the source of the pain which I had experienced in certain intercourse positions. Since childhood, a bone spur had grown from a lower vertebra and cut into my pelvic bone where it had created a false joint. As one side of the spur was 'fixed,' the other side was free to move, and with all the former ballet exercises, it had carved a groove in the bone. No wonder dance workouts were often painful. This abnormality meant my body was not in alignment, thus causing a mild spinal scoliosis with weaker muscles in one leg. This explained why my left leg had not fully supported me in ballet 'toe shoes,' and why I lacked strength no matter how hard I exercised. It also clarified why doctors had previously commented on my unusual internal alignment during pelvic examinations.

In hindsight, this back problem has worked well for me. After knowing the source of this physical disability, I joined a gym to strengthen all the pelvic muscles and kept up my usual health routines. I also began special core exercises in the hope it would help my spine and prevent any discomfort during sex. Since then, I have successfully continued this prevention path to accommodate the abnormality and have been able to preserve good physical strength.

My next health problem began with inter-monthly bleeding, which I thought showed signs of menopause. However, examinations resulted in a gynaecologist telling me I needed a hysterectomy operation as tests had revealed 'dodgy' pre-cancerous cells. This news did not faze me, because I liked the idea of saying goodbye to the monthly menstruation business. No more sanitary pads and tampons! *Yay!* In addition, I thought this operation would help my sex life. I was not sure how this would work, but I optimistically assumed it might give me better sexual experience. Therefore, I did not consider any negative side effects and almost looked forward to having the operation. The doctor asked whether I would harbour a sense of grief if I lost my uterus, or if it would make me feel like less of a woman. I happily assured him I was not that emotionally attached to my uterus, still felt feminine, and that I was delighted to have any unhealthy body part removed.

Marriage Problems

When facing this operation, it was my husband's attitude that caused disquiet. He was too occupied with his work to give support, and I got the impression my ill health was a nuisance factor. As he did not like hospitals, my only visitors were kindly gay/queer friends who brushed my hair, massaged my feet, and cheered me up.

In the following weeks, my parents came to visit to help me recover at home. After a couple of days, it was clear that my husband found their presence a problem. He could not tolerate the cheery demeanour of my father chatting in the kitchen each morning. They tactfully left, and I decided physically ready or not, I would get back to work and 'normal' married life. Physically, I felt weak and tired, but I was relieved my major health problem was now over. Emotionally, I developed a sense of isolation knowing I could not always rely on A.T. for support. In other words, he was not always going to 'have my back' in sickness if it was going to cause him any inconvenience.

What followed was a litany of work problems for my husband after he argued with his boss and had to find another job. After a brief time, the same thing happened, where he would just 'walk out' if management did not agree with his views. His next idea was to start his own business by using my savings I had put aside to assist for my son's wedding. Naturally, he was not happy with my reluctance to fully co-operate financially, despite receiving all my teaching salary to pay our daily living expenses. I also realised he was not comfortable with the closeness I had with my son and family, though we lived in separate parts of the country.

Good with the Bad

Revisiting this era reminds me that despite these challenging times, I was not totally in despair, as there were successes as well as problems. Here in this city, I continued to be inspired by the arts scene, and enjoyed considerable rewards in my work and extended graduate studies. Even parting from my son and family was tolerable, as we had that special symbiotic relationship that could exist despite any physical distance.

Human nature is often ridiculously optimistic, and so I put aside marriage fears when my husband suddenly announced he had another job back in my home state. This new vocation was in a different field of media, and he did not think there would be any of the former hassles with fellow workers, '*Who didn't know what they were doing.*' This felt like a new beginning, and I wanted to give our marriage a fresh start. The other telling factor was that my son's wife was pregnant, and as I was about to become a grandmother, being closer to my family was another good reason to move.

In all, there was too much happening to be thinking about our intermittent sex life. Along with his continual health worries, work, and money problems, I noted A.T.'s continued large intake of alcohol and cigarettes. Therefore, I hoped his tension would reduce in a new work situation and that he might develop a closer connection with my son and family. I was wrong, as it was not long before we had the first of many separations as his work and relationships continued to cause stress for everyone.

Trying to 'Save' the Marriage

Retelling the story, I can see I was on the wrong track by trying to make this marriage work. It was obvious my husband and I held fundamentally differing values, attitudes, and ways of communicating. Naturally, I did not want another marriage to collapse, as failing a second time was an unthinkable prospect. In fact, it was mortifying for two reasons. One, I could *not* blame the inexperience of youth for another failure, and two, it would also prove I had not learned any lessons from the past.

At this time, we attended a marriage counselling session. Here the counsellor advised us not to examine any past concerns or problems but to concentrate only on the present. '*Forget the past and start anew,*' she said. Because my husband was prone to angry outbursts, I was given the direction to not back down but stand up to his anger. There was no exploring the causes of his anger or techniques to find mutual understanding. This advice did not work, as he continued to get angry, and if I opposed him, he would sulk for days. As this silent treatment was so like my first marriage, I stopped confronting his wrathful outbursts, thinking it might cause him to cease communication all together.

Following the move to my home state, I at once obtained a good teaching position. As for my husband, the same pattern continued, and his new job inevitably failed. Undaunted, he decided on a career change from media to a general management position in the sporting world. The decision resulted in an agreed temporary separation where I was to stay in my teaching job, while he 'reinvented himself' by moving interstate once again. This idea suited me, as I could keep a degree of independence and see what would eventuate with his work.

Of course, I did not entirely blame A.T. for his problems with people and holding down a job. Although he was unlike my first husband in age and profession, they did have one thing in common, having both faced some family difficulties in their childhoods. A.T. did not ever have a good relationship with his biological father, which contrasted to my childhood experience of growing up in a fun-loving family environment. I was aware of this difference, and I therefore felt I could surely make an extra effort to sustain our relationship. It was easy to be confident about rejuvenating our marriage while living apart, where there was a tendency to only remember the positives. I therefore harboured unrealistic hopes for the future.

It was a delight to have a new rewarding teaching job and bask in the glow of being a grandmother. Therefore, I lulled myself into thinking that things would get better for A.T. too. Long phone calls convinced me that he had successfully changed direction by getting a good managerial position in a distant regional city. A.T. had a wonderful telephone voice and could write extremely witty and sentimental letters. This kind of communication kept alive the illusion that we could be a loving couple. While separated, I did not think much about the sex aspect of our relationship, and I just hoped it would inexplicably fall into place once we reunited.

Menopause

About this time, I noted obvious menopausal changes in my own body. In the beginning, the few hot flushes that occurred while I was interstate were not problematic. Being prone to poor circulation, I quite enjoyed feeling a warm body flush in what was a particularly colder climate. Later, after I moved to resume a busy teaching job, it was necessary to get regular sleep without the interruption of hot-flush symptoms. Fortunately, I was a suitable candidate for hormone-replacement medication, which instantly alleviated any symptoms of menopausal changes.[38] It was only a matter of weaning myself off the medication after a few years, and so menopause never became a problem. However, I hoped this body adjustment would aid any future sexual activity, and I welcomed the idea of having passed all the main physical milestones of womanhood.

Another Marriage Failure

Despite not wanting to leave my work and move further away from my son, particularly now that I had two grandchildren, I made a final attempt to resume the marriage. I persuaded myself that it was not A.T.'s fault that he had a chronic disease, and I was convinced the main cause of his former unhappiness had been work related. With a new career, I imagined he would become more patient with people, less irritated, and have a better empathetic partnership with me and everyone else.

Within three months of moving to join him, I could tell there were still ongoing problems. Although I managed to get teaching work straight away, he clashed with colleagues, and he was asked to resign. For me, it caused yet another crossroads decision, and we agreed to separate – yet again! However, this time I knew I could not sustain the lifestyle of following my husband from job to job anymore. By now, my parents were ageing, and my daughter-in-law needed help with the children, so I decided to devote myself to their care.

A.T. and I did not have a great emotional parting, and our separation just seemed to be a practical, common-sense solution. By

---

38 Information on medication for menopause can be found via the Australian Menopause Society (www.menopause.org.au). I have noted some types of menopausal hormonal therapy are safer than formally shown by the 2002/2004 studies, and some 'natural' herbal remedies can be harmful. Although hormone therapy worked well for me, it is always wise to seek professional advice.

now, there was not much sexual activity due his health, work stress, and my growing disquiet about our partnership. Anyway, we agreed to keep a distant friendship, so he left to live in his original home state to plan his next career move. Meanwhile, I returned to the family home to be a carer for my ailing parents and supply childcare for my grandchildren. I did not know how long I would be looking after my family, but at least this role was more pragmatic than trying to sort out my husband's life.

Being a Family Carer

Becoming a carer for the next six years created a mixture of sad and positive experiences. Sad, because it was a time of seeing my parents gradually fade away to their inevitable deaths. Most rewarding, because I was able to share that special last chapter of their lives in a meaningful way.

I felt closer to my father than I had ever been, and I recognised just how alike we were in our attitudes on life. He had an enquiring mind, was an excellent communicator, and still always put thought into action saying, *'Let's get off our backsides and do something.'* My mother remained her friendly, outgoing self, but I could tell she regretted not having some of her deeper ambitions realised. However, she was justifiably proud of her maternal role in always bringing a sense of unity to her extended family. As the eldest of her generation, she faithfully fulfilled the role of benevolent matriarch as well as being a devoted wife and mother.

The other insight was seeing the loving bond my parents still had with each other. I admired their closeness of love and friendship, and I still aspired to emulate their relationship. In fact, in their last days, they both suggested they wanted me to find true happiness with a loving partner. They could see that my second marriage was not in a happy situation, and so they encouraged me to think about the future.

Before my parents died and while A.T. and I were still apart, I made the decision to divorce – yet again. Deep down, I had given up on this marriage because of our different attitudes to work, colleagues, family, money management, and relationships. The partnership did not work as we did not combine well as a team. To me, the end of the marriage was evident when I remembered how I used to dread my husband's homecoming, because I feared the inevitable wave of stress when he came through the door. In fact, I think this is the litmus test of a partnership. That is, if you ever regularly dread opening the front door, something is seriously wrong.

I did not entirely blame A.T., as he had not experienced my kind of family life and had different expectations of marriage. Also, people easily aggravated him, so there were many occurrences of destructive battles with friends and workmates. Fortunately, we had an amicable divorce without any quarrels about money or possessions – thank goodness! Nevertheless, it was to take time before I could see why I had married this man, and to understand why I had the tendency to sometimes rescue people in an unhealthy way.

Reflection

On Being a 'Rescuer'
I learnt many things from my relationship with A.T., including trying to be helpful in the wrong way. As I have mentioned, in this second marriage I made the mistake of caring for my husband, to the point of becoming co-dependent. By co-dependent, I mean caring to the point of exhaustion, so I, was also in danger of needing care. I know now, over-rescuing others is not healthy, particularly if it

teaches people to lean on you too heavily. Psychology readings on the topic explained how people can come to resent their 'rescuer,' while the 'rescuer' can become exhausted with the effort. Armed with this knowledge, I am more aware of trying to give support in a much wiser fashion.

My tendency to rescue could have come from my grandmother, with whom I saved plenty of sick birds and animals. Then there was my hero fantasy world, where I flew from rescue to rescue, but I certainly did not get stuck in co-dependency as I did in my real-life relationships. Plus, in my daydreams, I expected caring to be equally reciprocated and imagined my 'Superman' would also save me when necessary. In real-life caring, such as towards my child, my students, or aged parents, I always felt rewarded and never burdened with the effort. In fact, I was delighted when my child became independent and could make his own decisions.

In both my marriages, I could see these men had latent talents, plus I felt I understood their past struggles and considered that through my wifely help, they would become more successful in life. I tried to protect their egos, manage everything on the home front, rescue with money, and readily excuse their failures. In the process, I ignored my own needs, used exhaustive energy, and did not set behavioural boundaries. In addition, I forgave or ignored behaviour that I should have challenged. In the case of my second husband, I explored every aspect of treatment for his chronic arthritis, instead of encouraging him to take responsibility for his own health. In fact, I almost 'lived' the disease with him by supervising his exercise, checking his diet, and organising the medical appointments. Particularly in the beginning, I was guilty of not helping him self-manage his own disease.

I am sure there were deeper reasons why I rescued in this way. Did I need love, admiration, validation as a good wife, or was it a guilty cover for my lack of sexual desire? It was undoubtably a mixture of all those reasons, along with being socially conditioned, empathetic in nature, and doing what I considered to be 'the right thing.' On the other hand, I wondered if I had been the type of chronic rescuer where I just needed to feel wanted by other people. All I know is, the results of this overinvestment in caring meant I pushed my needs aside and became burnt out. Although I tried to keep the marriage dream alive, inevitably there was the realisation that I had failed. As usual, my intentions were good even if the outcomes were not.

So, how did I rescue myself from being a rescuer, and how do I nurture people now? It was not until years later when I did a university master's degree in social counselling that I found a healthier way of helping people. Here, I learned more about the technique of 'actively' listening to clients until they had emotionally completed telling their often sad and painful stories. The important next stage was to help clients to formulate their goals and solutions towards self-healing. The only advice or help counsellors gave was through suggestions about how clients might achieve their goals. Certainly, a counsellor did not 'rescue,' but they helped clients with strategies to gain clarity and self-empowerment.[39]

I am still prepared to willingly help those in need, especially when there is no one else available. But I try to think about my deeper motives, set boundaries, and be aware that people should create their own goals. I had to remember it was important to step aside, so the person in recovery could experience their own power and exercise their own skills. In other words, walk with them and not 'carry' them. Instead of avoiding helping others, I can see my asexuality has put me

---

[39] There are websites that deal with aspects of 'rescuing,' including a description of the 'White Knight' syndrome. https://www.thoughtcatalogue.com > white knight syndrome

in a favourable position to extend myself more readily to those in need. Instead of supporting just one partner, I have the time and emotional readiness to care for family members, friends, and neighbours. As an asexual, I like to feel I can extend genuine love and care for others with an easy grace and expansive spirit. I now often recognise with a sense of wonder those moments of unselfish empathy between people. There is comfort in knowing that loving care and kindness can exist without sexual desire.

JOURNAL 14

A New Man and a New Life

Dear Journal,

This era presented another big leap into the unknown. I was now approaching a sixtieth birthday and wanted to have a home of my own, plus another chance for further study. First, I needed time to heal from a second divorce, recover from the loss of parents, and face a difficult departure from grandchildren if I were to move again to the city. Strangely, this era began with a new male friend who helped me in the transition back to city life.

A New Male Friend

Did my divorce clear the way for a fully enlightened future where I would realise my asexuality? Well not quite, as I promised my parents, I would not give up looking for the 'right someone.' Social pressure and family wielded an influence on me, and I still wanted to please people. With the social isolation caused by six years of caring and with the grief of losing my father, I rekindled the old imaginative dream to believe that some kindly, gentle man existed out there. I did not think about the sexual aspect, only that I wanted someone who would love and give me care. So, a few months before my mother died, a new male friend almost accidentally entered my life.

When I was on a one-day visit to the city, an acquaintance persuaded me to have coffee with a man who had just suffered the loss of his partner. Still being the 'rescuer' and having sadly just lost my own father, I agreed. The meeting was brief, as I needed to quickly return to the family home where I was still caring for my mother. Being eight years younger than myself, this man had a reserved personality and a love of history. The coffee 'blind date' went well, and despite his obvious social shyness, we managed to share an interesting conversation about books, agriculture, and many topics covering the natural environment. Immediately, it felt like a brotherly connection, though I did not believe I would see him again because of the physical distance between our places of living.

The new quiet friend (I will refer to him as P.S.) and I exchanged letters and a few phone calls, which he followed with a surprise visit to my hometown. My mother was delighted to see me with a male friend, and she enjoyed his discussions about local history. In fact, she liked his brief visits, as they were a welcome distraction from her own sadness and physical ailments. At this time, she was grieving the loss of my father, and a failing heart was sapping her energy. Therefore, it was natural for me to turn to P.S. when my mother also died. He was able to help with the aftermath of dealing with the distribution of my parents' belongings and helped in my transition into a new phase of life. A part of me wanted to stay near my son and family, but I also wanted to relocate to the city where I could create a new home for my country family to visit. Other desires were to explore fresh study/work challenges and have the new partnership with P.S. as mutual support.

Reasons for Seeking Another Relationship

There were quite a few emotions that clouded my understanding at this time, which was why I again entered a relationship that underneath I felt was going to be supportive, but this time with quite different boundaries.

The possible reasons for this relationship were…

- o To share the grief for the loss of my parents.
- o To support my feelings of sadness when parting from my son's family.

- To gain emotional help and encouragement in starting a new life.
- To fulfil a promise to my parents that I would try to find someone.
- To give me someone to support (rescue?) who had lost their partner.
- To provide help as I was suffering physical exhaustion and backpain.

At least I knew we would *not* consider marriage and agreed that our financial affairs were to be strictly separate. I now wanted to keep a strong degree of independence, so I thought that a L.A.T. relationship might work. (That is, *'living apart together.'*) This meant keeping a loyal connection where we could enjoy holidays together, enjoy visits to our separate homes, and share social outings. Subconsciously, I sensed such a partnership would create a comfortable emotional distance for both of us. More consciously, I figured this man was not likely to fly into rages or impinge on my independence. Looking back, I am sure this friendship served a valuable purpose in a time in our lives when we were both suffering personal losses.

Positives of the New Friendship

At the time, many aspects of the friendship worked well. P.S. was a slim, healthy man who was moderate in all things and a skilled mechanic. I knew his social reserve was a natural part of his personality, so I could ease any of his social discomfort, and I instinctively knew when he wanted me to do the talking. I understood his reticence and knew I could cover his communication difficulties of dealing with party banter. I knew how to 'work the room' and speak to everyone in social gatherings. Therefore, I did not see his natural shyness a problem as we complemented one another in many other ways.

P.S. and I had many interests in common, and being an avid reader, he displayed a good historical knowledge. Although he did not appear to be artistic, he appreciated dance, music, and visiting libraries. This meant he was always willing to accompany me to movies, or to the theatre and art galleries. He was also keen to explore other countries, and I instinctively knew he would make a good travel companion. In retrospect, I will be forever grateful P.S. came into my life when I was making this move back to city life. His practical aid and calm presence were just the kind of support I needed. It was a busy time with the challenges to get a job, deal with my parents' estate, enrol in a university course, and buy a small city unit – a first home that would be totally mine.

Therefore, the friendship grew slowly, although I soon came to realise that sex was important to him. In fact, he sensibly regarded it as the 'glue' in a relationship. So, I decided to try and sustain this part of the intimacy and use all in my power to make it work. I did not discuss my indifference to sex, as I thought it was something I needed to sort out within myself. In the meantime, I tried to be warm and loving without admitting to him I had to seriously negotiate anything sexual, both physically and emotionally.

I am sure P.S. knew that I was different and often said I was 'an enigma.' He could not explain what he meant, but he sensed I wanted him to love me more on an emotional level than physical. Also, he knew I was self-reliant, and there was a part of me that liked creating a life on my own. It was not long before I came to believe he needed a different type of woman; one who could better fit with his need for a more physical relationship. Nevertheless, I felt sure that if things did not work out in an intimate way, at least my new friend would always be a brotherly companion. He was clearly supportive and the kind of mate who would respond in a crisis and be there for you if necessary. Because I only wanted a congenial relationship, we soon drifted away from trying to be an intimate couple. Later, I was brave enough to 'come out' to him about my asexuality; he kindly tried to understand, but it was a concept he found especially confusing.

One of my main decisions after moving was to gain a university degree in psychology and counselling. I knew sexuality would be one of the main subjects as well as examining grief and loss. The grief topic became enormously helpful in accepting the loss of my beloved parents, and I was able to learn much more about sexuality. All the while, I felt sustained by a vague hope that my new university social science studies would reveal some new sexual insights. At this point, I still did not understand why sex never naturally seemed to enter my head, and I had not found the source for my constant lack of desire. I was sure this next study phase would take me a step further towards understanding the complexities of sexual human behaviour.

Reflection

Academic Sex Studies

When I enrolled in the sexuality subjects of the university course, I thought I knew a reasonable amount about sex but imagined there would be new knowledge about sexual diversity. Also, I was interested in any psychological research that could enlighten me as to why I did not have a 'natural' need for sex. The studies did present a wider understanding relating to some sexual orientations, but it also included some disturbing data about child abuse and rape. Then, there were some humorous experiences, such as visiting an adult sex shop.

Attitudes Towards Orientations

One revealing exercise displayed our feelings and attitudes towards different sexual orientations. We had to stand on an imaginary graded line numbering from one to ten (one being low tolerance through to ten representing high acceptance). In response to different questions, we moved to our selected position on the line according to our beliefs. When asked, *'Are you heterosexual?'* I stood at position nine because I preferred close relationships with men. To the question, *'Do you understand and tolerate other orientations such as homosexuality?'* – many of us stood at positions nine or ten except sadly, some only rated their tolerance at one or two. This was my first experience of seeing sexuality as a spectrum.

Bisexuality

From this kind of exercise, I could see the sliding scale of acceptance when fellow students (including myself) did not know where to place themselves. For example, I did not understand bisexuality, and in my ignorance, thought that fundamentally you had to be either heterosexual or homosexual. During the course, my bisexual fellow students enlightened me about their orientation, and I came to understand their 'fluidity' by being in the middle of the sexual spectrum. The two bisexual students (one male and one female) in my tutorial group gave heart-rending descriptions of love and loss with both their respective male and female partners. I had no doubt as to the depth and sincerity of affection they had experienced and could fully understand how they were genuinely bisexual. In fact, I envied their ability to love people from more than one gender.

Paedophilia

Naturally, the most upsetting topic was paedophilia. None of us could wrap our heads around this aspect of sexuality, and I felt physically ill even thinking about it. At this point, I felt sorry for sex counsellors if they had to deal with this type of perpetrator. It was also disappointing that our lecturer on this topic centred attention on the *identification* of a podophile, but they did not provide any research as to how this awful type of sexuality developed in the first place. I would like to see more work on the *prevention* of paedophilia, by understanding how it forms in a person and finding what medical or psychological means could be employed to deal with this addiction. However, I do note more scholarly articles researching into the causes of paedophilia are beginning to appear online. Despite wanting to accept everyone's sexual orientations, any sexual practice that produces physical or mental harm needs serious attention so preventive measures can be implemented.

Sexual Acceptance

Other than harmful sex, I like to believe that a variety of orientations can contribute to the positive development of our human race. For example, in my experience, most gay/queer teachers use their creative abilities to present interesting lessons, have a sensitive understanding of their students, and readily understand those who feel different or isolated. I believe people's sexuality can translate into having unique talents to care, educate, and bring creativity to others in a specific way. For example, I have noted how gay/queer writers and journalists can make space in their lives to study, travel, write, and inform people in a way that would be almost impossible if they followed the lifestyles of many heterosexual families.

Rape

The other area of concern was the topic of rape, where the lecturer simply said that rape was about power and not sex. I found myself agreeing that exerting power could be part of the need for control, although I thought that sexual *'turn on'* must play a part. I concluded the sex was the power 'weapon' of domination, while it also created an arousal for the perpetrator.

I can fully understand the bravery, anger, and frustration that led to the present global '*Me Too*' movement. Here it is not just rape but uninvited sexual attention and intercourse without consent. At present it is a sensitive time while the social rules of sexualised conduct are undergoing serious review. Until new etiquette for male and female behaviour becomes normalised, all men in work and social settings need to be thoughtful about the interpretation of their behaviour. This new awareness is a reminder of past times when I just ignored inappropriate sexually motivated advances from males. I considered it good manners not to complain or speak out, so always quickly removed myself from the situation and pretended it did not happen. Now, I would say something, either politely, with humour, or a seriously firm refusal, depending on the situation. Even at this time, the legal system can still be brutal for a victim of rape. Prosecutors and investigators can cause more harm to victims who are already wounded through the often psychologically damaging examinations.

Rape as an Assault

I have often wondered how I would cope if I was ever raped. Once, in a seminar on personal safety, a police officer asked this question and then strongly expressed her views. She insisted that such an act perpetrated on a person without consent would be a *physical assault*, and she recommended that we mentally treat it that way. Framing the attack as a '*violation on one's deep inner spiritual well-being*' could cause ongoing psychological problems. Despite the normal fear, anger, and physical pain of such a crime, it was stressed that it would not be healthy to carry the burden of shame, guilt, or loss of trust in relationships for the rest of one's life. So, to reframe the attitude to such an assault she recommended:

> *Make up your minds here and now that you would not allow such a crime to cause chronic loss of inner self-respect, and it is most important to create a strong philosophy against such a possibility. Do not let it be an attack on your spirit, but see it as a violent physical attack.*

In other words, we had to 'rehearse' our attitudes of resilience and inner resolve, even though such a crime might never happen to us.

Asexuality and Correctional Rape

Although lecturers did not mention asexuality during my later studies, I became horrified when reading about the idea of *'correctional rape'* for asexual people. This is where someone forces sex upon them as a 'cure.' To me, it would be also unacceptable to propose that even a loving sexual act might be a 'cure' for asexuality. Then again, as an asexual, I might more easily equate the notion of rape as a physical assault, rather than a permanent psychological wound. However, I would feel extreme anger and sense of disrespect. In any regard, this type of crime would not diminish my need for justice, although I would hate the idea of it letting it destroy my spiritual joy in life. Of course, I would be more affronted if the rape occurred with the purpose of 'curing' my asexuality and therefore became an attack on my sense of identity. Sadly, I have encountered an asexual young woman, where correctional rape destroyed her sense of ever again wanting romantic touch or embraces.

Visit to a Sex Shop

Without a doubt, the most unforgettable academic task was a practical assignment given to all students in our tutorial group. The tutor asked us to visit a sex shop and buy an article to bring for our next tutorial discussion. Up until now, we had managed to analyse all sexual matters with a certain degree of sophisticated maturity. Therefore, it was interesting to see how this challenge raised nervous insecurities about entering a place totally devoted to sex. Just for fun, I contacted another academic friend saying that I wanted her help with this unusual assignment. She willingly agreed but was obviously gobsmacked to find it was all about sex-toy shopping. Mind you, I had previously visited one of these places in a frantic search for a red feather needed as a stage prop. But on that occasion, I had no interest to browse or examine any other products for sale.

The shop visit was certainly a fun experience. Two friendly young women assistants greeted us and talked about the items as if they were normal everyday objects for sale. The shop seemed normalised too, as it was set out like an ordinary general store with sections of ornaments, board games, racks of magazines, shelves of oils, perfumes, DVDs, clothing, and shoes. Then, there was a section that displayed what looked like articles from an animal pet shop with heaps of leather and chain. The most puzzling display was an array of battery-operated gadgets, with no indication what they were for or how they were used.[40]

A closer inspection revealed the ornamental coffee cups were decorated with copulating cows, the chess game pieces were all sexualised, and the magazine covers displayed lots of female breasts and buttocks. The displayed clothing designs covered little flesh, the high-heeled shoes were like stilts, and the 'pet shop' articles looked most uncomfortable as if intended for human restraint or punishment. Of course, a considerable number of the gadgets were

---

[40] I applaud adult shops that are elegant, stylish, or have sharp/clean modern décor, rather than the old dark and sleazy places that used to exist. Also, I dislike shop names that suggest sex is sinful or dangerously secret.

penis shaped – so many, that they caused an unintended impact on our brains. After absorbing so many images of penises, travelling home in the car we saw them everywhere in the shapes of pine trees, picket fences, roof installations, and chimneys! We even had to stop the car when our uncontrollable laughing made it dangerous to keep on driving. This happened after deciding that even the directional arrow sign painted on the road also looked like a penis!

As I had to buy a product for demonstration, I settled on a vibrator that looked like a plastic cigar. At least it was cheap, and after testing the vibration on the back of my neck and shoulders, I knew that it could at least massage other parts of my body. Because I could still achieve the deeper muscle contraction 'core-gasm,' I instinctively knew I would probably be repurposing or discarding this 'toy' after the required tutorial viewing.

The tutorial itself was hilarious, with gadgets humming all over the place amid hoots of laughter. Many students reported that they found the idea of walking into a sex shop (or sneaking) quite nerve-wracking. It was a sign that most found the idea of sex was a *'naughty but nice'* human function that inspired feelings of secret delight. As prospective counsellors, we were aware that future clients could raise sexual problems, so we needed to face our own reticence around the many complex aspects of sexual behaviour.

Our subjects covered a variety of topics on sexuality, including sexual counselling, sexual assault, addiction, adolescence sex, pornography, pregnancy, contraception, child abuse, the sex industry, and cultural/gender diversity. But concerning gender diversity, the topics only included gay/queer, lesbian, and bisexuality, with nothing about transgender or asexuality. Therefore, these sexual studies certainly extended my knowledge, yet did not enlighten me about my own lack of desire. Nevertheless, the course gave me further understanding about the fact that sex could be a separate desire that is not always associated with feelings of love.

Separation of Sex and Love

I knew sexual drive could be directed towards a desire for physical satisfaction alone. But how did this fact apply to me? Being an asexual meant that I still had a desire for love, and as my journals show, I have always been 'in love with the idea of love.' This only compounded my dilemma of wanting love without sex, which was why I tried so hard to be sexual. Up until the age of forty, I thought mutual sexual intercourse was supposed to be an act of deep love. However, I did accept that some men turned towards prostitution services for sexual gratification. But that sex could be just for fun was something I had not always considered.

In the 1970s I remember being surprised when a formidable, single, older woman told me she and her occasional lover enjoyed 'fun' sex romps in her bed. At the time, it shocked me that she would have a liaison with a married man, just for a bit of carnal gratification. Of course, I now know that a majority of sexually experienced people enjoy sex as a physical encounter without the need for sustained love. It seemed people could enjoy *'empty-of-love'* sex like pleasurable sport, such as a stimulating tennis match with a few good games, and it is all over! Also, I often heard the phrase 'making love' which, I imagined, meant having sex to confirm a deep personal bond and wanting to be in total union with someone. To summarise, my ideas on sex/love came to the following conclusion…

- *Sex* – entails desire for physical contact that is more of a mechanical operation to satisfy physical pleasure, and where the body is an object of desire.
- *Love* – is wanting a deep sense of emotional fusion with a partner. I am sure such a love-partnership would entail

feelings of surrender, trust, and a mutual empathy. Therefore, I can see why artists use their mediums to give expression to the all-consuming passions of heartfelt love.

So why would people want sex without loving intentions? There are obviously reasons for wanting sex other than expressing ongoing love and/or lustful desire. A few such purposes could be:

- physical release
- stress-relief after a dreadful day
- as an antidote for grief
- to enhance a celebration
- as an inducer to sleep
- just for fun
- to demonstrate forgiveness (In fact, I know of children who were conceived as a result of 'make-up' sex after an argument.)

I acknowledge there exist desires for a particular type of sex, including the pain/pleasure principal, or where people want to explore forms of domination. These kinds of practices might be satisfying for some, but I doubt if they would result in an equally *balanced* feeling of being *'as one'* with a partner. Hurting, restraining, or dominating areas of sexual activity would be off my list, even if I were a sexual person. Then there are those previously mentioned negative reasons where there is use of sex as punishment, or without consent as in rape, or where there is a dominating unequal power over another. For me, these are scenarios I want to leave in the realm of adult movies and *not* in real life. Then, there other strange areas of sexual arousal which I think are weirdly mysterious, such as attraction to objects. However, my attitude is one of indifference, *except* where they cause harm or demean animals or people.

Motivations for sex exist deep in one's psyche, and how would one even know what a partner is really thinking during intercourse? Thank goodness my partners could not read my thoughts of *'You can cope – it will all be over soon.'* Or, could they have been thinking about some gorgeous rounded-in-the-right-places 'celebrity star' while having sex with me?

I know my main aims for engaging in sex were twofold; to fulfil my partner's expectations, and to get a sense of loving acceptance for myself. In my emotional world, feelings for connection and physical love *were* separate, as sexual desire was never part of my experience. Hence, I behaved enthusiastically towards sex when it did not reflect my inner desires. Although I could control my own orgasms and leaned towards emotionally connecting with males, anything physical was a separate issue. Because I was trying to *'make love'* without sex – it was really an act of deception for both me and my partner.

Conclusions – Sex and Love

I was looking to feel loved by a man with a pretence of enjoying sex, so there was a separation between my outward behaviour and inner self. Romantically, I harboured the happy-ever-after ideal, where the two forces of sex and love would one day combine. I am sure no one marries with the intention to divorce and to separate after the lustful stage of hormones subside. It is not just sex that helps couples through the tricky times but having that *'I-have-got-your-back,'* loving friendship.

Meanwhile, as an asexual, and if I were in a heterosexual partnership (and this is a big 'If'), then coping with sex would need a *huge* love element to motivate the act. Why? I think that such a big physical gesture would be to express a *big* emotional feeling. There are some asexual people who can feel sexual desire, but *only* when they deeply love the other person. My thoughts about the separation of love and sexual desire have again caused me to reflect about the question of *'what is love?'* At least one thing is clear: there are various sexual/love emotions that can be separate or exist together.

JOURNAL 15

Living Alone

Dear Journal,

Once again, I transitioned into a new life after my mother's death, where I moved to the city, but this time to buy my first home. Finally, at the age of sixty, I was able to contemplate living in a space where I had complete control of my environment. In the process, I developed a comfortably friendly distance between myself and P.S. (my quiet friend), who recognised my growing need for independence.

Lone Experience

What followed was a period of feeling truly liberated without having to care for anyone other than myself. This meant I could do what I liked, and I did everything! I studied philosophy, became a tutor, and engaged in part-time work in schools and dance studios. For social activities, I stayed connected with friend P.S. and kept close contact with my son, daughter-in-law, and grandchildren. My city pad was also a wonderful place for the family to enjoy city visits and became most important for grandchildren when they enrolled in a nearby city boarding school.

To my amazement, the following years whizzed by, and it was not long before I was facing my seventieth birthday. At this age I still vaguely wondered if I should have a closer male partner to share life within my older years. Obviously, I tried to listen to conventional wisdom about old-age loneliness, but at this point, I was not so enthusiastic about even pursuing a 'living-apart-together' relationship. To my satisfaction, I finally realised I was far more contented being alone and experienced a certain delight in living on my own. Although I was not enthusiastic about having a special partner, I would still have one final helpful almost-a-relationship experiment.

The Friend Who Inspired Self-Realisation

After halting the intimate side of the relationship with my quiet friend P.S., I became acquainted with an interesting person who lived in a nearby suburb and regularly visited the same shopping centre as me (I will refer to him as B.E.). Once we had a few accidental meets at the local coffee shop, he made some friendly overtures towards me. He was different in terms of a shared sense of humour, similar political views, and had the qualities that I thought would be the basis of a great, fun-loving kind of friendship. But B.E. also implied that sex was an important aspect of his life, so I did respect his honesty.

To pursue any intimate relationship with B.E. would have entailed my old ritual methods of coping with any sexual encounters. It quickly became obvious we would both value a casual long-term friendship much more than a short-term sexual relationship. Besides, I realised that an experimental sexual union at this stage in life was a probable waste of time, and that we both needed uncommitted personal freedom. So, we became long-term friends, and, in the meantime, he helped me to discover something new about myself!

Lack of Fantasy

As usual, every relationship resulted in valuable personal lessons. It was easy to discuss sex with B.E., and he once raised the topic of sexual fantasies. This became one of those 'lightbulb' moments, when I realised I did not have a natural sexual imagination. I had flights of fancy of being a clever spy, brave hero, or brilliant performer – but nothing that involved sex. Here, I began to appreciate I was different, and thus it became a major step in accepting my own individuality and knowing I was not like other people.

A New Contentment

It was good to finally see that platonic friendships were the best for me and recognise that the happiest times in life had been when I was single. That is, single but with rewarding work and a few caring, supporting relationships. Although I felt relieved about giving up any idea of searching for a life partner, I did not realise that my inner contentment of living alone came from my asexual self. Rather, I thought that I had arrived at a state of self-acceptance through life experience, and it was probably because I was always more interested in the arts than sex.

The other confirmation came from doing some maths that proved despite years of exploring heterosexuality, I had spent most of my life without it. Including the two marriages and some eras of seeking sexual activity, the actual time of being spasmodically sexually engaged was extremely little. This means, from the age of twenty-one to my present age of over eighty, time engaged in active sex only added up to seven years. That amounted to over fifty-three happy years without sex!

'Pity Sex'

Thinking about my past intimate friendships, I still marvel as to how I managed the sexual side of those relationships. My partners had often commented that I apparently enjoyed sex, so obviously my acting ability had succeeded in not making me appear frigid. For me, it was always a sincerely motivated act, one that secretly harboured the prospect that my pretending might become reality. In other words, I held onto a *'fake it until you make it'* kind of mentality. At least most partners viewed me in a pleasing way, and I hope they did not detect I might be performing *'pity sex.'* (That is, a woman engaging in sex with a man only because of his desire.) On the other hand, I always felt sadness, as feigning sex never felt right, and I vaguely knew I was not expressing my real self.

To summarise, living alone and feeling truly autonomous meant that I began to question myself in a more detached way. I knew I was enjoying a high degree of contentment while becoming aware I did not have the same desires as other women. I was happy in my solitude but was not sure why, which was a bit puzzling. Puzzling, because as a friendly person who liked other people, I had a degree of guilt about liking my satisfying state of semi-seclusion.

The other thing, which remained in my thoughts, was those questions of fantasies. It had been the interesting conversations where B.E. had raised the topic that made me wonder more about this creative side of the human imagination.

Reflection

On Sexual Fantasy

It was a revelation to realise I had no memories of sex-related fantasies. At times, I had certainly deliberately tried to imagine and plan for sex, while not naturally drifting into a free-floating fantasy world. I realised I did experience some nightly dreams of meeting charismatic strangers, and I also concocted daydreams about being a hero or spy.

Nightdreams

In a recurring dream I would imagine meeting a male while travelling (like ships that bump in the night), and we would both sense a unique bond. Our parting would leave us with the feeling we had gone through an uplifting experience. This stranger was someone '*who was on the same page*' in terms of attitudes to life, and I would imagine this meeting would forever remain in our memories. The dream-person was always male, slim, and intelligent. I would know he was unavailable as a prospective partner, and that he was only a chance visitor in my life. Our intuitive bond was only ever conversational, though often in a scenic outdoor setting. In analysing these dreams, I conclude they must have been about wanting an emotional connection out of need to feel some kind of platonic intimacy.

Daydreams

Daily news bulletins often inspired me to daydream about rescuing a missing person. On lone walks, I invented scenarios where I would use my remarkable powers of detection and observation to find missing persons or track down perpetrators. Usually, I would imagine informing authorities anonymously, thus enjoying the secret knowledge that I was the unknown saviour. I guess this idea stems from the DC Comic book Superman/Clark Kent characters?[41] But, with inner reveries like this, it is no wonder I became a 'rescuer'!

Then again, I had day and nightdream images where I wore a classic suit and performed office tasks with impressive efficiency. Here, I am typing without mistakes, thinking clearly, making quick decisions, and only pausing to drink large mugs of coffee. I am sure these kinds of achievement-based dreams came from the office scenarios in film and television. There was also another imagined scenario, where I would pretend a large audience would be watching me perform spectacular physical feats, or dance movements with an excellent degree of skill. (I do this when in a strenuous exercise class where I need extra motivation!)

---

[41] DC Comics Inc is one of the oldest USA comic book companies having first published in 1937.

The Purpose of Fantasies

I believe I could not have happily existed without the ability to imagine and fantasise. I am sure flights of imagination helped me as a child in relieving the boredom of constant illness, the lack of playmates, and unpleasant situations. (As mentioned before, I had created a fictional childhood playmate.) Fantasy was also a method of rehearsing for events in my real life by imagining and 'trying on' the emotional states of fear or delights of success. So many of my adult achievements in dance, drama, or writing began in the pretend games of childhood. I am sure fantasy has helped me in terms of creativity, also in reviving a positive emotional mood or releasing stress.

At times, I particularly liked holding pretend conversations with people who had wronged or upset me. These were most satisfying, where I expounded my grievances with great eloquence and imagined their reactions of shame or sorrow. When I did confront such people, I usually said little, or decided the altercation was not even worth addressing. Then again, when rehearsing for a stage performance, I would imagine the scenes and reactions of an audience; all of which I am sure created better results once I stepped onto the stage.

Reasons for Sexual Fantasies

Although my sexual fantasies have always been non-existent, I know they support the human need for procreation and intimate connection. As often reported, such fantasies enhance desire for sex, rehearse for a sexual encounter, or explore satisfying sexual practices that one may not contemplate doing in real life. There are many other reasons for fantasy, such as 'virtually' exploring diverse types of partnering, enhancing foreplay, gender experimentation, or having sex in a variety of unusual settings. We often hear of sex (both real and imaginary) in toilets on airflights with references to the 'mile high club' – but knowing my efforts to use any plane toilet, I can only marvel at such a feat! Then again, some people may prefer fantasy to the intimacy of a real partner, to relieve loneliness, or where a life-situation prevents normal intercourse.

Stimuli and Sexual Attraction

I have often been surprised by the variety of external stimuli that can inspire sexual attraction and fantasy. What excites the senses, coupled with a physical reaction, can be instrumental in acting as a personalised sexual stimulus. Whether it be the feel of leather, touch of satin, sight of a breast, smell of perfume, taste of alcohol, sound of a particular song, or experience of beauty in an environment that incites sexual tension. When reading dance history of the 1800s, I was fascinated by the sexual excitement of men who flooded to the new form of classical ballet performances. Here, they could see the previously covered naked ankles of the female dancers who now dressed in shortened floating tulle costumes.

Having a heightened unexpected sexual encounter can create a lasting fantasy with a deep desire of wanting to repeat that experience again. Once, a friend and I were approached by a slightly inebriated man at an art exhibition. Later, after drinking more wine and viewing some paintings of nudes, he began to suggest he imagined my friend and me in bed while he watched. The poor man saw the stunned looks on our faces, then embarrassingly explained he had experienced such a situation many years ago and could not get it out of his mind. In the face of our shocked laughter, he quickly excused himself never to be seen again! After this weird incident, I wondered whether men have visual fantasies of *past* encounters, while women tend to dream of a *future* handsome beau?

Of course, there is the external stimulus of pornographic film, erotic literature, or a glossy magazine where the images 'speak' intimately to the observer. Although this sort of sexual incentive never did work on me, I can understand how such images may excite some people. What is difficult for me to understand, is when fantasy translates into reality, such as a man who wants to expose his penis in public, peek through windows, or act on deep desires towards objects. Some time ago, I had a regular 'flasher' who continually upset my peaceful enjoyment of walking in a nearby public park by exposing himself, particularly if I happened to be walking alone. Fortunately, a plain-clothes policewoman eventually caught him in the act and then found him pleading, *'Please don't tell my girlfriend.'*

Summary – Fantasy

I am sure the use of imagination and fantasy is a good thing for creativity, whether it be in the arts, the design elements of our lives, or enhancement of sexuality. It is an important part of our human experience; nonetheless, I can see it as problematic where fantasy becomes a controlling addiction, or where it crosses boundaries into some form of harm or cruelty.[42] From having an imaginary friend, thinking of dramatic scenarios, or creating dance movements, fantasy is a key factor in my inner visual world. On the other hand, it was strange to know I did not have sexual fantasies like other people, a fact that did not make me feel sad – only different.

---

[42] Many websites including Psychology Today tackle the broad topic of fantasy as it applies to creativity, sexuality, and mental health.

JOURNAL 16

♥

How I Found Asexuality

Dear Journal,

Here, I can relate a memorable happening in my life, when all the pieces of my inner sexual self just fell into place. It came sometime after I had virtually given up on the idea of living with a partner. The searching for a male life-companion had ceased with the realisation that I was more than content with my own company. In fact, it was a relief to no longer feel the need to search for love. I was learning to love myself and was quite satisfied with the affection from friends and family.

Yes, something in me had changed, and I am sure this was nothing to do with ageing factors. As I said, my happiest memories were those times in life when I was living alone and pursuing artistic dreams. Finding my lack of sexual fantasy had only endorsed the idea that friendship was more important than sex, and highlighted how I did *not* equate sex with either fun, pleasure, or ecstatic love. So, these factors combined into creating a contented knowing that I was satisfied with my life. At last, I was looking to myself for my own happiness and stopped bothering to compare myself with other married couples. I still did not know anything about asexuality, but I had reached a happy point of satisfaction about being single. This new contentment was not particularly age related, as I felt a new youthful vibrancy that came with the relief of allowing my sexual unease to evaporate. Seeking sexual love had been all too hard, and without any truly uplifting experiences, I just let go of the old marriage dream.

A LIFETIME OF BEING AN ACE: MAKING ASEXUALITY VISIBLE

For the next few years, I existed in this peaceful state, and by not dissipating energies on fruitless relationships, life began to feel more rewarding. Without the anxiety or guilt of sexual pretending, I was more able to concentrate on artistic pursuits. Also, I felt a greater sense of outreaching affection towards my fellow human beings, and even found more humour in my daily life. My new sense of well-being also manifested itself in renewed physical vigour and stamina, so despite approaching my eightieth decade, I was feeling healthier in every way. But little did I know things were about to become even better.

AVEN and Asexuality

Having grown into a sense of serenity about myself, I was not looking for relationships or actively researching the topic of sexuality anymore – so coming across the AVEN website was a glorious accident.[43] I just happened to open the website while seeking out what the word '*asexuality*' meant. Here, I read a definition of asexuality, and there for the first time, I had an instant recognition of my sexual orientation. I was stunned! There were paragraphs, words, descriptions – all describing ME, plus revealing a whole community of people just like myself!

My reaction was to read, reread, sit in silent shock, pace the room, and read again. It was an indescribable '*Ah-ha*' moment to finally understand I was asexual. In all, that discovery gave me quite a buzz! There were also some online asexuality tests, which absolutely

---

[43] I have referred to David Jay, the founder of the AVEN website, several times. You can find further information about him on Wikipedia and through an interesting radio interview on YouTube.

confirmed my discovery.[44] The tests resulted in a high indication of my asexuality. One report said:

> *You may find that you have quite low or no interest whatsoever in having sex and/or you experience a lack of sexual attraction to anyone. You may still desire romantic relationships, but you do not feel the need to have sex. Moreover, you are likely to avoid situations in which you may be propositioned for sex and may find sexual intimacy feels unwarranted in the context of intimate relations or connections.*

The relief was enormous. I was 'normal' in the sexual world; I belonged to an estimated 1 percent of the population. (However, it is probably a much higher percentage because asexuality is still an often unacknowledged, and hidden orientation.) Although I was basically more contented with myself and I felt good about life, now that my asexuality was clear, it was exhilarating. Never mind all the past time and effort looking in the wrong places and forcing myself into married-life directions – I now had the answer. There is nothing like the joy of inner knowing when you have discovered a deep truth about yourself. No doubt, this finding presented an instant knowing that I had always been this way.

Thoughts raced such as: '*I knew I was different,*' '*No wonder I never felt in step with my peer group,*' and '*Of course, this is why sex had not been on my mind.*' Now there was the thrill that only new knowledge could bring, and a sense of vindication about my lack of sexual desire. At last, I had found not just the imaginary elephant in the room; it was more like the unseen mosquito that had annoyed me

---

[44] There are a few free tests online, where one can see the types of questions that are generally asked, including www.idrlabs.com > asexuality

most of my life. It was as if I had been trying to fill a hole that did not even exist!

AVEN Website Discoveries

During my first visits to the AVEN website, I had dived into the basic sexual definitions and the varied ways of being asexual. It was a comfort to read how asexuality was *not* a choice or caused by a physical or psychological disorder. I also knew that I was not suffering from any trauma or did not hold negative views of sex; it was just that I did not desire or even bother to think about intercourse. I had only ever thought about sex in a deliberately rational way, such as a subject to be researched.

The most comfort came from feeling legitimised as an asexual person – not just because I now belonged to an exclusive group, but because I could accept myself as uniquely normal. Better still, I felt like a rather rare and exceptional human being. Most importantly, I was delighted and thankful to be asexual and certainly would never want to be any other way. The worst thing would be for someone to suggest that I needed '*fixing*' or had '*missed out*' on something special in life.

AVEN Forum for Older Asexuals

I began to delve into the on-site forums where members posed questions about their sexuality under varied headings. There was one forum for older asexuals, so that was the section I first explored. Here was the question of '*How old were you when you found the answer to your sexual confusion?*' After some more reading, I realised I was one of the oldest.

I expected postings to be mainly from female asexuals, so it was surprising to see quite a number written by males. To be an asexual male in a sexualised world, I could see as being especially problematic. In this era, any male not wanting sex would be decidedly 'uncool,' and it would not be an easy topic to negotiate with a girlfriend or discuss with his regular peer group. Also, it would be hard for an asexual male to physically satisfy a sexual female, as I imagine faking sex as I did could be extremely difficult for males.

Asexual Symbols and Cake

The AVEN website introduced me to symbols and language of asexuality, which gave me a sense of belonging to a new community. There was a lot of mention of cake, growing from the popular asexual joke about *'preferring to eat cake than have sex.'* Being a savoury lover, I do not like the taste of cake, and the images of large, gooey, welcoming cakes to new members were slightly off-putting. Rather, I could say I would sooner dance or eat chocolate any day than have sex.

'Ace' Meaning Asexual

Asexuals use the term 'Ace' to describe themselves. I do not mind people calling me an 'Ace,' as it is a reminder of card games where an ace is usually a winner. The asexual symbol is often the ace of spades, with romantic asexuals tending to use the ace of hearts. Thus, for me, I prefer to use the ace of hearts because my leaning towards wanting to experience love is a core aspect of my asexuality.

The Asexual Flag

The other emblem to create a sense of belonging was the asexual flag. This flag has horizontal bands of black, grey, white, and purple with the following meanings:

- black = asexuality
- grey = grey-asexual (the area between being sexual and asexual)
- white = sexuality of all other people who are not asexual
- purple = community

The Black Ring

The other signifier of asexuality is a black ring on the middle finger of the right hand. I knew wearing this symbol would not spark much recognition by anyone, knowing how few people knew about asexuality. Despite this, I decided I would occasionally wear one, just to give me some secret satisfaction of knowing my place in the gendered world. Besides, since 'coming out,' a comment about my black ring has often led to explaining its significance, so it has sometimes been a successful way to introduce the asexual topic.

AVEN Website – Going Online

There were many positive emotions in finding the AVEN online community. At first, I was hesitant about joining a discussion forum, but I finally found the confidence to contribute comments about my age and how long it took to recognise my asexuality. It was the discovery of AVEN that motivated me to record my experience of how asexuality became '*visible*' to me, so hence it invoked the idea to embark on this writing project. Without a doubt, AVEN contributors have been both a source of inspiration and encouragement. For me, it was a significant goal to inform people about asexuality in the hope that they, too, could become accepting of this valid way of being. I also hoped asexual people would gain some comfort in the knowledge that my years of searching had been worthwhile. In fact, I had found that being different to most of the population was a good thing.

AVEN as Comforting Support

David Jay, who is himself asexual and the remarkable founder of AVEN, will always have my heartfelt gratitude. Finding the AVEN website and asexual community has been a reliable source of comfort and has truly enhanced my place in the world. Whenever I feel misunderstood or have been the butt of negative asexual reactions, I always return to the AVEN website to recapture the feelings of understanding and support. I know if ever I truly felt alone, then AVEN would be my first port of call for that sense of like-minded connection. Luckily, the transformation of my inner world has meant I do not often need extra emotional support. It is also a comfort to see other countries beginning to develop groups and organisations to educate and advocate for asexual people.[45]

2021 Better Together Conference

Just when I was hoping to meet other asexuals in person, I was delighted that a LGBTIQA+ conference was to happen in my home state. This 2021 Better Together Conference was organised by the Equality Project and had extended an invitation to everyone to take part, including asexuals and allies (that is, all folk of any sexual persuasion). The main aims of the conference were as follows...

> *In order to facilitate a conversation about LGBTIQA+ rights in Australia, we need to have a platform to share our ideas and experiences and build bridges between our diverse communities.*

In my enthusiasm, I spontaneously applied to present a session on my experience of being an elder asexual titled 'A Lifetime of Asexuality – Making It Visible.' I was delighted when my application was successful, and the report of my big public 'coming out' will be recorded further on.[46]

---

[45] In Australia there is the recently formed Ace & Aro Collective AU (https://acearocollective.au) which can also be found on Facebook (AceAroCollectiveAU).

[46] The 2021 Better Together Conference report is in the Appendices along with information about the Equality Project Australia – a LGBTIQA+ organisation that delivers support and policy for the queer community.

First Public Asexual Lecture

A few months after my AVEN research into asexuality, I attended a university meeting where a guest speaker was lecturing on the historical concepts of love and romance. This was the first lecture where I heard any mention of asexuality in a public forum, and it was gratifying to hear an academic confirming that this orientation existed. Not only did she verify asexuality but spoke of it as normal and having always existed. Her extensive research covered the topic of sexuality from the historical, cultural, physical, and emotional perspectives.

Being younger, this woman had grown up with a naturally broader understanding of asexual matters and had been brave enough to re-examine diverse types of sexuality. Her study included the historical and cultural attitudes relating to ideas about marriage and romantic love. After the lecture, when I asked what had motivated her research, she made it clear that as an asexual herself, she wanted to explore the topic. Unlike me, she obviously acknowledged her asexuality much earlier, and therefore had developed a happy acceptance of herself at a younger age. This chance meeting gave me a role model of someone who could live as an asexual both with confidence and high self-regard.

That Word – 'Normal'

It is noted above the word '*normal*' is often used when talking about asexuality. Throughout my own writing and research, I also often use this word, as it does convey my intended meaning, that asexuality may be unusual, but is an acceptable (normal) way of being. Normal is a neutral kind of word inferring that something is average, permissible, and healthy in comparison to the majority. However, normal is a word that seems to change in application as new knowledge becomes available, or values and attitudes change.

Therefore, we hear statements about behaviour 'becoming normalised,' or in these Covid times, hear the phrase 'the new normal' as we change our actions to prevent viral spread. The concept of normal is also connected to the word 'spectrum,' where there are different degrees of normality. Indeed, 'on the spectrum' has proved to be a useful phrase when describing the diversity of sexual 'normality.'

Education About the Sexual Spectrum

The AVEN website presented valuable information about the myriad aspects of asexuality, along with the many types of asexual experience. At first, the complex variety of categories were frustrating, and I had a desire to either simplify or ignore such a detailed analysis. Despite the problem of navigating asexual categories, I did come to appreciate our human diversity and that no two people are the same. After some initial difficulty, I found my way through the different asexual classifications, which I will now endeavour to summarise and reveal where I think I fit on the asexual spectrum.

Reflection

The 'Asexual Spectrum'

At first, I did not have the patience to sort through all the asexual categories, although when I did, it helped to classify myself. Trying to understand all the diversities within just one type of sexuality was another reminder about the complexity of our sexual human nature. Within every distinct sexual orientation, there is a spectrum of difference and degrees of desire. This creates a clearer understanding of the range of sexual alternatives. For example, I consider myself at the lower end of the spectrum with 'no sexual desire.'

Firstly, I came across the terms where asexuals considered themselves as belonging to grey areas or being a demi-asexual. Then again, asexuals could have different tendencies in relation to romantic attraction. In other words, asexuals can experience varying degrees of attraction or desire in wanting to connect with another person. Secondly, I could see how asexuals can also be romantically inclined. Here is a brief list of a few asexual varieties:

1. *Grey-asexual*: People who are somewhere between asexual and sexual. Although feeling asexual, they do have sexual desire on rare occasions.
2. *Demi-asexual*: An asexual person who will have sex, but only when there is a deep emotional love in the relationship, and where it often takes a long time for such a bond to develop.
3. *Romantic tendencies*: Relating to gender or non-gender where there is attraction, yet with no desire for sex. Some of these were...
    - *Heteroromantic*: Meaning feeling romantically attracted to the other sex.
    - *Homoromantic*: Having attraction to the same sex. For example, an asexual female can feel romantically attracted towards another female but not want the intimacy to culminate in sexual expression.
    - *Biromantic*: A romantic attraction to either male or female gender.
    - *Panromantic*: A romantic attraction to a person without gender being important.
    - *Aromantic*: Meaning not attracted or wanting romantic relationships at all.

My Asexual Category

At first, I could not bother to give myself a label and thought just the term 'asexual' was enough. After browsing a few of the categories, I became curious to analyse what descriptive label might fit my sense of asexuality.

Although appreciating my own female gender, I do have more of a romantic attraction to males, mainly because of their communication style and direct manner. This means I like the male tendency towards action, resilience, and their often-practical approach to problem solving. I am also aware I seek the maleness in myself, as I want to embrace some of that male confidence, power, strength, and single mindedness. This ideal was clear in my childhood daydreams, where I became a female superhero wanting to lead equally with a man by my side. Working as a team, I imagined the combination of our complementary skills would win the day.

Therefore, despite being female in gender, I have some male characteristics as part of my personality. Of course, in terms of dance, I have always appreciated male/female partnerships where the different physical attributes complement each other. But I am not a 'homo-asexual,' and as said before, I could never imagine embracing females, having always admired the more androgynous physiques of the dance world.

The Asexual Classification

I decided my label was a *heteroromantic asexual* except that like demi-asexual people, I do feel the need for an emotional love-connection, even in a close friendship. So, being a *heteroromantic asexual*, I can feel a degree of romantic attraction towards males while wanting a loving but *nonsexual* friendship. Confusing? Maybe. But there it is!

Despite the complicated detail, such labels helped to define my unique asexual orientation, highlighting that like everyone else, I am a complicated human being. It also raised the question of what is meant by 'romantic attraction' and how it differs from love. This topic will take some thought, and I aim to tackle it in another reflection essay further on.

Fluidity

Often, I come across the word *fluidity* as applied to bisexuality or alternative gender preferences. Alternative gender is where a person expresses themselves sometimes as male and other times as female. In terms of asexuality, it could relate to grey-asexuals where there are rare occasions when they might move towards being sexual. Then again, it could describe the type of asexual who would consider sexual encounters, *only* if she or he felt a deep loving bond. Despite having past sexual encounters where I may have appeared '*fluid*,' I really was not, and I know my behaviour was not in tune with my true basic desires. In other words, I was faking the sexual connection and not at all being fluid.

One could use the word '*plasticity*' instead of '*fluidity*,' but here I use '*fluid*' in terms of different attractions or responses within certain types of sexual orientations or genders. I would use the word '*plasticity*' if describing how the brain changes, such as when adjusting to environmental change or learning new skills.

Other Terminology

I note there were terms relating to attractions associated with a desire to be connected to certain types of people. Here I will mention a few that I know apply to me. My love of dance always meant I noticed both males and females who have the aesthetic build of a dancer. Hence, I know I tend to feel what is called '*aesthetic attraction*.' On the other hand, this attraction can quickly fade if it becomes obvious the person's personality is incompatible with mine.

Another type of attraction is more academic, where I want to be with people who are impressive because of their intelligence. This is called *'sapio attraction'* (meaning to be wise) and occurs when one feels stimulated by a clever person's enthusiasm for knowledge. However, I find this sort of attraction can also dissipate if he or she has other undesirable traits. Once, I held a maths lecturer in high esteem, as I admired his academic ability and needed to understand his lectures on statistics to pass an exam. When asking for extra assistance, he was more than willing to oblige but also wanted to stroke my long blonde hair and make sexual innuendos! He instantly lost my respect along with any *'sapio attraction,'* and I passed the exam *without* his help.

There is also the term *'biophilia'* applying to those who feel deeply attracted to beautiful surroundings in nature. It is known that some people like to have sex in outdoor places, although for me, it would infer a general delight in the natural world. I always wanted to be a landscape painter, as the elements of weather, colours and shapes, or animals in their natural habitat are a constant fascination; so I do tend to be a nature lover.

Wanting to Talk About Asexuality

Despite this nuisance of sorting out terminology, it helped me to understand what kind of asexual I was. It was also a help towards the next stage of my asexual journey when I developed the urge to 'come out' to other people. Why? Initially, it was the actual elation of understanding myself and wanting to share that feeling with others.

Then there was the sobering thought of knowing there would not be a single soul who would casually say, '*Oh yes, I always thought you were.*' 'Coming out' meant I had to be prepared to face disbelief and cope with the obvious comments, such as '*Oh, but you never met the right person.*' With a degree of bravery, I decided to proceed and deal with any criticism as graciously as possible. So began the process of 'coming out' which will be the subject of my next journal.

JOURNAL 17

The Process of 'Coming Out'

Dear Journal,

As an asexual person who had decided to come out, I considered how it might affect my relationships; particularly those who thought they knew me well and would struggle to accept me in the same way. Nevertheless, I decided to put aside anxiety and disclose my asexuality for two reasons...

1. It felt personally liberating to reveal the truth about myself.
2. There was the genuine hope of helping people (including other asexuals) to understand that this was a positive and genuine type of sexuality.

However, I was still apprehensive as to how close friends and family might react to such a revelation. Also, coming out may not always be desirable, especially where it could be hurtful or too emotionally disturbing for someone to hear. I was conscious that revealing my asexuality should not always be about making me feel better about myself.

Fears of Rejection

I also wondered if people would think I had physical or psychological problems, not take me seriously, or conclude it was something to do with my older age. The comments I expected were...

- 'But you are now that age when hormones have reduced.'
- 'Of course, you never did meet the right man.'
- 'There could be a physical or psychological reason for your lack of desire.'

- o 'You grew up in an era when sex was taboo – so you are probably inhibited.'
- o 'Perhaps you harbour some sort of guilt or shame about sex?'
- o 'You must be having me on – you're joking!'

Admittedly, the first three points seem to 'support' my asexuality – although not the last three. I admit to being post-menopausal and not meeting exactly the right man, and I did have some minor physical impediments to sex. On the other hand, I have never felt generally inhibited about sex, and I do not believe sexual intercourse is either sinful or shameful. Certainly, I would not be inclined to tease, joke, or trivialise any asexual orientation.

At this point, I had absolute confidence in my own judgement and was convinced beyond all doubt that I *always* had been asexual. In fact, I had even played 'devil's advocate,' by looking at reasons to discredit my own asexual theory, and to thoroughly examine my own biases. I did this by brainstorming all my past life experiences that could been seen as a *cause* of my asexuality. Conclusion? Every potential explanation *against* being an asexual did not apply to me. Why? Because as far back as I can remember, I *never* developed any sexual interest or sexual desire like most other people. In conclusion, I did not feel shame or think being asexual diminished me in any way, nor did I feel any sense of loss.

'Coming Out' For Other LGBTIQA+ Groups

Disclosure of oneself as an asexual is unlike many other LGBTIQA+ people, as most queer orientations are known in the public arena. This means that most gay/queer people do not always need to explain much about the nature of their orientation – except intersex people, who are born with a combination of male and female sexual anatomy. In this regard, asexual, intersex, and some gender-related orientations are often 'invisible' to the public. With asexuality, there is nothing much – no behaviour – to reveal!

Of course, one does not forget the often-terrible tales of homosexual instances of societal or familial rejection. In fact, some young gay/queer guys used to seek my friendship as a replacement mother or sister because their family had shunned them. Homosexuality, along with many sexual variations, entails behaviour that society can harshly judge from cultural or moral points of view. Then again, I spare a thought for those who come from religious or cultural domains, where revealing their true sexuality would ostracise them from family and community as well.

'Coming Out' to Different People

Disclosure to diverse groups of people is still an ongoing challenge. With friends I gave small hints in conversation, and with greater public awareness about LGBTIQA+ issues, it became easier to talk about the included 'A' for asexuality. As mentioned, wearing a black ring on the middle finger of my right hand (one of the asexual symbols) also often helped to introduce the topic. Overall, I found raising the issue casually and naturally seemed to be the most comfortable approach.

The main reactions I experienced were twofold.

1. Relating to my earlier choices of men to marry.
2. My elder age.

So often I got the expected comment... '*You never met the right man.*' In fact, no heterosexual man would have been right for me! Of course, some people reminded me that I was now older, and I should realise it was natural for my sex drive to have diminished. I could tell it was hard for them to understand I never had a '*sex drive*' in the first place. Overall, people were polite, respectful, and outwardly accepting – maybe because I was obviously delighted about my new sexual orientation and did not need their sympathy.

Family Members

Raising the topic with my son was easier than expected. He always viewed his mother as being a creative, alternative type, who questioned many things in life. Therefore, he did not react as if it was important when I mentioned I was writing about asexuality. With two almost adult sons of his own, he lived in a world where cricket and football scores were far more interesting than the non-sex life of his mother. As his wife was an easy-going modern woman, she, too, had always been accepting of what I did with my life. So outwardly they did not react with much overt surprise or concern.

Parents

Although my parents were deceased before I realised my asexuality, I often imagined how they would have received my new sexual revelation. Despite knowing they were a loving couple who enjoyed a normal heterosexual relationship, I am still sure they would have accepted my orientation, as throughout their lives, they always encouraged me to be true to myself. If they could see I was happy, I am certain they would have been understanding, and even wanting to 'come out' to them in my imagination is a testament to their attitudes of loving acceptance.

Former Partner

The hardest experience was 'coming out' to my former partner – the 'quiet friend.' Here, I worried he could think it was somehow his fault and that I had not welcomed his initial sexual advances. The worst feeling was my guilt in knowing that in our first year when we set out to be intimate, I had pretended to enjoy sex and at times encouraged his advances. On many occasions, I would give him a spontaneous hug, and he would take this to mean that I was trying to instigate sex. These memories made me feel uneasy, but nevertheless I did raise the topic, with my only comfort being that it was never my intention to deceive. I took him to a hotel bar, ordered a beer, and told him I was writing about asexuality and why. He appeared too stunned to say much at the time, and I wondered if he considered it an excuse to move away from our platonic friendship. Later, I sent him a written statement emphasising that in no way was he to blame for my sexual disinterest. He never spoke of this again, but we continued to communicate as old friends. In fact, I suspect he was relieved to know our relationship had quickly become platonic because of me and not him.

'Coming Out' to the Public

My first public 'coming out' was online to the AVEN asexual community. This was easy, as I knew there would be immediate acceptance, but also difficult in not knowing my audience. At the beginning, it felt weird typing my thoughts into cyber space to unknown people, as it was not like conversing with Facebook friends. In the past, I was accustomed to communicating with 'live' audiences or speaking face to face with those I knew or professionally trusted. The variety of online people were male, female, older like me, much younger, depressed, lonely, curious, questioning, or also like me, enthusiastic about their asexuality.

Through reading their thoughts and experiences, I felt accepted and happy to share a little of my experience. I realised, as a much older person who had waited such a long time to find my asexual self, I had a unique story to tell. It was then I felt inspired to write these journals for my internet friends and wider audiences. I also hoped that any sort of writing might advance knowledge about this usually unacknowledged orientation. In addition, I knew these journals would have the bonus of further clarifying asexuality for myself, and indeed, this has proved to be true.

The Defining Stages of Coming Out

Understanding my sexuality has proved to be an interesting process with defining *stages* that actually spanned many years. It entailed not just 'coming out' to other people, but also 'coming out' to myself. In my younger days, ignorance prevailed, as I thought sexual desire would develop as I grew into adulthood. In fact, self-knowledge and revealing my sexual self is still an ongoing process, as I continue to prepare to speak at conferences and draft this book.

To summarise, after puberty I went through the following stages that would lead me towards my present sexual understanding.

1. The first stage was '*noticing.*' I noticed as a teenager I was not reacting to sex the same way as my friends.
2. Then followed the stage of '*comparing*' myself to others, and wondering why they were excited about exploring methods of kissing or petting.
3. This led to the behaviour of '*pretending.*' Here I began to model behaviour to match with my school friends when it came to sex and relationships. I feigned delight if I received a letter from a boy or fabricated excitement if a boy held my hand.
4. The hardest thing was that I did not even know I was being untrue to myself. This was the awful stage of '*acting in ignorance.*' Therefore, the need for love and belonging found me adopting a 'boyfriend' and accepting his proposal for marriage, because I thought it was the right thing to do.
5. After and between marriages, there were stages of serious '*sexual research.*' Vaguely, I knew something was not right, so then I began to educate myself about sexuality.

THE PROCESS OF 'COMING OUT'

6. Eventually, after years of spasmodic sexual investigations, I came to a kind of *'self-acceptance'* about my own natural way of being. This meant that I stopped trying to connect with a partner in any physically intimate fashion and became content with enjoying platonic friendships.
7. Finally, there was the relief in finding the truth of being asexual. Along with this liberation was a sense of *'integration,'* meaning that all parts of myself came together into clear focus with a renewed self-identity.

To summarise, there were seven stages, including *noticing*, *comparing*, *pretending*, *acting in ignorance*, *researching*, *accepting*, and then the final sense of *integration*, which felt like a 'union or inter-fusion' of the self. It was like the stages of grieving but ended with a happy acceptance of findings rather than the sad acceptance of losses. In all, 'coming out' has been, and still is, a positive experience.

So how did things change and what were my reactions after 'coming out' to people? It is interesting to note that along the way the outcomes were both positive and negative.

Reflection

After 'Coming Out'

Personal Change

After uncovering my asexuality and 'coming out,' I know I have changed. Why? Because now I do not have that 'anxious spectre' in my head reminding me of a possible sexual deficiency. Without that inner tension, I now enjoy a sense of release and feel more open to the world.

I am sure others see this change in my demeanour. When celebrating my eightieth birthday with four other women of the same age, we contemplated the changes in ourselves over the years. The age-transformation was obvious with hair colour, and where gravity had its effect on our bodies. Despite this natural aging, there was the comment that '*We're all just the same as when we were young.*' After a slight pause, one friend looked at me and said, '*Except you of course.*' Searching for the word, she finally decided on '*exuberant.*' '*Yes,*' she said, '*you are far more exuberant*' – to which all agreed. Without a doubt, I knew I was showing the renewed kind of vitality that comes after an emotional burden has lifted.

Positive Changes

In terms of the positives of coming out, I know there have been beneficial changes relating to my emotional well-being, physical health, and social interactions. The following lists relate to all freedoms I noted since my asexuality became visible.

Emotional

Coming out has created the following stress releases and emotional changes.

- There is the emotional relief of not worrying about my lack of sexuality.
- Without anxiety, I have a greater focus on everyday tasks and projects.
- I am aware of a greater understanding of human individuality and diversity.
- Being less anxious, I have more 'headspace' to think about broader global issues.
- I have a greater appreciation of humour and readily see the funny side of life.

THE PROCESS OF 'COMING OUT'

- There is a positive sense of self-awareness and the ability to be self-deprecating.
- I am more self-forgiving about my human failings and mistakes.

Physical

Since 'coming out,' aspects of my health have improved, for two main reasons.

1. Lack of stress has created different physical preferences, so I do not care if I develop muscle instead of just being aerobically fit. I have given myself permission to look and be strong, so therefore I reach for the heavier weights these days.
2. Regarding alcohol, I always aimed to be a careful social drinker, remembering my first ballet teacher who taught her dancers how to 'ride' their drink. This meant slow sipping to make a drink last an hour followed by a glass of water. After memories of needing at least two glasses before sex, I now lose the taste after one standard drink. But I still have a glass on rare occasions, believing my father's rule – '*a little bit of everything does you good.*'

Social

Since learning about asexuality, I now have far more self-understanding.

- I do not need to be social because I think I 'should.' There is no need to pretend that I want a male partner or take part in 'make believe' flirting behaviour.
- I love social solo-dancing without a partner, but it is still magic if a man chooses to join me, but only where the dance motivates him rather than wanting me.

- o I can now acknowledge a preference for isolation. This does not mean I want to be a total recluse, but I recognise the desire to spend regular time alone.
- o I still like stimulating environments and social occasions (particularly if dancing is involved), as well as a need for silent spaces.

Being Happy Alone

I must admit to moving away from some former social endeavours, as my preference is to spend more time at the writing desk, and I no longer need to be a pretend member of the social sexual world. Indeed, one of the few positives of Covid restrictions was the added excuse to avoid events that no longer held any interest. This does not mean I am antisocial or want to avoid being with people. Rather, I tend to be a tad asocial, where I like solitudes for work, reflection, creative planning and critical thinking. I am also consciously meeting new people and ideas through literature, film, and study research. So despite being a little asocial, I am constantly intrigued and fascinated in my fellow human beings.

Emotional Balance

Although for many years my own emotions were confused, I now feel a new kind of contentment. However, I cannot expect everybody to feel the same degree of inner balance, and at times I need to watch impatience with people whose sexual emotions seem to cloud their rational thinking.

Regret

There is a touch of sadness that I am retired from teaching. As a teacher, many students told me they felt supported and inspired in the subjects I taught. In fact, I wish I had realised my asexuality earlier, as I am sure I would have engaged with more humour and further encouraged my students' unique individualities.

Post-Traumatic Reaction

I admit to a very mild degree of post-stress reaction to my years of unrecognised sexual confusion. Occasionally, there is still a disturbing, recurring dream where I am with a shadowy, male figure who I know I am supposed to please in a sexual way. There is a painful mental struggle of wanting to escape without hurting his feelings, but at this point I usually wake with absolute relief.

Summary

Overall 'coming out' has been more than worthwhile, except so many people raised the following questions – *'What is the cause of asexuality?'* and *'Is there a biological reason?'* These questions have also intrigued me, as there could even be an evolutionary purpose. Therefore, the next journal entry will delve into the asexual research and plausible scientific causes of asexuality. I think it is only natural to wonder what primary genetic or physical elements could have created my unique sexual orientation.

JOURNAL 18

Scientific Asexuality Research

Reasons for Scientific Research

Although I am deficient in scientific knowledge, I do have a curiosity to understand the causes of certain phenomena, particularly where it has a unique effect on human lives. In terms of human sexual development, it is interesting to consider the complex interaction of genetic inheritance, what happens in utero, and social/environmental factors that all must have an influence. Sexuality is beginning to attract more research, but I am sure there are still many areas to be explored. Nevertheless, I looked for any asexual studies via the usual digital-information pathways.

After conducting internet and library searches, I found little information as to any rational explanations of asexuality. This was disappointing, and I would have liked to see more information for the following reasons...

1. I want to better understand the causes of sexual diversity.
2. I personally would like to see science confirm my claim to being an asexual person, rather than just relying on my own self-reporting.
3. To confirm asexuality is *not* a disorder (a claim which I do not believe).
4. It would be satisfying to have proved that asexuality served humanity in some way. (Note: If we were all asexuals, there would be few humans at all!)

In asexuality, research could occur in multiple areas, knowing that many interrelating factors can shape human behaviour. Such study areas would possibly need to include the physical, psychological, social, historical, and cultural, as they all have some impact on our different sexual preferences and desires. I am sure any sexual/gender/relationship exploration could help in many areas such as...

- Helping women and men strive for equality in relationships.
- Assisting men to show and communicate emotions.
- Supporting marriages through difficult stages.
- Understanding sexual crimes and rehabilitation of perpetrators.
- More fully protecting the victims of sexual misconduct.
- Understanding and treating addiction related to sexual behaviour.

I believe further research into sexuality could uncover the reasons for distinct types of sexual attractions, including asexuality. Any investigation into asexuality would supply another lens through which to understand the mysteries behind all sexual orientations. Although I am curious about the probable causes, at this point, I doubt that any scientific research could change my feeling of 'rightness' about my asexuality. Nevertheless, I do believe in the methods of scientific theory. Therefore, the following possible areas of research come to mind.

Physical Research

Genetics

My first question was how our inherited genes might have something to do with asexuality. To me, the study of genetics is a fascinating field with genes (over 20,000 of them) being the basic units of our heredity. So far, I have not found any answers relating to asexuality in this area. However, there seems to be a consensus that genes with their unique DNA are an important contributor to sexual behaviour.

Epigenetics

This research area examines how and where genes are 'expressed' and turned on or off by 'nature' of our biological development, or through the 'nurture' in our environment. What chemical changes result in genes turning off or on? Despite the notion that manipulation of genes could cure disease, I would not want this research to 'cure' asexuality or alter core gender or sexual orientation, as I absolutely want to keep my asexual uniqueness. In the case where sexuality is an addiction that causes physical or mental harm, then one might be agreeable to such a method of eradication.

Chemicals and the Brain

Circulating chemicals are an interesting part of sexuality, and I realise just how many are involved in sexual attraction and the neurochemistry implicated in mating.

The chemicals, such as pheromones, can explain the often sudden stages of...

- o attraction
- o desire
- o lust or intense attraction
- o the idealisation of the loved one
- o those all-consuming and overriding passions.

Then there are questions to how the sex hormones of testosterone, oestrogen, progesterone, the feel-good dopamine, the joyful mood serotonin, pain-reliever endorphin, the love-bonding oxytocin, or the nurturing vasopressin might work in our bodies.

Therefore, I am sure we could learn more about these incredible substances, such as how to encourage them to work for our relationships.

Recently, a nasal spray for women has become available. It is a synthetic peptide to improve the neurotransmitter activity in the brain to restore the chemical balance and sexual desire. This sounds excellent for those females who are genuinely suffering from 'hypoactive sexual dysfunction disorder' (HSDD). Here, the important word is 'suffering,' inferring there is real distress for women who have a defined physical or psychological cause for their difficult sex lives. Although some medics might easily mistake me as having HSDD, I am certainly not in distress and would not seek medical treatment. However, I am delighted when research helps anyone on the sexual spectrum, and when they want to recover their former sexual desires.

Animal Research
Research in animals has revealed varied levels of sex drives and yet similar hormone levels. It was reported that some healthy male animals were *not* sexually interested in the females of the same species, but when assessed, these males had a normal healthy amount of male hormone. This suggested the brain receptors did not absorb the chemicals in the usual way. Ergo, does this mean that asexuals could have an adequate amount of hormone, except for some reason, may have different brain receptors?

The existence of such animal displays of asexuality are confirming as they run contradictory to the idea that asexuality might be a psychological problem. If behavioural issues cause asexuality, such as fear of commitment or a repression of sexuality, then this theory cannot hold up, because animals are supposed to be incapable of these kinds of emotional reactions. However, this rests upon the assumption that humans and some animals have similar causes for sexual difference. Evidently, research into the mating habits of sheep and voles are revealing the complexity of the brain and chemicals involved in sexual performance. It is interesting to consider that animal studies could shed light on our human behaviour.[47]

Internal Brain Size

In humans, some scientific studies found the brain size of heterosexual women and gay/queer men were similar, both with *symmetrical* right and left hemispheres. There were also findings in straight men and gay/queer women, where their right hemispheres were both *larger* than the left. These similarities also related to the activity of the amygdala, which is the source of basic flight or fight emotions. This suggests it could be biology and not environment that creates the core of sexual orientation.

Brain Plasticity

Plenty of mystery still circulates about the workings of our amazing brain. We now know it is 'plastic,' so one can create new skills by developing new neurological pathways.[48] This type of relearning could possibly ignite or alter certain sexual behaviours, but I doubt whether one could relearn or unlearn sexual orientation or change the deep core of the brain. To use a computer analogy, one might change the brain 'software' but not the 'hard drive' that exists on a more basic level. I will admit to bias here, as in looking to understand the cause of asexuality, I am not looking to see if I have a 'disease.'

---

[47] This information was found through varied internet sites that report scientific studies on animal mating behaviour. Even if the technical details are difficult to understand, usually the abstract and conclusions of the study can be understood.

[48] Book on brain plasticity – *The Brain that Changes Itself* by Norman Doidge (2008, Scribe Publications). Note that recovering stroke patients use brain plasticity to regain physical abilities.

SCIENTIFIC ASEXUALITY RESEARCH

Physical Body Types and Asexuality

When reading about possible physical traits, I found questions as to whether asexuals follow a body type. There were suggestions that physical attributes could have been contributing factors. For example, if one was shorter or lighter than average, or when the onset of puberty occurred. There was also a proposition that an underdeveloped body could mean menstruation began later in an asexual female. In my case, I do confess to being small in height and have always been on the light side, with my weight showing only minor changes over the years. Then again, I was physically underdeveloped when I began early menstruation at the age of ten, so in my case, this theory does not fit.

Asexuality as a Medical Problem

Although I am concentrating on asexuality as a lifelong orientation, I do acknowledge it could develop after a medical episode or following a trauma. But in these cases, I presume there *was* a former existing sexual desire – unlike myself who never ever felt anything. I will acknowledge my physical problems such as childhood bronchitis, early menstruation, a spinal bone spur, childbirth scarring, along with the normal menopausal hormone adjustment. My listed physical restraints could look to be enough to cause asexuality, not to mention my problematic marriage relationships. I admit these factors could have *reinforced* my asexual position – but, as stated before, I do not believe they were the cause. However, it is accepted that for some people, a loss of sexual desire would require treatment.

Reasons for Psychological Research

As a normal sex drive can affect the brain, it follows that sex can be a formidable motivator of behaviour. From noting moments of sexual passion in books and film, I can see that, for the characters, all thoughts of future consequences do not appear to matter as sexual desire becomes the main overriding force. On the other hand, an asexual person without such overriding passions could therefore have a vastly different mindset. As a result, I suggest they may have a more generalised loving focus that extends towards many people, and not just one partner. Sexuality is such an important basis of the human experience, and any ongoing research would be valuable in understanding how it affects the expression and control of our emotions.

The deep-seated nature of sexuality can create both positive and negative emotions, that in turn, give rise to inner happiness or mental distress. Although I see asexuality as basically positive as a minority orientation, it, too, can cause loneliness, anxiety, depression, and a sense of non-identity. Let us hope research and education can support in avoiding mental stress by dealing with negative attitudes towards people who are different, so allowing all forms of sexuality to be more normalised. From the AVEN website, I also see where heterosexual people have reached out to the asexual community to understand why their partners are not interested in sex. Therefore, I strongly believe behavioural research into sexual behaviour can help everybody.

Asexual Education

As I have said, sexuality activity does not always define sexual orientation, as asexual people can engage in sexual situations, despite it not reflecting their inclinations. This can occur when they are trying to satisfy partners or behaving according to cultural expectations. In my case, I was usually trying to please a partner and show affection, while being desperate not to show sexual indifference. Hence, for me, extensive information on sexuality diversities would have been helpful during my early questioning years. Also, because asexuality is a *self-reported* type of orientation, it can only be supported by good research, whether it be qualitative, sociological, biological, or historical.

Qualitative Research

Whereas most scientific research consists of statistics and numbers, I found qualitative research to be slightly different. However, with less numerical data, it was not devoid of scientific methods for gathering information to make it as free as possible from bias and able to reach valid conclusions.[49] Methods included observations of behaviour, in-depth individual or group interviews, open-ended questionnaire surveys, and secondary research from literature, existing data, or filmed recordings. This way, evaluations could give reasonably accurate interpretations and perspectives of human behaviour. In fact, as reported in a former journal, I completed some qualitative asexual questionnaire tests online, all of which reassuringly confirmed my asexuality.

Sociological Research

At any age, it is interesting to reflect on the changes in society that relate to so many aspects of our lives. These changes include fashion, technology, global trends, economics, and our attitudes towards sex. I am sure there are many beliefs about sex practices, marriages, and relationships that do not always reflect what truly happens. The history of marriage is a fascinating topic, showing how patriarchal power, religion, politics, economics, law, property ownership, and culture all have an influence.

Understanding gender and sexual orientation from a social point of view still has a long way to go to counteract outdated conventional

---

[49] See qualitative research methods used in the areas of human behaviour in Wikipedia and other scholarly papers online.

ideas. Here are only *some* of the gender-biased comments I have heard:

- Women take jobs away from men. (I still hear that from older males.)
- Marriage should only be between a man and a woman.
- A child needs a mother and male father who are the biological parents.
- Gay/queer marriage is not normal, despite it being legal in some countries.
- Women are not as academically inclined in science/mathematical subjects.
- Women invite sexual advances by how they dress.
- Traditionally men should be church leaders (no female cardinals or Popes).
- Men should not cry or be emotional.
- Men are insulted if told they are behaving like a girl.
- Women cannot fight at a warfront.

Cultural expectations can control and limit both males and females to behave in a certain way. The need for community acceptance and feeling equal to other people can be an enormously powerful force. Because I did not understand the sway of social influences, it took me a long time to understand who I was, or why I made certain life choices. So, I hope research into sexuality can change our behaviour to give us greater freedom to be ourselves.

Historical Research

As well as social research, a historical view of relationships can be enlightening in comparison with our present-day culture. In the past, marriage arrangements grew out of a variety of purposes, such as for…

- the bargaining of females in tribal situations
- the capture of females after conflict
- aiding biological genetic strengthening
- bringing about political alliances
- the gaining of property through inheritance
- Historically, love has taken on cultural elements of...
- the heroic (saving the damsel)
- dying for love (Romeo & Juliet)
- love as chivalry (courtly love)
- following expected conservative behaviour (the mannered Victorian era).

Throughout my life, there has existed the conservative view of sex in the 1950s to the freer love notions of the 1960s, and to now in the twenty-first century, where there is more readiness to embrace LGBTIQA+ orientations and gay/queer marriage. Regardless of cultural changes, continual research and education can only help guard against the many historically narrow views of gender and relationships.

♥

Reflection

Sex and Evolution

Evolutionary Effects of Asexuality
I like the idea that gender and sexual-orientation diversity could be a key part of our human development and survival. In this random universe, I am sure a wealth of sexual differences (including asexuality) have a place in the complexity of human evolution and survival. Diversity, I believe, is necessary for natural selection, with both nature (what is genetically inherited) and nurture (what

develops from an environment) being factors in the creation of human individuals, thus making each newborn unique.

Therefore, I question how asexuality and other unusual orientations could contribute to human development. Despite asexuality obviously not enhancing human reproduction, it may be theorised that some non-productive asexuality may *indirectly* and subtly aid reproduction and create certain advantages, such as by…

- o influencing heterosexual siblings, giving them a greater urge to reproduce
- o an asexual person having time to give extra parental/family support
- o the existence of gay/queer and asexual people, to create a reproductive advantage for others – such as in the female line of gay/queer relatives, where there can be a greater propensity for reproduction to occur
- o people being attracted to the other sex by firstly being comfortable with asexual or gay/queer friendships
- o assisting in a world of climate change and pollution, where global population may need limitation.

Naturally, these are only vague ideas, where research could provide answers as to why sexual minorities exist, and what purpose they might serve. There are some scholarly articles on sexual orientation in relation to evolution, including the idea that non-conceptive sexuality can strengthen social bonding for survival.[50] However, universities may not lean towards such research, as I suspect funding might be prioritised into other areas of greater economic benefits. Besides, there is now an understandable focus to

---

[50] https://theconversation.com/homosexuality-may-have-evolved-for-social-not-sexual-reasons

research Covid viruses, vaccines, and climate change. On the other hand, the AVEN website shows a continually expanding list of sexual research projects with requests for participants to contribute.

From my limited scientific comments, the only way I could contribute to such research is to offer my asexual journals to any student who may glean something from them. Nevertheless, for survival, humans need to focus on many levels for health and well-being. As well as dealing with climatic and pandemic issues, governments also need global cooperation and science-based education to support good mental/physical health. This is because I believe people can better survive if they have rewarding relationships and a chance to be heard.

JOURNAL 19

Asexual Relationships

Dear Journal,

I often hear the question as to how asexuals can manage relationships, given that many of them do *not* want to live entirely alone. Indeed, some do desire a family life with a partner and children. Here, I undertake the challenge to suggest what kind of relationships might be possible for asexual people – including myself.

Asexual Relationships

Given my present age and life experience, a live-in relationship is something that is certainly not on my present radar. Nevertheless, I think about the emotional needs of other asexuals, especially after reading of their loneliness and relationship concerns. Indeed, quite a few younger asexuals have voiced their anxiety about being alone for the rest of their lives.

Whereas I lived in hopeful ignorance, they are more aware that without sexual desire, searching for a loving partner is going to be a challenging task. This is a dilemma for many asexual people and why many wanted me to write about how I survived and coped with intimate relationships. I *did* survive, but not without making bad decisions because of my lack of asexual knowledge. Therefore, I struggled unnecessarily through some stressful partnerships. I like to think younger asexuals could be more enlightened than me, and rather than a fruitless search for an unsuitable marriage partner, they could entertain several types of caring relationships.[51]

Possible Asexual Relationships

In terms of long-term relationships, I believe asexuals could negotiate several satisfactory solutions. Everyone deserves to love and feel loved, and although it is probably more difficult for an asexual person, I am sure that loving relationships are possible. Some asexual relationships would be atypical to the majority, but if they were acceptable to the people involved and did not cause harm to anyone else, then why not!

Here, I can imagine a few types of asexual relationship options such as…

- An *asexual couple* could naturally engage in a loving relationship, and if they were a male/female couple, they may have sex occasionally in order to have children. Again, they could avoid sex and conceive in some other way.
- Asexuals could *marry a heterosexual*, but with the understanding that the sexual partner might seek sexual satisfaction elsewhere (see section on polyamory), or the couple could negotiate sexual interaction in a way that was mutually acceptable.
- An asexual could form platonic family relationships with a *heterosexual couple* and share co-parenting responsibilities for the couple's children.
- There could be a marriage where a *male has two partners*, one sexual and the other asexual, with the two wives ideally having a sisterly type of relationship. (See section on polygamy).

---

[51] This New Zealand website contains interesting insights on asexual relationships. https://asexualitytrust.org.nz >Asexual people and relationships

- o Or an asexual person could enjoy a *life alone*, along with a wide range of friends, family members, and activities that satisfy the need for loving friendships and a rewarding life.
- o An asexual might *remain single* and obtain relationship satisfaction through devotion to an organisation or career that serves others in the community.
- o Asexual artists, musicians, or dancers can often find devotion in *creative* work and replace sexual love with the satisfaction of creative endeavour. (I noted that in the past, many ballet and music teachers were single females who never searched for a partner.)
- o In the same vein, some people might feel fulfilled in devoting themselves to *academic* writing, study, or research, or even challenging *sporting activities* to replace close relationships.

I am sure there are many more options, and I would hate to think being an asexual meant not having opportunities of love with another person. On the other hand, the need for relationships is unique for everyone, and so some asexuals (like me) could happily prefer to lead a semi-solitary life. However, finding the right partner and a loving friend can take time, so there is the need for more asexual meet-up groups through social media. Some asexual sites are now developing, although the pool of available people is small and vastly spread by distance over states and countries. This means meeting in person is not easy, but healthy friendships through internet communications would be better than nothing.

Polyamory and Polygamy

It could be easier in cultures where polyamory or polygamy are normalised for asexuals to have relationships. I know some of these practices exist in the world, and I accept such relationships could work, but I would consider three main conditions to avoid any possible jealousies or mistrust. These are...

1. Do no harm and sincerely aim to promote mutual well-being for everyone involved.
2. Operate within the bounds of respect, clear communication, and genuine affection.
3. Be prepared to review and reset emotional boundaries when necessary.

Polyamory

This practice is defined as when there is more than one intimate relationship, but with full knowledge and mutual consent of everyone involved. Acceptance of polyamory varies, depending on religious views, governmental laws, and whether (as in some countries) adultery is illegal. In other words, people can have close relationships (intimate or otherwise) with more than one person.

Polyamory does not mean cheating or secretly having sex with multiple partners at the same time. It also does not mean an 'open relationship,' where there is a seeking of other sexual experiences outside the agreed partnership arrangement. As I understand, true polyamory is consensual between all people involved and consists of mutual love, trust, respect, shared agreements, and ongoing communication.

Being an asexual female, I think a polyamorous situation would be acceptable with one proviso. The stipulation being that I admired and respected any others who were providing sexual satisfaction to my partner. Naturally, for anyone prone to jealousy, intimate arrangements could be quite challenging and achieving mutual agreement would be easier said than done. As for me, at this stage, I am far too solitary to live in a group situation.[52]

Polygamy

As most people know, polygamy is the practice of men who are married to more than one wife at the same time. ('*Polyandry*' refers to a woman who has multiple husbands.)

I once met a man who had four wives according to the custom of his culture and religion. He confessed to being happy with this arrangement as each wife had a special skill and family function. One loved cooking, another loved childcare, one liked gardening, and the other enjoyed sex. (However, I did not speak to his wives!) Again, as an asexual I could cope with this kind of arrangement from a sexual point of view, but I would probably apply for the childcare role. As said before, such arrangements would entail personal compatibility with a high degree of communication and negotiation for an agreeable family life.

After recent years of studying the variety of relationships that occur around the world, it does not faze me if people have two or more partners. For me, such arrangements would ideally include mutual compromises with all persons involved, although I could not entertain the use of power, control, or emotional abuse.[53] In such relationships, I would also not feel comfortable where there existed any underlying deceit. I am sure ongoing situations with multiple partners would require regular negotiation and re-examination about emotional needs and behavioural boundaries. This is because people's desires, feelings, and personal circumstances usually change

---

[52] The Psychology Today website discuss polyamory in some detail.

[53] Rules relating to open relationships: see websites such as – www.genevaconventions.org/open-relationship. Note: I have not summarised de-facto arrangements, where there can also be more than one relationship.

over time. Also, in group relationships, individuals would need to be comfortable within their religious, moral, and philosophical beliefs.

Sex Workers

I would like to acknowledge the 'professional' sex workers who can supply a safe and caring service to many people. For example, they often help those with disabilities who cannot easily seek a sexual partner, or heterosexuals who have an unwilling asexual partner. Plus, I am sure there are many other reasons why people who are unable to have their sexual desires satisfied in a safe way seek out professionals in the sex industry. I also note that sex workers have been regular supporters of LGBTIQA+ rights and have always taken part in the Mardi Gras. Here, I do not condone the darker side of the sex industry where there is no protection against the abuse of sex workers and where they work in unsafe, unhealthy conditions.

Asexuality and Other Cultures

If relationships have the main elements of care and affection, I respect the right for human beings to live accordingly within their own culture. Here, I admit to having limited experience in meeting asexuals or LGBTIQA+ people from other countries with distinct beliefs and governments. One could only imagine the cultural challenges some people (particularly girls) experience and where religious groups do not accept any form of gay/queer orientations. Therefore, I am concerned when countries deny asylum to asexuals who want to escape emotional suffering and persecution. Some governments do not realise that other cultures could find such asexual orientations most unacceptable. In some societies, being married and having a large family is the expected practice. Therefore, both asexual males and females try to flee these obligations.

Asexuality and Disability

I also have concern for asexual people who cope with physical disabilities as well as sexual differences. Sexuality is still a part of their lives that needs understanding, particularly as the disabled often experience omission and alienation in so many areas. Therefore, asexuality could also add to their isolation, as without that sexual energy, it could be harder to seek personal friendships. I am sure everyone wants to feel loved and respected, so I hope health practitioners and family members acknowledge both the sexual and non-sexual orientations of disabled people.

My Relationship Possibilities

Although my inner emotional life is better than it ever has been, I like the idea of being flexible and open to having close relationships. At my age, having a deeply intimate relationship is most unlikely and not something that I even consider. While platonic relationships are preferable, I do not want to hide behind asexuality as an excuse for avoiding loving partnerships. Who knows, there may be another asexual person out there waiting to connect with me, or I could be involved in a strange kind of coupling where the inclusion of a platonic companion could be desirable. Despite my present state of single contentment, I would not like to be dogmatic and say, 'No,' to such relationship possibilities. Life can always throw up unexpected changes and new dimensions, so even at my mature age, I keep an open mind about the future.

From experience, I know I can manage and survive sexual encounters, even within unsatisfying relationships. Therefore, I wonder if I could have sustained a relationship with a man if I deeply loved him. Would I have 'put up' with sex under these circumstances? This idea certainly takes a stretch of the imagination, and fortunately I never found myself in this situation. But I would be happy in a close, loving friendship with a male homosexual couple. This way, I could partake in a loving, caring role while enjoying their male approach to life, with big lashings of fun but no sex.

Asexual Relationships – The Positives and Negatives

What would be the positive or negative effects within asexual relationships? Here one can only guess, keeping in mind that as an asexual person, I naturally want to lean towards beneficial influences. So, to avoid bias, I will try to imagine both positive and negative reasons as to how asexuals could give and receive through their loving partnerships.

Positive Effects in Asexual Relationships

(I have made some of the following points before but will repeat here for the purpose of summarising.)

- o There is a healthy human need for a variety of relationships – so within the formerly described polyamory or polygamy situations, it would be beneficial to have an asexual person as part of the relationship group and so help to remove any sexual jealously.
- o Asexuals can have flexible lifestyles without the ongoing efforts of needing to keep sexual relationships alive, resulting in more time to spend with people in the wider community. (This means they can readily serve, advocate, and spread loving kindness towards a wider scope of people.)
- o As an asexual, I am sure I can undertake more community care projects, with my time not taken up with caring for a partner. Consequently, I am watering neighbour's gardens, volunteering to help people with documents, helping in history research, and checking on elderly neighbours. These

actions are not chores because I gain satisfaction in advocating for people other than myself.
- Employers could welcome asexuals to positions in the professions of teaching, nursing, and allied health, such as therapeutic massage, counselling, or any profession involving care relationships – particularly where non-sexual physical touch is involved.
- In my case, I often wonder whether my past devotion to students and clients was more single minded, because I did not have the constant emotional pull of sexual desire.
- When I did engage in working with all-male groups, I felt acknowledged and respected as an instructor rather than as a female. I wonder if this acceptance was because of my lack of sex pheromones or my lack of response to theirs?
- Again, I can only speak for myself, where I know my freedom from often demanding family domestic routines gives extra time for other commitments. So, asexuals could have more time and inclination to focus on arts, science, or projects that require long-term devotion and concentration. I hasten to add that I am sure having more time to spare did not make me any more creative or wiser than sexual folk!
- I believe asexuals make excellent friends because they often exhibit...
  - A wisdom, through having dealt with life changes and a search for identity
  - A readiness to accept others and be more tolerant of people who are different
  - An ability to self-reflect and engage in reflective listening
  - A readiness to help and advocate for others

Negative Effects in Asexual Relationships

- I know asexuals can use heterosexual relationships to relieve loneliness despite not being fully prepared to have close intimacy. Therefore, there is a danger of leading someone to falsely believing they have the prospect of sexual encounters which does not happen. How do I know this? Because I have been guilty of a similar type of behaviour – even though it was not my intention.
- Asexuals can become 'rescuers' in an unhealthy way both for themselves and others involved. This can happen because asexuals sometimes need friendships or want affection, and their care can develop into co-dependency. Again, I say this, because at times I was guilty of such behaviour.
- Asexuals who *reveal* themselves can feel a strong emotional negativity about their future relationship possibilities. When this happens, they can become isolated and lonely after being judged or criticised about their admitted asexuality. Maybe if I had 'come out' earlier, I could have experienced some of these negativities to a greater degree, but I know they exist through reading comments from distressed asexual people on the AVEN website.
- Some people say they accept a person's asexuality, and yet in romantic situations test the boundaries with sexual gestures. This is unfortunate, as it could result in a *romantic-asexual* wanting to avoid future romantic settings and so become an *aromantic* as well as asexual. This did happen to me in a mild way, but I was determined not to let it spoil my enjoyment of intimate settings – so my romantic desires are still intact.
- Within relationships, unacknowledged or misunderstood asexuality can cause untold psychological suffering. In one

recent conference presentation, an asexual researcher relayed many instances of coercive emotional abuse. Here she reported where asexuals had experienced belittling verbal behaviour, physical violence, rape, and even threats that their partner would commit suicide if they did not engage in regular sex.

o As mentioned before, insensitive people can harass asexuals by inflicting *'correctional rape'* on asexual victims, where an enforced sexual encounter is supposed to function as a cure or punishment for not being a willing sexual partner.

All this analysis raised other ideas about the complexity of sexual relationships, particularly in terms of the *energy* of attraction. So I began to think about what creates a dynamic force in relationships, which I explore in the following reflection.

Reflection

On Sexual/Emotional Energy

While in Melbourne in the 1980s, I enrolled in a graduate diploma in Human Relationships Education studying how gender, sexuality, race, and physical/psychological development affected connections with other people. This course also highlighted how our relationships affect each other, and how we have a linkage of people, just like a family tree, who have connected us emotionally and not just biologically.

Energy of Attraction

As a result of noting past emotional connections, I understood how some family members, friends, acquaintances, teachers, and even idolised artists all had an effect in creating my self-identity. In my case, parents, aunts, my English tutor, ballet teacher, plus the distant admiration of some famous people were among those who influenced and shaped my attitudes to life.

These inspirational people all had a special attractive *energy*, which has made me think about *sexual energy* in relationships. Without the diversion of sexual desires and with a platonic kind of loving energy, I am sure asexual people can create a unique kind of attraction. What do I mean by sexual energy, and how would it compare with the energy of asexual people?

Sexual Libido Energy

I can sense this energy when vibrant, confident, sexual people walk into a room and create an aura of attraction. They can create sparks of interest from others just through eye contact, physical gesture, or posture, and probably with strong pheromones along with other pleasure chemicals playing a part.[54]

Asexual Energy

From my experience, I must give out a friendly vibe of energy in appearing approachable and trustworthy. Often virtual strangers will treat me as an ally, confidant, or instant helpmate. So often, I can become the instigator of a would-be sexual encounter when they ask, '*Can you help me meet that attractive woman in the corner,*' or I become the ear of a stranger's sad tales of lost love or life events. So, I think I must put out a different sort of 'love' energy, coming from a natural vibe that invites people to engage with me on an amicable, platonic level. But I do not consciously or actively seek such communication.

---

[54] The website – https://hms.harvard.edu > love and the brain – gives a good summary of the body chemicals which are produced from feelings of lust, attraction, and attachment.

Sexual Incompatibility

People have told me, and I have read website statements, where some married couples say they are sexually '*mismatched.*' A lack of sexual knowledge may prevent a couple from understanding why they legitimately have differing sexual energies and desires. Where such an unbalance of desires exists in a relationship, I like to think these couples could find sexual compromises or alternative arrangements that would be acceptable to both parties. Such alternatives could be an agreement of what degree of sexual intimacy the asexual person could manage, or whether it could be permissible for the sexual partner to seek satisfaction elsewhere. Everyone has their own idea of how often they would like intercourse – from wanting unlimited sex to only once a month. As for me, when I was married, I could only manage the ability to cope with sex about once in ten days, without starting to feel anxious about having to 'perform' if it were wanted more frequently.

Suggesting to a partner that they might be on the asexual spectrum would be a delicate matter. The non-sexual partner could be defensive and need reassurance that they were not unlovable as human beings. Nevertheless, having truthful discussions about essential boundaries in a relationship or coming to a new emotional contract would be tricky. In this case, a good counsellor would be helpful; that is, if you could find one who understood asexuality! I am sure compassionate communication is the key in all such sensitive negotiations, along with considerations of how and when such discussions took place. Sadly, the other alternatives are living with unspoken and hidden ways of coping or bringing the relationship to an end.

Renegotiation in Relationships

I do not think it is simple to create openness for positive compromise and to be prepared for renegotiation of sexually committed relationships. Easier said than done, as compromise or a new partnership contract should create *mutual gain* and not a just a *loss* for one or the other. From my experience, all relationships change over time, for many reasons, and so the wants and needs of a partnership also can require periodic re-examination.

Reasons for changes in a relationship could include physical, cultural, or personal issues that begin to intrude into the couple's lives. In the past, I found effects on my relationships came from often unexpected changes in health, work, or challenges to my basic values. For example, when I struggled with health issues, or my husband kept changing careers. Then there were times when my partner dealt with people in a way that did not agree with my standards of kindness and respect. Certainly, these often-unseen challenges did not help towards keeping an emotionally balanced relationship. Consequently, I never really succeeded in having crucial conversations or redefining emotional boundaries.[55]

Present-Day Marriage

The divorce rate shows that many monogamous marriages become tired and unhappy without any revitalisation. It is hard to expect one person to give all the desired elements of stability, safety, excitement, mystery, friendship, and sexual adventure. All this creates a huge expectation for monogamous marriages that are supposed to last a lifetime – so no wonder they often do not last!

---

[55] Recommended book: *Crucial Conversations: Tools for Talking When Stakes are High* by Kerry Patterson, Joseph Grenny, Ron McMillan & Al Switzer (2002, McGraw-Hill Education).

Sometimes I wish marriages were renegotiated affairs set in realistic terms of lovingly negotiated contracts of five-to-ten-year spans. At certain stages, couples could decide to part, stay, or discuss future expectations in their marriage. Such a contract could also contain pre-arranged fair property agreements, so any settlements could be more easily achieved. These kinds of pre-nuptial arrangements may reduce much of the grief, loss, and emotional harm often experienced when couples undertake division of property or childcare arrangements. Partners might also put in a greater emotional effort if they wanted to maintain their marriage into the future. So, maybe anniversaries should also include a private ritual of recommitment.

Future Marriage

I believe there could be hope for a new kind of marriage that has an emotional and philosophical kind of contract. Today, when often both spouses work, I have seen where young couples appear to have equal financial say, and where domestic and family chores are divided in a collaborative way. They seem to conduct their lives as a genuine team with the display of intimacy that can only grow where there is equality. If the emotional role of males and the accepted income capacity of females grow, then married commitments may again become a more realistic long-term commitment.

Where marriages fail, I like the phrase '*conscious uncoupling*,' referring to where couples aim to leave each other in a respectful, calm, and kind way instead of in the often-stressful states of despair, anger, or revenge. Then of course, there is the considered ongoing care of children, with expectations of change negotiated for their best long-term benefits.

With all this heady thinking about relationships both sexual and non-sexual, I have so far avoided tackling the concepts of love and romance. Once I was teaching a class of teenagers where we were discussing human behaviour, and one student asked about the concept of love: what did *'being in love'* mean, and how would one know if they were truly *'in love?'* *'Let's talk about this love stuff,'* she said.

So, my next journal entry will try to explore this most vital of emotions. I will admit it has taken a long time to think through what constitutes love in all its forms, as it is the most frequently used word when it comes to talking about emotional happiness.

JOURNAL 20

♥

Learnings About Love

Dear Journal,

Thinking about love was not just a matter of recalling past emotional events, but also trying to tease apart the feelings that create this positive kind of emotion in all its varied forms of expression. So, I will now challenge myself to examine what the concept of love has meant to me over the years.

I would hate to think how many times I say the word 'love' while knowing it does not describe the exact quality or intensity of feelings. I can love my son, love a film, or love eating ice cream, demonstrating that I use this one word and apply it to everything and everyone. Therefore, I will try dissecting these different 'love' type of emotions, including the notion of romance, to get some clarity of meaning.

The concept of love has demanded much of my amateur philosophical thought, and I have consumed many lectures, sermons, films, magazines, and textbooks, all of which made pronouncements about love in its many forms. Despite all I have heard or understood, love has been tricky to explain – even to myself.

Often, I have been frustrated when wading through complicated philosophical, social, or physiological discourses on love and friendship. In the process, I often became lost in the many threads of meaning, complex sentences, or academic jargon. Hence, in expressing my own thoughts, I tend to use dot points to create clarity. It is not my intention to sound as if I am preaching, knowing that everyone has their own wisdom about the meaning behind emotions.

So here goes! Firstly, in my thinking about love over a lifetime, I realise it went through about four stages of gradual comprehensions. These covered my understandings of love as experienced in relationships, through philosophy, friendships, and sex and romance.

Stage 1 - Love as Expressed in a Variety of Relationships

My first lessons in love to about the age of twenty-one were...

- Recognising love within a role, such as between parent and child.
- Realising that there was a sexual kind of love as it existed in marriage.
- Understanding sex could be just for its own sake and without love.
- Loving someone as in a sustaining friendship.
- Knowing of the existence of love between people of the same sex.

In more detail...

- I firstly understood love as related to the roles in life such as in parenting, being a sibling, teacher, colleague, or friend. *Example: My earliest loving relationships were with my mother, father, aunt, grandparents, brother, and first teachers. Later I experienced this kind of love in a deeper way once I had a child of my own.*
- I gradually began to understand the notion of sexual love. *Example: Where girls talked about boyfriends and alluded to sexual excitement, or in the 1950s films that showed a discreet sexuality, as did the romantic novels and the example of my parents.*
- I came to realise there could be a separation between love and sexual desire.

> *Example: Late in my teens, I understood some men visited prostitutes just for sex while still appearing to love their wives.*

- Later, I began to identify the difference of *'being in love'* with the yearning of sexual desire and *'loving someone'* where there was an everlasting bond. Here, I *rationally* understood the yearning of sexual desire, though I did not feel it. Also, I saw the lifetime love that existed between devoted couples.
  Example: The deep friendship-love that sustained my parents' long marriage.
- My parents fortunately explained homosexuality and were accepting of gay/queer men. Oddly, it was not until my early twenties that I heard the word 'lesbian' or understood what it meant.
  Note: It took the suicide of my father's friend to raise the topic of same-sex love and desire. However, it has taken many years to understand the diversity of love couplings in the gay/queer world, including my own asexuality.

Stage 2 - Philosophical View of Love

In academic studies I adopted innovative ideas about love through the previously mentioned philosophical writings of Paul Tillich and his four ways of viewing love.[56]

1. Altruistic, noble love – coming from feelings of profound awe and respect. I felt this kind of love through my admiration of talented artists, charismatic leaders, or people who showed great qualities of talent and humane values.
   Example: I had this type of awe and high respect towards my

---

[56] The love philosophy relating to agape, philia, eros, and libido is from the writings of the German American philosopher Paul Tillich. (Here eros refers to the 'mystery' of attraction.)

high-school English teacher, my dance teacher, and many other educational mentors. (This can also be the kind of 'Agape' love expressed by religious people when honouring their God.)

2. Platonic/friendship-love – as expressing large doses of sincere kindness and care. The kind of love as extended by friends whose love encourages others to be their best selves.

   Example: My former journals have given many examples of these kinds of supportive and encouraging friendships. Currently, I have friends with whom I debate the questions of life and share big doses of humour. They also encourage my creative projects and genuinely want to me to succeed.

3. Libido/sexual love – relating to the physical desire for sexual intimacy. I admire this sexual aspect of love without wanting to explore it myself, but I recognise it is a vital ingredient of most partnered relationships.

   Example: Sexual love is expressed everywhere! In human behaviour, conversation, advertising, media, written word, and the arts.

4. Mysterious force of love/empathy – that is attraction to another person. It is difficult to explain why one can feel a certain emotional pull towards another person. I knew this attraction often happened, along with the innate desire to be kind to strangers, being that lovely quality of human empathy to help those in need. I also think this attraction can be tenderly romantic but not in an ardent, amorous way.

   Example: I always liked the films starring the actor Gregory Peck and was bereft when he died. There was something about the kindness in his face, tone of voice, and general demeanour that I found attractive. (Although I never imagined sleeping with him!) I also marvel at the innate empathy between young babies when they cry in unison if one is upset. Then there is the magnetic pull when people can mysteriously relate to someone across a crowded room.

Summary

For years, I was happy with this philosophised version of love as emanating from four emotional sources –

1. The high admiration for another.
2. The need for security of friendship.
3. Physical sexual desire.
4. The mystery force of attraction.

To combine all of the above aspects of love towards another person would seem to say… I admire you, I want to be bonded to you in lasting friendship, I physically desire you, and I feel almost magnetically attracted to you. Therefore, I decided real love would consist of a degree of all four of these elements, of respect, friendship, sexual attraction, and mysterious desire.

Love as Friendship

In the above analysis I do not have the sexual libido-love, so it is the 'philia' friendship-love that strongly applies to me as an asexual. This means that platonic friendship is my greatest source of *intimate* love experience, and I have already examined this in one of my earlier reflections. Because friendship is such a valued part of my love experience, I will reiterate some thoughts about this abiding kind of affection, where a high degree of intimacy can occur – even without sexual closeness.

As I have said, I do not think society values friendship enough, and *'just friends'* always sounds dismissive of this type of relationship. So, here I will summarise some of the loving aspects I have found in friendships. I delight in…

1. Sharing the intimacy of eye contact.
2. Loving the intimate moments of mutual understanding.
3. Enjoying the shared empathy of humour.
4. Responding to each other with compassion.
5. Displaying encouragement towards reaching personal goals.
6. Sharing each other's problems and/or ideas.
7. Negotiating mutual understandings and compromise.
8. Delighting in encounters that bring a sense of fun and joy.
9. Understanding each other's flaws and mistakes with forgiveness.

This kind of friendship-love can spill over into the climate of life, meaning that....

- It 'lights my world' knowing a friend is there.
- I feel more embracing of everyone and everything.
- I feel more secure, stronger, and more prepared to act on personal goals.
- Often, I become more creative after sharing ideas with a friend.
- I certainly see more humour in life after sharing fun experiences.
- It enhances learning through verbalising ideas in a safe environment.
- It may not be like other people's love experience where they enjoy love with sexual anticipation or in the ecstasy of intercourse, but it fully satisfies my emotional needs.

Friendship, the gratitude of being alive in this world, and satisfying work are quite abundant rewards for me.[57]

Stage 3 - Understanding Romance and Sexual Love.

What Is Romance?

Much later in life I considered the concept of romance, and how it might be associated with love. Eventually, I decided 'romance' consisted of three main aspects.

1. Romantic, as referring to the ambiance that helps produce the attraction between people. Therefore, it can be a created special atmospheric space that encourages emotional connections and is a precursor to courtship or friendship.
2. I also equate romance as a part of the mysterious attraction of '*eros*' as previously described in the philosophical love analysis.
3. Romance can be conveyed through speech, touch, and loving gestures.

Examples of Romantic Attraction

To me, romance has always suggested visions of an atmosphere to inspire love. Therefore, I like to believe there are special elements that create romantic allure that can motivate love. Examples of romance can be seen as...

- o A mysterious 'force' that creates attraction between people.
- o An emotional appeal towards another and wanting to be in their presence.

---

[57] 1. David Jay's talk on YouTube, Asexuality, where he speaks of friendship and connection; 2. I tackle the idea of having a friendship to yourself further on in the reflection on self-love.

LEARNINGS ABOUT LOVE

- ○ An enhancement of feelings that could lead towards sexual or platonic love.
- ○ An attraction to the idealised or heroic person where there is a touch of awe.
- ○ An atmosphere (either natural or deliberately created) with a sense of alluring/artistic qualities – such as 'romantic' scenes with images of candlelight dinners, picnics in a park, glasses of wine, log fires, and the cliché of walks along a sunset beach.

Yes, I like the idea of romance as a set of appealing feelings or settings, but does it always go hand in hand with sexual or long-enduring love? In the desire for loving friendship, I am sure one can experience the exchange of romantic gifts and gestures without wanting sexual intimacy. Therefore, romance and sexual love are concepts which can exist separately. In fact, I like to believe I am a romantic at heart.[58]

Stage 4 - Defining Love as a Complex Mixture of Feelings.

Finally, I recognise there are varied emotional ingredients that are bound up into creating what we sense as being love, thus making it more understandable as an inter-dynamic flow of feelings between two people. That is, love is a combination of *several* emotions that create this positive, interactive flow. To use a scientific analogy, the realisation made me feel I was getting down to the smaller particles that constituted a magnetic energy of love and desire.

It took a long time to see 'love' as being a mixture of several feelings that were all wrapped up in this one word. For years I thought real love was ONE big, magical, separate emotion until the

---

[58] There is an account of romantic attraction at https://wikipedia.org/wiki/Romantic_love

'lightbulb' moment occurred. From some unknown source, I began to see love as a *'bunch of feelings'* that flowed back and forth like an ever-flowing energy field *between* people, creating an exchange of positive emotions. I will term these feelings as the *'ingredients'* of love. So, what are some examples of these so-called ingredients that I think creates the emotional exchange we call 'love'?

- A feeling of wanting and wishing to be in the presence of a loved one.
- A preparedness to actively care by listening to each other.
- Feeling a need to respond with loving verbal or physical communication.
- Having a sense of sharing mutual ground of understanding and equality.
- Feeling safe and able to express one's true self in each other's presence.
- A knowing that you have each other's back and support.
- A sense of encouragement towards each other to achieve personal goals.
- Sharing basic values and having genuine respect for each other.
- Having an important level of readiness to forgive and accept each other's flaws.
- Using elements of a play-based approach to solving problems.
- Shared humour with fun and laughter that releases anxieties.
- After a time, having those shared memories of history and life-adventures.
- A sense of becoming your authentic self within the relationship.

- o   Other feelings that I have overlooked![59]

The Behaviour of Love

To summarise all the above, I feel the behaviour to sustain love includes paying real attention to your partner/friend, listening to each other, putting yourself in the other person's shoes, and then acting accordingly. I am tired of the phrase 'having a conversation' without mention of actual outcomes after the talking is done. To me, the loving words should lead to the behaviours that bring love into a living reality.

Being a Nice and Kind Listener

I have noticed the most loving people are genuinely *'nice and kind'* in their demeanour. Nice and kind are two simple, almost boring little words, although to me, they best explain behaviour I most admire in people. I am sure the demanding work in love lies in the niceness of active listening and a kindness in action. I admit that active listening is difficult for some people who are more often worried about what they want to say.

Again, I have been in wordless relationships where we only tried to 'sense' each other's feelings, and where there was not the bravery for either person to put those feelings into words. Body language and facial expression can communicate so much, but without loving expressions and conversations, I cannot always 'see' what people are thinking.

The Love Process

Although I understood the desires and needs for love, I now recognise the sensation of true love is like an inter-energy dynamic. By inter-energy, I mean like a positively charged force that happens

---

[59] Emotional love needs summary – www.healthline.com > emotional needs relationships.

between oneself and the beloved. I view this loving process as vibrant, much like the flow and power of a dance, and therefore in constant change.

When I have experienced small degrees of love within a platonic friendship, I feel more confident, vibrant, and able to tackle life without fear. Friendship really does inspire me to be my bravest self. Also, in loving moments, there is a shared intimacy that I want to last forever. I may not have experienced long-term sexual relationships with the intensity of libido-love, but my moments of shared intimacy and sustained friendships have more than sufficed.

Reflection

Self-Love and Universal Love

Having explored love as existing between two people, I began to think about *inner* self-love and the *outer* love of being in the world and universe. Firstly, self-love was something I had ignored, thinking loving myself seemed a bit narcissistic. Secondly, that marvellous larger feeling of loving life was something I had not truly recognised or acknowledged.

Self-Love

Do I have a healthy friendship towards myself? It took years to be truly sexually conscious and develop a sense of inner freedom. By sexually conscious, I mean the searching for sexual understanding, and by '*sense of freedom,*' I mean feeling free from anxiety that something within me was not right. So, for years I did not have a genuinely happy self-regard.

For a long time, I felt guilty about being happily alone where there was no pressure to show sexual love. So, I marred my past joys of friendship with an underlying anxiety and lived by the fears of how I '*ought to*' and '*should*' behave. Sadly, the fruitless sexual searchings only created a hidden dislike of myself. My first real sense of self-worth did not come until I knew I was an okay asexual human being. Therefore, all my journeys only led me back to myself, but with a new wisdom as expressed in T.S. Eliot's famous words:

> *'We shall not cease from exploration*
> *And the end of all our exploring*
> *Will be to arrive where we started*
> *And know the place for the first time.'*

Now, as a recognised asexual, I feel lovingly alive, albeit not in the same way as other people. But I do feel more self-contentment and at last 'like' who I am in a way that is not ridiculous self-love.

The reasons why I now feel better about myself are as follows...

- I like the 'patient' me who can finish large projects that last for a lengthy period.
- I can accept the tendency to rescue, but with a greater ability to set boundaries.
- I am more aware of the spirit of kindness towards other people and myself.
- It is easier to enjoy the ability to see humour in difficult circumstances.
- I am more prepared to make mistakes, even if errors can still cause frustration.
- I can appreciate my efforts to keep fit and care for my body, not just for dancing but for healthy living in older age, and so be still useful to others.
- I understand that although I like to be alone sometimes, I am not antisocial.
- I like that I am curious and want to learn more about the world.

    o   I am pleased I have a 'big picture' feeling about the planet and universe. Meaning that while I do not understand physics and science, I like that I have somehow come from a small speck of stardust in the cosmos.

The Inner Selves

Sometimes I imagine my different personality facets as a group of inner identities. These change from time to time, but now I acknowledge there are about seven parts of me that come to the fore in certain situations. The team of seven are:

1. The '*Wise One*' who expresses universal love and decides on moral action.
2. A '*Ms Curious*' who encourages the seeking of new knowledge.
3. The '*Loving One*' who wants to be nice and kind towards myself and others.
4. The '*Teacher*' who likes to impart knowledge.
5. A '*Fun Spirit*' who is creative and humorous – much like an inner child.
6. The '*Dancer/Mover*' who is dynamic and desires to be expressive.
7. The '*Adventurer/Warrior*' who is strong and resilient.

These parts of personality usually engage together – so I could be adventurous, fun-loving, and learning all at the same time. Yet, sometimes I become aware that I am not quite emotionally balanced by not engaging with enough humour or realising I feel the need to dance more. In this way I can use my seven aptitudes for self-reflection if something is felt to be missing in life. Here I am not referring to 'multiple personalities' where there are extreme changes in behavioural identity and memory resulting from trauma.[60]

Feeling Love on a Big Scale

After writing about self-love, I am conscious of feeling love in a universal way. Since the asexual realisation, I am more aware of the world around me and feel in tune with love as a broader experience-phenomenon. I can only believe this has come about through feeling free of inner stress. Thinking about this kind of expansive emotion gave rise to two questions...

1. How does one define this sense of love on a universal scale, or having oceanic feelings of love?
2. Without sexual love, can asexuals more highly develop other forms of love through a sublimated or transmuted process? (Relating to a conversion of sexual energy.)

Universal/Oceanic Love

Universal love definitions online reference those feeling-moments of radiance, love, and harmony for everything and everyone.

Often, I feel a sense of positive emotions in a universal way. Just as some people describe their religion as *pantheism*. That is, the belief in a God who exists in all things. At times I feel a similar connection towards everything in the world around me. For example, when I see children at play, hear birds conversing, listen to music, or the moment when I recognise a student has just mastered a skill. On these occasions I feel a thrill that is almost visceral.

Then again, there is the absolute delight of witnessing or partaking in dance when music, movement, and emotion merge together. There are other times, too, when I feel more than a 'pang'

---

[60] For additional information – https://www.healthdirect.gov.au > dissociative identity disorder.

of joy of what I can only call an *'oceanic experience'* when I feel *'at one'* with the world around me. By the term *'oceanic love,'* I do not mean a mystical trance in a religious sense, but those moments of experiencing an all-encompassing wash of feelings that leaves one feeling it is wonderful to be alive. It reminds me of the phrase *'everything is as it should be,'* when in a moment of clarity, I feel a profound sense of beauty in the world.

I can describe this oceanic love physically as a tingling or pleasant gut-twinge, with the emotional reaction of needing to smile for no reason! Music, dancing (either watching or doing), genuine laughter, or being aware of a moment of beauty in the natural environment can all inspire this kind of love experience. There are many examples of these 'shiver-with-delight-moments' – so here comes another list!

Images of Loving Moments:

- Witnessing married couples who have been together for many years, still showing devotion in old age, even when one partner has advanced dementia.
- Watching a pas de deux in Swan Lake where the dancers meld with Tchaikovsky's music, making 'virtual' love visible in motion.
- Sunsets, the dome of the Australian blue sky, beach coastlines, shapes of trees, and the farmlands surrounding my country hometown.
- Reading descriptions of nature in a novel where words become a painting.
- Hearing any music that inspires me to move or just stand still in awe. Example: 'Spiegel im Spiegel (Mirror in a Mirror)' by Arvo Pärt.

- The times when performing on stage and feeling a connection with the audience by their rapt silence and not just their final applause.
- Watching 'Wanderer' butterflies dance together in my nearby park.
- Viewing the rhythmic gait of horses quietly making their way across a field at sundown for a final drink from the river.
- Remembering the grace of my parents as they waltzed – especially the flow of my mother's ball gown.
- Watching a young child's delight playing with what we see as insignificant objects.
- Remembering moments of understanding a concept, idea-sharing, shared laughter, or when everything came together in truthful recognition. For example, when I suddenly understood my own asexuality, or when I simultaneously laugh with friends.

Indeed, having these love experiences in so many things, I wondered whether my asexuality caused a transference of love to other areas of life.

Sexual Sublimation and Transmutation

Being an asexual, the idea of love transference was an appealing consideration. For example, when a person has loss of sight, their hearing becomes more acute. I therefore asked, if sexual desire is missing, does that make other kinds of love more intense? I pursued this idea because it seemed to justify asexuality as having a positive effect on humanity. So, I pondered if there could be a psychological substitution, where the energy of sexual love either became '*sublimated*' or '*transmuted*' to make other kinds of love more intense?[61]

Sublimation

I looked up the word '*sublimation*' to find it meant channelling negative and unacceptable impulses into behaviours that are positive, yet socially acceptable. For example, having a cup of tea instead of lighting a cigarette. It came from the Freudian psychological view of mental well-being, as a '*defence mechanism*' to reduce anxiety from unacceptable urges. Here, the word sublimation did not fit with asexuality, as it is not an unacceptable urge causing anxiety, nor is it socially unacceptable in relation to behaviour as it is unseen. Then I researched the word '*transmutation.*'

Sexual Transmutation

The definition of '*sexual transmutation*' revealed the idea of a creative life-force energy that can convert into energy of another nature. For example, where physical exercise can transmute or dissipate sexual energy. Again, many people have careers taking over their lives where the energy of work activities can take the place of sexual desire. But any transference of the 'non-energy' of asexuality cannot change into another kind of energy when none exists in the first place!

Love Transformation

Therefore, although this idea of sexual energy did not fit the asexual person, I wondered whether the *energy of desire to love* could spill over into other areas of life. Anyway, I decided to create my own terminology. I call it *love transformation*. I like to believe asexuals can

---

[61] Assessment of transmutation and sublimation by Robert Assagioli, an Italian proponent of humanistic transpersonal psychology.
(https://kennethsorenson.dk > transmutation-sublimation)

transform their caring emotions into other areas of living. Because there is little research on asexuality and love transference, I can only give observations about how I feel love has changed and intensified in my own life. This relates as to how I use my time and what engages my attention, now I have the freedom from past personal soul-searching.

Time, Focus, and Attention

These days, worries about sexual relationships do not occupy my thoughts or influence decisions. As a result, I have more time and energy to apply to creative work, meaningful friendships, and community service. Family members often comment how I attract people in need and seem to have continual care projects in the local neighbourhood. Perhaps any extra urge towards doing kind deeds comes from my asexual way of being. However, I am still anxious about the things I *ought* to be doing on a global scale, such as paying more attention to poverty, refugees, or climate change.

Having examined the positives about love, the other important aspect can be found in a phrase, often used by a friend. She would sign her emails '*With love and laughter from...*' Therefore, my next journal will raise the topic of humour and the positivity of laughter in life.

JOURNAL 21

Humour and Asexuality

Dear Journal,
Having exhausted the love topic, my other most important ingredient for life-survival has been humour. I am not a comic, except having the delight of knowing what causes my genuine laughter and taking comfort from recognising humour, even in times of tribulation. Through taking a 'tongue in cheek' view of myself, I can also more easily cope with trying situations, and even smile at my past fruitless attempts of heterosexual behaviour!

Also, I am sure humour plays a strong role in sexuality and love. My mother said she always wanted to marry a tall man who was a musician and certainly not a farmer. But she married the shortest little farmer she could find. Why? Because he was an intelligent broad thinker and had an appreciation of the arts, but most of all because he had a wonderful self-depreciating sense of humour. I have met many other people who found love and laughter sexually attractive.

Before going to sleep, I usually take in some YouTube humour on my phone. For me, the best way to finish the day is in tears of hilarity, as it works better than a sedative. Therefore, I can think of no better way to complete my asexual journals than end with the idea of laughter.

Asexuality and Humour

Belonging to a minority group may not seem to be a probable cause for humour, but there are fun ways to counteract any fears or anxieties. Therefore, I relish in any amusing activities, including joking with others, reading funny books, watching comedy via film or social media, and noting any of life's absurdities that happen in daily life. Thank goodness my parents encouraged humour, were always relating entertaining stories, regularly took me to see comedic movies, and surrounded me with love and laughter in equal doses. Although I was asthmatic where too much laughing or crying made me breathless, I still choked with delight when my father related his absurd stories and anecdotes.

The humour I have always admired is the self-depreciating kind, where people tell jokes against themselves, or retell events of things that had gone wrong! My family abounded with such tales of farm events, usually with stories of animals who had not behaved according to expectations. For example, when the pigs ate our airborne flying kites that were tied to a fence, or how a snake visited my mother in the outside toilet causing her to make an undignified exit, or when Father leaned over an electric fence and shocked himself into the cattle yard, only to be menaced by an aggressive bull calf. All crazy happenings that held the elements of anger, danger, frustration, and fear – but we laughed anyway!

It was not until I studied drama that I realised just how comedy is born from tragedy. Anything comical has stemmed from life's frustrations, calamities, unexpected incidents, human mistakes, or odd accidents. No wonder the emblem of the theatre consists of the two masks of both comedy and tragedy. In fact, when life gets too overwhelming to the point of being ridiculous, my only antidote is to look for and acknowledge the humour.

The distinct types of humour I really enjoy are...

- o the ironic moments in life
- o self-depreciating anecdotes
- o revelations of surreal/illogical situations
- o the use of word play

- observation and imitation of life's surreal moments
- describing life-frustrations and experiences
- odd moments of weird synchronicity
- physical humour – but not too ridiculously slapstick
- the silly and nonsensical such as in Monty Python or the Goon Show
- the presentation of topics that are usually taboo, like sex
- the revelation of formerly unspoken truths
- the revelation of two meanings in double entendres
- the repeated or 'running' joke

While recording in these journals some of my most difficult sexual moments, although serious at the time, now seemed amusing in retrospect. For example, many of my ridiculous attempts at being sexual could all be fodder for a stand-up comic. Humour has always been my antidote to cope with failures and to help accept myself in a more forgiving way. When it comes to sexual humour, I do understand and appreciate sexual jokes, with the one proviso that they do not undermine other people. I was surprised at one suggestion that asexuals may not always 'get' sexual humour, although, as an asexual, I do laugh and recognise such jokes quite easily.

Living in a sexualised world has meant that over the years of digesting films, books, and conversational sexual innuendos, there is not much I do not 'rationally' understand. In fact, I often make sexual jokes or references myself; perhaps because they do not titillate or make me squirm with embarrassment. However, what does make me squirm is when humour becomes a way of putting people down, and over the years there has been a sad abundance of anti-gay jokes. Thank goodness brilliant gay/queer comics now grace our screens and stages.

Yes, I enjoy the art of the joke, the surprise twist, the opposing ideas, the play on words, the recurring gag, and how the comedian can lead your mind down one path, and then shock you into another. Comical techniques reveal the human misunderstandings, the tragic, human mistakes, foibles, and fears that can all be a wonderful source for humour. I could not believe a film about a funeral could be funny until I saw one and bought the DVD so I could watch it again.[62]

For me, humour also informs and illuminates ideas. I totally admire stand-up comedians and just marvel at their skill to reveal our human foibles. Soon after the AVEN website revealed my asexuality, I heard a joke about it. On one occasion, a comedian surprisingly included an asexual joke in his routine, which caused me some interesting reactions.

The Joke

The comedian said, '*Asexuality was like belonging to a book club and not reading the book.*' He acted out the dialogue of a book club member saying to an asexual, '*What did you think of the book?*' Then, taking the role of the asexual, he looked awkward, twisted himself like a pathetic child, and said, '*Oh, I haven't actually read it.*'

From this joke, I concluded it was amusing for someone to belong to a book club if they did not like reading. Ergo, an asexual trying to belong in a sexual world when they did not want sex, was equally as strange and object of amusement.

At first, I reacted negatively, as at the time, asexuality was still new for me, and I was not ready to have fun poked at my new-found orientation. It also reminded me I had been guilty of trying to join the sexual world under false pretences, so maybe the joke only

---

[62] UK film, *Death at a Funeral*, an MGM 2007 black comedy directed by Dean Craig.

pointed out my own painful truth. (Which of course is an excellent function of humour!)

Such a gag would not worry me now, as I do not mind being 'sent up' if it is in a non-hurtful way. Indeed, I feel concern for comedians these days, as many topics can verge into touchy areas of political correctness, so I do not want to become overly sensitive to jokes about my orientation. However, I deplore those anti-gay jokes that aim to 'punch down' or diminish others in any way. At least in this case, the comedian included a joke that gave some recognition about asexuality in the public arena. Recently, I have heard other asexual jokes that I quite like, such as one about an asexual woman saying, '*I just want a man to sweep me up in his arms, take me to the bedroom, lay me on the bed, and then clean the house while I am asleep.*'

I also smile about my computer junk mail, where 'asexuality' is obviously not a word understood by people who write algorithms. After looking at sexual and asexual internet sites, an algorithm software must have concluded by my gender-confusing email address that I was a male and looking for sexual help! As a result, I continually receive offers to correct erection problems or am propositioned by many sexy women wanting to date or massage me!

Despite a few awkward moments of coming out, I take more delight in not taking myself too seriously. Indeed, seeing the funny side has been one of the greatest survival techniques to sustain me over the years, and my renewed, relaxed asexual self has been able to laugh a lot more easily.

As well as humour, I will mention other kind of behavioural techniques that have helped me through periods of deep anxieties or to control signs of exhaustion and burn out. (For example, when my stress-symptoms became short crying fits that erupted suddenly without obvious reason.) Hence, my next reflection will be about defensive mechanisms which have helped me with feelings of anxiety, chronic stress, or burn out. Everybody has their own ways of coping, so the following notes are only what has worked for me.

Reflection

Survival Techniques

Journal writing about humour reminded me of other tricks to relieve any inner stress caused by traumatic events or negotiating life's more demanding daily challenges. Why are such techniques necessary for me, or anyone for that matter? The reasons why I need these deliberate moments of escape are because…

- I am responsible for my own happiness and do not expect people to make me happy.
- As an asexual, I need to find ways to counteract any risk of loneliness.
- My mind needs rest and intervals of play if I am to complete big tasks.
- Play-type of activities can induce creativity.
- I need to avoid exhaustion or burn out.
- With good self-care, I relate better to others and do not need to lean on them.
- Attention to all-round health eventually saves both time and money.

Recording these mind-over-matter ideas does remind me to always pay attention to emotional equilibrium and recognise *when* and *why* stress is creeping up on me. I also need to remember to use my stress-releasers regularly and with some priority, so I can prevent anxiety before it happens. '*Prevention*' is always my go-to word when it comes to health.

Of course, I know there are the usual methods recommended for relaxation. These can be yoga, massage, a long bath, swimming, exercising, and walking in the park. However, all these practices require time management, adjusting schedules, and planning, not to forget travel and money. Although I have used all these relaxers, I like methods that are easily achievable and pay attention to what I am thinking and feeling in the present moment.

So, what are the body/mind techniques that I can undertake within the confines of home? Here I will list the coping skills that I use to help my physical state, thinking processes, and feelings. I know I need to pay attention to those '*ought/should*' anxieties, particularly when trying to reach self-imposed goals or reacting to anything sad or negative.

The Physical

Directions and reasons why I need to do the following…

1. Straighten the posture – so spine is in alignment and tall as possible without strain.
   Why? Because of bad neck and spinal positions when using media appliances.
2. Breathe more deeply – feel ribs expanding!
   So good to do this, particularly after all the Covid mask-wearing in public.
3. Shut, then open eyes, and deliberately take notice of things around me.
   Long hours of computer-work mean the eyes need a change of focus.
4. Smile at nothing and put a pencil in one's mouth to force the mouth muscles into a 'smile' position!
   Unlike frowning, smiling puts the wrinkles in the right place.

5. Do a bit of low vocal humming for breathing and voice exercise.
   I would hate to get that 'old lady' voice through lack of vocal cord use!
6. Walk through the nearest park or where there are trees.
   Walking is the antidote for prolonged sitting at a computer.
7. Only use the muscles required for movement and relax the rest.[63]
   For example, do not tense muscles that are not necessary when typing.

Play-Based Physical Activity

Moments of free-play allow the brain to have a recess. These kinds of play are not time-bound, but are spontaneous, unplanned, and do not fit with any important purpose. This sort of activity is fully engaging, absorbing, and utterly engages the attention. Except it is not useless play, as these fun distractors are brain-releasers that can revitalise and assist in the more serious tasks. As we often note, after taking a break, one suddenly finds problems can be solved. The other thing is that play can subtly improve brain and mental health as you are engaging in learning without any stressful demands. My playtimes sometimes include…

- o Doing some drawing, doodling, or learning how to sketch cartoon characters.
- o Trying to remember how to play the recorder (only when the neighbours are out!).

---

[63] I use the Alexander Muscle Release technique to reduce physical muscular stress. (Fredrick Matthias Alexander – Wikipedia) Alexander's principles concentrates energy into the working muscles while relaxing other muscles not needed for action. (Preventing muscular over-use and tension.) Note: This technique relates to muscle use and does not cure diseases as some people claim.

- Learning a couple of contemporary dance steps on YouTube.
- Playing a game of Candy Crush or solving a Wordle puzzle on my phone.
- Sending a fun message to those more distant friends or relatives.
- Drafting a silly poem for a friend.
- Take in a movie or a dose of either Netflix or Stan.
- Playing with great-grandchildren.
- Making a creative list or brainstorming about future projects on paper.

Controlling Thoughts

Making sure the 'Wise' part of me has control here!

1. Are my thoughts negative, or do they tempt me to stray off-task? If so, then I should try to *'thought stop'* by any means such as:
    - Substituting with a positive thought or image. *(This is not easy.)*
    - List any negative thoughts and sort them later. *(I have lists everywhere.)*
    - Look at the source of negativity and see if it is fear based. *(It usually is.)*
2. If it is a fear-based worry of what *'might'* happen, then I could…
    - Dismiss with humour if it is unrealistic or return to it later if it was valid.
    - Take some action for a real fear, even if it is just writing a plan.

3. Remind myself that visualisation helps. For example, if typing a difficult piece, I imagine how good I will feel in that smug state when I get the job done.
4. Here I repeat my father's wise direction of the three 'Dos.' That is…

    - Do the worst job first.
    - Do it at once.
    - Do it well (that is to the best of your ability).

Acknowledging Feelings

I try to remember, *'thoughts create feelings and feelings create thoughts.'* The following ways of coping are my usual 'go to' options.

1. Acknowledge with gratitude all comforts I have in my life.
2. Congratulate myself for what I have achieved and do not look at the task as being too big. (Chop it into small bits, delegate, or call in the experts.)
3. Visualise future success without putting pressure on myself about precise finishing dates, allowing time for fun life events to intervene.
4. If feeling overwhelmed with a problem, I remember to…

    - Say to self, 'This too will pass.'
    - Consider other people who have bigger problems than mine.
    - Remember the skills I can use to overcome obstacles.
    - Face the fears and bravely dive into the crux of the dilemma.
    - Be patient in getting to the solution.
    - Take short breaks when doing big tasks.
    - Use background music to get in the right mood.
    - Verbalise problems with a friend or colleague.

o Delight in rewards for work completed.

Note: In movies there is a constant use of alcohol to commiserate or reward any moment of high drama. It is only the characters that are pregnant or are recovering alcoholics who drink water. So, alcohol needs a special health consideration and control in real life! Some years ago, cigarettes were seen as the stress-releasers, which have now lost popularity for good reasons. Despite alcohol always being used as a stress-release, I think it should be mainly used to enrich joyful celebrations, or to enhance creative ideas for a worthy cause. (Such as exploring new concepts and designs for a theatrical production or fund-raising initiative.)

Brainstorm Charts

Being a visual person, creating brainstorm charts on a large sheet of paper also works for me before making a sensible list. One can create these charts on a large sheet of paper, with an image or word of the main idea or topic placed in the centre. Then, from that central image or word, there are 'branches' of themes that relate to the topic with simple phrases relating to that strand of thought. The page finally looks like a crazy tree of ideas, and yet from this mess, one can recognise the main goals. As my mind does not work in a linear fashion, these weird charts help sort out the priorities for action.[64]

Conclusions About Coping Strategies

Fortunately, all the mentioned coping skills have come to the fore when I was grappling with relationships. By turning my mind to other things, I often saved myself from misery and was able to keep hopeful that one day, I would find answers to my various life problems. Fortunately, along the way I have not experienced any real

---

[64] I found the use of these 'Mind-Map' charts through books by Tony Buzan, who is a leading authority on matters about the brain and learning.

bouts of deep depression – only a few healthy crying bouts under the shower!

I know that everyone needs to find their own techniques for emotional self-care to prevent chronic anxieties from taking control. Laughing until I cry by watching comedy, engrossing myself in a film, reading a book, or dancing are the best remedies for me!

On this happy note, my next and final summary journal will bring all these asexual musings to an end!

JOURNAL 22

Summary and Outcomes

Dear Journal,
In recording my asexual story and reflections, I have felt rewarded by gaining clarity about my inner self. At last, I have put to rest any messy anxieties and can bask in the real me.

Why Did I Try Journal Writing?

Although I have a theatrical background, I did not want to write about my lack of sexual life just for dramatic effect or to get attention. In fact, there was trepidation in journal writing, knowing just how much I had caused my own inner turmoil.

That said, my asexual explorations have been rewarding. Finally, I have achieved a measure of self-forgiveness about the marriage breakdowns and can more easily live with those past unwise decisions. It has also given me an opportunity to re-examine beliefs about love, religion, and relationships, and it has been liberating to 'stand outside' myself and understand asexuality more clearly. There is now no 'drive' for me to continue the unproductive search for belonging, and I can accept I am still a flawed human being, but one with a degree of inner contentment.

My Hope for Other Readers?

It would be a bonus if my journals were able to advance knowledge and acceptance of asexuality in some small way. Also, I hope it raises questions for and further thinking about concepts such as…

- o what is romance?
- o the diversity of sexual behaviour

- marital expectations
- the different forms of love
- health and the science of sexuality
- the importance of humour and self-care

It would also be my wish that readers would feel the encouragement to be accepting and compassionate towards themselves and confident enough to question the prevailing social norms.

The Invisibility of Truth

Journal writing has reminded me that I can never truly know other people by what they do or say. No one ever really understands why people behave in certain situations or knows what happens behind closed doors. For example, I remember all the people who expressed total surprise when I became a divorcée, as to them, my marriage had only reflected the 'happy couple.' In the same vein, you can live with someone and yet never know their deepest thoughts or true motives.

Keeping things hidden can be hypocritical, such as those who preach Christian beliefs yet secretly and knowingly abuse others. In my case, I had pretended to have sexual desire towards men when I did not. No wonder my favourite form of drama was working with masks; that was what I did in real life. For years, I had been engaged in camouflaging my asexuality by wearing the sham mask of a heterosexual. The only masks I wear now are for Covid!

However, in my defence, I *did* have feelings of loving affection despite being sexually ignorant. It is a relief to admit I have unwittingly 'lived a lie' and yet forgiven myself. At times, I still think about these romantic occasions with men I tried to partner and hope they sensed my loving regard for them. Yes, there are still some moments of sad regret.

Reasons for Writing About Asexuality

Writing journals or 'coming out' about asexuality was not overtly necessary– so again, I question why did I bother to do it?

To summarise, there are a few main reasons, but for my own sake, I wanted the 'true me' to be visible. Plus, I am proud to be able to label my sexuality and belong to a unique community. My other reasons are:

1. To help other asexuals, who may fear loneliness or mistakenly believe there are no opportunities for loving relationships.
2. To encourage more honest examinations of our human relationships through education, research, communication, broader thinking, and greater flexibility towards sexual diversity.
3. I care about other people who are existing in unhappy relationships, in which asexuality could be an unknown factor. In knowing about this orientation, it might help towards understanding the incompatibility of sexual desires.
4. To encourage others to be true to themselves, and not be like me, where I had been unknowingly guilty of *'self-infidelity'* by not being authentic. That is, being unfaithful to my true self.

Political Concerns

There appears a constant need to re-examine the many areas of policy affecting our new inclusive approach to sexual orientations and gender. These include governmental laws, legal public records, medical manuals, school curriculums, and the dictates of some church organisations.

Currently, there are concerns regarding the following issues...

- Gender in relation to changing gender on birth certificates.
- Education and curriculum in schools.
- Religious attitudes that negatively affect sexually diverse people.
- The need to change medical diagnostic manuals where new sexual knowledge has not been taken into account.
- The need to address legal concerns regarding making conversion therapies illegal, medically altering binary genders before children are old enough to give consent, or the legal responsibilities relating to the procedures of transgender.
- The responsibility to tackle sexual abuse in other countries where the World Health Organization and global human rights approaches could bring influence on sexually related issues that cause suffering.
- Inclusion of asylum seekers who are avoiding sexual persecution and cannot live freely in their birth country because of their true sexual orientation or gender.

Those who fight for justice are remarkable, and often dedicate a lifetime of doing the following arduous work, such as...

- Knocking on political doors over many years.
- Writing countless submissions.
- Working to engage community support.
- Educating for public awareness.
- Organising conferences to air concerns and promote action.
- Using their abilities to look for different pathways to implement change.
- Advocating for those with multiple disadvantages who cannot speak for themselves. (I have met people who are

disabled, transgender, and recently arrived from a different country.)

Thank You, David Jay and AVEN

Thank goodness there is an online site creating a platform for asexual knowledge and communication. The AVEN website has given not just education but also a focus and a community to help endorse a sense of belonging. No wonder it took so long to find out about asexuality, as until the internet extended our world, I only had books and a limited library research to look for the elusive sexual answers. Therefore, I reiterate a big thanks to David Jay, the creator of AVEN, that I finally found my happy default non-sexual position.

Other Writers on Asexuality

I am grateful to others who have shared their valued insights and wisdom on asexuality. At first, other than reading internet sites, I did not delve into any authors, as I did not want other people's analysis to influence my own thoughts. Why? Because I wanted to sort out my own sexual confusions before testing conclusions against the wisdom of others. It is only during the latter journals that I was ready to read how other authors interpreted asexuality, and I began with two excellent books I found referenced when scanning the internet.

So, what did I uncover? It was a joy to have my story confirmed by their writing, where they endorsed so much of my own experience. Therefore, I will recommend and list these special books in the bibliographical section.

'The Now' – My Present Relationship to Life and Love:

I believe that as an older asexual, with my lifetime of self-searching, I can now celebrate sexuality.

I want to endorse attitudes that accept the individual uniqueness of our human race and the need to be honest in our relationships.

SUMMARY AND OUTCOMES

I would also celebrate if science could prove that human sexual diversity was a necessary part of human evolution. Just as we need special vitamins and minerals in our diet for health, I like to think we need special, distinct kinds of sexuality to enhance human life.

I like the idea that the passions of sexual energy and love can spill over to into areas such as the arts, sport, writing, or any activity that helps others.

In conclusion, I feel privileged to be a 'witness' for my asexual orientation and to speak up for those of us who are sexually different. I hope everyone finds that elusive loving relationship with themselves and delights in their uniqueness of being.

An asexual poem 'To Love'

> *Love image – a flowering spirit in the mind*
> *Engulfing all – every time*
> *The energy – that stab-twist in a heart*
> *The light – a warm-glow of an eye*
> *The breath – indrawn-gasp of awe*
> *An ocean wave – lifts and curls*
> *A loving hug to life – a whisper in the ear*
> *I, a small lantern – so good to be here!*

Of course, Shakespeare wrote the best lines in the play *Hamlet* about being authentic...

> *This above all: to thine own self be true*
> *And it must follow, as the night follows day,*
> *Thou canst not then be false to any man*

All I can say is, '*Bless the asexuals, who can bring their life-energies to be lovingly expansive and so benefit everyone and everything in their world.*' Therefore, I embrace all sexuality and take delight in my own asexuality. Indeed, I feel the sun on my back!

Davina A. 2022

Appendices

2021 Better Together Conference Report
The Equality Project Australia
Bibliography

2021 Better Together Conference Report

♥

The two words which set the tone of the conference were 'safety and bravery.' I am sure everyone felt safe and accepted within an atmosphere that encouraged both truth and bravery.

Overall, it was a humbling experience where so many brave individuals spoke of their experiences in overcoming personal pain. I heard stories about discrimination, and the difficulties of feeling accepted as valued human beings, despite sexual differences.

I admired the tone of the conference where such a diversity of people felt welcomed, including asexuals, sex workers, intersex folk, and allies. (Allies are people who strongly support the gay/queer community).

The opening session was awe-inspiring, with many people giving short speeches about their orientation and experience. Not only did they speak their truth with grace, but they also revealed the many multiple and layered complications that occurred in their lives. For example, having a unique sexual orientation, plus coping with other challenges such as having a disability or being a refugee, immigrant, or an Indigenous person.

The conference included various caucuses where separate groups could talk about their unique orientation and situation. These sessions where important in raising concerns and need for positive change in many areas. For example, policy changes to support LGBTIQA+ folk through governmental, educational, medical, or media arenas. As well as changes in policy, participants suggested the need for greater public education about gay/queer life challenges and the continual need for support groups. I attended two caucuses, one on advocacy for issues that can confront gay/queer people without family support, and the other for asexuals.

In my own asexual presentation, the audience was respectful and most attentive. Although I am self-critical, I admit to enjoying the experience. My session touched on topics such as...

- o Asexual invisibility.
- o Definitions of words such as orientation, gender expression, and attraction.
- o Being asexual in a sexualised world and use of pretense.
- o Finding the Asexual Visibility Education Network website.
- o The process of 'coming out' including the negatives and positives.
- o Understanding the concept of love and asexual partnerships.
- o Future action in terms of research and outcomes.

As this conference was organised through the Equality Project, which is the body that informs on all matters relating to the LGBTIQA+ community, I have included the following information about their policies.

The Equality Project Australia

♥

This is an Australian organisation who created the LGBTIQA+ Policy Guide to ensure that lesbian, gay/queer, bi+, transgender, gender diverse, non-binary, intersex, queer, asexual, and aromantic people and their families experience real inclusion and realisation of their human rights in Australia. The Guide is an overview of the most important needs experienced throughout Australian LGBTIQA+ communities.

- Fairness: 'The conviction that all Australians have the right to live in a just and transparent society while being protected from the abuse of power in all spheres.'
- Human rights: 'The fundamental rights that recognise and respect the intrinsic value, self-determination, and dignity of all persons.'
- Equality: 'The ability of all Australians to choose and pursue the same opportunities as others without experiencing significantly more barriers than any other person.'
- Intersectionality: 'An acknowledgement that people are inherently multi-faceted, both in terms of their status within LGBTIQA+ communities and a wide range of other important attributes, and that human rights should apply to all parts of a person.'
- 'Yogyakarta' Principles Plus 10: Additional principles and state obligations on the application of international human rights law in relation to sexual orientation, gender identity, gender expression, and sex characteristics, to complement the Yogyakarta Principles recognising…

- 'The needs, characteristics, and human rights situations of persons and populations of diverse sexual orientations, gender identities, gender expressions, and sex characteristics are distinct from each other'
- 'Sexual orientation, gender identity, gender expression, and sex characteristics are compounded by discrimination on other grounds including race, ethnicity, indigeneity, sex, gender, language, religion, belief, political or other opinion, economic and social situation, birth, age, disability, health (including HIV status), migration, marital or family status, being a human rights defender, or other statuses. (http://www.yogyakartaprinciples.org)
- Self-advocacy: 'Policy that is developed by and with the people with lived experience of the phenomena associated with that policy will be more likely to define those phenomena, engage complexity, and propose effective solutions than policy that is developed mostly by agents who speak and work on behalf of people with lived experience.'

Website: For further information, consult the website – www.theequalityproject.org.au

Bibliography

Asexual Visibility Education Network (AVEN) – founder, David Jay (www.asexuality.org)

Anthony F Bogaert, *Understanding Asexuality* (2012, Rowan & Littlefield).

Julie Sondra Decker, *The Invisible Orientation: An Introduction to Asexuality* (2015, Skyhorse Publishing).

Betty Friedan, *The Feminine Mystique* (1963, W. W. Norton).

Germaine Greer, *The Female Eunuch* (1970, MacGibbon & Kee).

Marilyn French, *The Women's Room* (1977, Simon & Schuster Summit Books).

Simone de Beauvoir, *The Second Sex* (1949, Vintage).

T. S. Elliot, *Four Quartets* (1943, Harcourt).

Acknowledgements

Organisations - people - activists - past intimate partners - readers

Firstly, thank you to David Jay and the AVEN website for creating the forum where I was able to rediscover myself and thus feel honoured to be an asexual person. You taught me that I was not only normal, but that I was both extraordinary and unique.

A sincere thank you to Kate, Gary, and Roy for their interest, support, and encouragement in the writing of this book. As authors, you clearly understood the complexities of writing and encouraged me to keep on task.

An extra thank you to Kate for your excellent work in all aspects of publishing.

A deep appreciation of the professional work undertaken by readers, editors, and cover designers.

A special thank you to Paul for the patient work in correcting all those silly errors one's brain does not recognise.

I wish to acknowledge the Equality Project Australia for their support of LGBTIQA+ people and for organising the 2021 Better Together Adelaide Conference, where there was a welcomed inclusion of all asexual folk.

The Better Together Conference also gave me the opportunity to meet other asexual people and applaud those tireless activists who raise awareness of the asexual orientation.

I wish to acknowledge those kind nameless men with whom I tried to engage in past intimate relationships. Thank you for teaching me about myself.

Finally, I humbly acknowledge my readers in the hope that you gain something from my experience and celebrate your own sexuality.

About the Author, Davina A

Originally from a country community, Davina A has been a dance, drama, and communication teacher in schools, community groups, and tertiary institutions. In addition, she has been a medical secretary, administrator, and public speaker. Her writings include war stories for the Australian War Memorial, with a historical record of agricultural farming invention being accepted by the National Library in Canberra. Academic studies include a graduate diploma in human relationships education and a master's counselling degree in social science, with a focus on sexuality and gender. Since 2017, this 'Asexual' author has concentrated on making her sexual orientation 'visible' and supporting LGBTIQA+ causes. Her asexual research and writing has strengthened the belief that sexual diversity is to be celebrated in all societies.

- o M.Scs. (Counselling) University of S.A.
- o Dip.T. B.Ed. (ACAE) now University of S.A.
- o Grad Dip. Movement & Dance, Grad Dip. Human Relationships Education (MCAE) Melbourne

Davina is a member of a small collection of authors, known as the Midnight Authors, who write to bring pleasure, insight and variety to adult readers (fiction and non-fiction).

https://www.midnightauthors.com

www.ingramcontent.com/pod-product-compliance
Lightning Source LLC
Chambersburg PA
CBHW072340300426
44109CB00043B/1972